Raising Brooklyn

Raising Brooklyn

Nannies, Childcare, and Caribbeans Creating Community

Tamara Mose Brown

NEW YORK UNIVERSITY PRESS
New York and London

NEW YORK UNIVERSITY PRESS
New York and London
www.nyupress.org

We gratefully acknowledge the Feminist Press of the City University of New York for permission to reprint material that appeared in *WSQ: Women's Studies Quarterly*, "Mothers in the Field: How Motherhood Shapes Fieldwork and Researcher-Subject Relations," Vol. 37, 2009.

Library of Congress Cataloging-in-Publication Data

Brown, Tamara Mose.
Raising Brooklyn : nannies, childcare, and Caribbeans creating community / Tamara Mose Brown.
p. cm.
Includes bibliographical references and index.
ISBN 978-0-8147-9142-4 (cl : alk. paper) — ISBN 978-0-8147-9143-1 (pb : alk. paper) — ISBN 978-0-8147-0935-1 (e-book)
1. Nannies—New York (State)—Brooklyn. 2. Public spaces—New York (State)—Brooklyn. 3. West Indians—New York (State)—Brooklyn. I. Title.
HQ778.67.N7B76 2010
302.3'4089960729—dc22 2010033741

New York University Press books are printed on acid-free paper, and their binding materials are chosen for strength and durability. We strive to use environmentally responsible suppliers and materials to the greatest extent possible in publishing our books.

Manufactured in the United States of America
c 10 9 8 7 6 5 4 3 2 1
p 10 9 8 7 6 5 4 3 2 1

Contents

Preface

My desire to understand how paid childcare providers use public places emerged from my experience as a scholar suddenly plunged into motherhood. While not a paid childcare provider, I am a mother of two toddlers and have spent many hours of many days in public places while caring for children. After giving birth to my first child, a daughter, in 2004, I began gravitating to the public park three blocks from the apartment that my husband and I rented because I had been socialized to believe that that is what you do when you're a new mother. Even though my daughter was far too young to appreciate the playground activities made available to her, I continued visiting the park on a daily basis (twice a day once my son was born a year later) to break the monotony of days filled with graduate coursework, diaper changing, multiple feedings, and hours of talking to this little creature who could only stare back at me and gesture. At first, it did not strike me as odd that some park users were either adult Latina or Filipina caregivers with small white children, since I had just come from Los Angeles, where this was a familiar sight. Once I became a regular Brooklyn park user, however, I was intrigued by the familiar West Indian accents I heard from the many black women caregivers using public parks. I recognized those accents, for I had grown up in a Trinidadian immigrant household in Canada with a father of African, Indian, English, and Irish ancestry and a mother of African, Indian, Carib, Spanish, and French ancestry. Both identify as mixed race, as do I, but having lived in the United States for the past nine years, I am racially identified as black, as are my children—similar to the caregivers I encountered.

After frequenting the parks for some weeks, I began to notice that these Caribbean-born women and their charges were, in fact, the primary users of this park during weekdays. Although I had lived in the area for over a year before my first park visit, I realized I had never seen any of these women living in the neighborhood. I wondered where these women lived and why they came to these parks in such large numbers to take care of children whom

I assumed to be other people's, an assumption I later found to be correct. After all, I had found an Italian American part-time babysitter who lived in a brownstone building where she had been raised next door to the brownstone my family was renting at the time. Would there not be enough babysitters available in the neighborhood that families could call on? Further, I questioned the reasoning of having a West Indian babysitter who might bring a different ethos to a home and to a public park that was generally not in a West Indian community. Other questions came to mind: Were these women comfortable working in a predominantly white neighborhood? Did they feel safe there? Did they socialize with other West Indians, seeking refuge in their own culture during the workday? After asking myself these questions, I decided I had to investigate.

I began to see that the use of public places by West Indian childcare providers was related to matters of race, ethnicity, immigration, political economy, and transnational motherhood. Further, my research led me to topics involving care, culture, globalization and its effects, and issues of urban gentrification.

As I encountered West Indian childcare providers over a three-year span in public places, discussed everyday activities and shared food with them, or simply allowed my children to play with their charges, I became more aware of the significance of West Indian childcare providers' frequenting of public parks. Something more than simply getting out of the house and going to the parks with their children brought these women to such public places in neighborhoods that otherwise they might find unwelcoming. They were creating a distinct community to make their workweek more manageable. I then discovered that most of these "sitters" or "nannies," as they call themselves, lived near Flatbush Avenue, one of the major West Indian ethnic enclaves and shopping districts in Brooklyn, which was at most seven major street blocks away from the area in which their employers lived. This fact awakened me to the role of gentrification in the employment of these women.

Simple walks down the street with West Indian babysitters in a gentrifying Brooklyn neighborhood slowly turned into note-taking events, interviews, and observations of social networks being developed. In this book, I provide insights into a social world that has been written about extensively, but without reference to the human relations that babysitters form to help stave off some of the frequently noted isolation felt among paid childcare providers.[1] I show how these childcare providers create community through the use of what sociologist Georg Simmel calls "sociability." This sociability that Simmel and subsequent sociologists have studied as a way of understanding social groups creates a structure of interactions that people regulate by and for one another in public places.[2]

Through this lens I developed an appreciation for the women I studied as they worked long hours in what appeared to be a community of culture.[3] These childcare providers appeared to enjoy their jobs more when they had opportunities to express their culture during their workday. They measured their job performance, not by some standard given to them by their employers but by the cultural standards set within the West Indian enclave, a standpoint that ultimately allowed them to assert their own autonomy. Spending time at the park with my own children throughout this period and seeing the multiple ways West Indian childcare providers got through the workday helped me to reconnect with my own culture and changed my life in ways that go beyond this book.

Acknowledgments

This book is the result of social interaction at its best. I am indebted to the participants in my research, including the West Indian childcare providers I have come to know since 2004; their employers, some of whom were dear neighbors; those who work tirelessly at Domestic Workers United to fight for the rights of all domestic workers in New York; and others I interviewed.

I offer my gratitude to the Graduate Center at City University of New York for the initial funding that helped move this project along. I am also grateful to Barbara Katz Rothman, Philip Kasinitz, and William Kornblum for their commitment to this project, their help in deepening my analysis throughout the years, and the enthusiasm for qualitative research that they shared with me. I am deeply thankful to professors Mitchell Duneier, Nancy Foner, and Sharon Zukin for their critical comments on earlier drafts of this work and for pushing me to connect sociology to the everyday experiences of living and working. At the Graduate Center, I was lucky to meet Andrea Siegel, Lauren McDonald, and Colin Jerolmack, who all gave their time to review various chapters that would later become part of this book. Joanna Dreby encouraged me all along the way and has served as a role model for mothers who defy the odds of academia. I am especially grateful to the sociologist Erynn Masi de Casanova from the University of Cincinnati, who has tirelessly looked through various iterations of this book and subsequent articles. She is an amazing scholar, my dearest friend and my rock.

At Brooklyn College, City University of New York, I would like to thank Carolina Bank Muñoz and Greg Smithsimon, two of my current colleagues who read drafts of chapters and the entire book. They were supportive, allowing me to bother them with questions and giving me the confidence to make this book become a reality. I also benefited greatly from the support of our chair, Kenneth Gould, who has supported this endeavor in many ways that go unnoticed.

At each point in this book I received the support, encouragement, and motivation necessary from my editor, Ilene Kalish. I am grateful for her vision, her commitment to this book, and her role in pushing me to stay focused. I also thank all of the anonymous reviewers for their careful comments and for challenging me to think more critically about my writing and research. I hope to know who they are one day so that I may thank them in person.

My dear friend Sharon Edwards piqued my research interest in the West Indian population in general—I thank her for all of our long discussions about being a Canadian West Indian and how this shapes our social world. As for all of my friends who are mothers in Canada, Los Angeles, and New York, who have long heard of this book and wondered what I do for a living—here it is, and thank you for waiting for it!

My deepest thanks and love go to the people who were with me throughout this process from the beginning. I thank my parents, who have given me the strength to know who I am as a person and the freedom to explore many avenues before entering a career as an academic. Their teachings of West Indian culture and love for literature have had a profound impact on my research as well as my life. I hope to pass that along to my children in the way they have with me. I thank Alyssia and Matisse for filling my life with energy and unwavering love and for being part of this book in so many meaningful ways. Most importantly, I thank my husband, Jason Brown, for allowing me to write in peace by taking our two children out to Prospect Park every weekend for hours at a time while I was writing the initial drafts of this book. He has given me the perspective to see what I do as a way to capture our social world with passion and make my findings accessible enough to make the work worthwhile. His support means everything.

Finally, I thank all the mothers, fathers, and childcare providers of Brooklyn who have allowed me a window into their world. While I am sure some may disagree with my analysis, I am reassured in knowing that our struggles with work and family are more similar than they are different. Let us support one another in the future and attempt to understand each other in ways that go beyond the superficial.

Introduction

The Neighborhood

Most mornings around 9:30 a.m., after eating breakfast, showering, getting dressed, and giving a quick send-off to my husband, I feed my kids, get them dressed, and prepare a diaper bag, then walk my one-year-old son and two-year-old daughter in their double jog stroller across the highway bridge and another five blocks to the park. As I arrive at the second block, after walking by a local bakery, I pass a three-foot-high Mother of Mary statue embedded in the front stoop of a brownstone home that prompts me to say a "Hail Mary." Like the good Catholic my mother always wanted me to be, I say my Hail Mary to clear my conscience. With the fresh smell of coffee and chocolate croissants on my mind, I continue along my path in this once predominantly Catholic, Italian neighborhood toward one of Brooklyn's oldest public parks. As I look at my surroundings, I am reminded of the changes that are continuously occurring in the area.

This newly gentrified neighborhood has a high density of three- to five-story brownstones on almost every street. Many of these buildings are under renovation by the incoming, mostly young white upper-middle-class professionals who are buying homes for close to and often over one million dollars or renting homes or apartments for several thousand dollars a month (at near-Manhattan rates). Where once lunching on pizza was the choice for many in the midday rush hour and sitting on your front stoop was the main form of entertainment, I now find organic paninis with vegan options and a "mommy and me" yoga class on every block. The "Grups" (yuppies or hipsters, a term inspired by a *Star Trek* show in which a virus killed anyone who demonstrated the signs of the aging process) are everywhere.[1] Their fashionable white iPod earplugs, over-the-shoulder messenger bags, and T-shirts that appear torn at the seams yet cost well over fifty dollars indicate the Grups as the newest cultural group in Brooklyn's gentrifying neighborhoods. Where is the older generation? I see evidence of the once-dominant ethnic group in the form of older Italian men in collared dress shirts with front-pleated slacks and worn dark-colored shoes. Some congregate along the perimeter of the park to engage in regular discussions of daily events or to find out when the next bocce ball tournament will take place. Others can be seen chatting through the dimly lit doorways of Italian social clubs adorned with signs stating "Members Only" that practically demand a peek from passersby.

I usually arrive at the park around ten o'clock. I enter through the open gates of the basketball courts just off one of the main shopping streets, directly across from an Italian restaurant, a pet store, a local grocery, an insurance company, a senior center, and a laundromat. I walk diagonally across the basketball courts, typically empty during that time of the weekday, past the fenced-in bocce ball alley to my right, and through the second entrance of a fence that separates the recently painted courts from a large courtyard area where a statue stands to commemorate those men who gave their lives in World War I. Twenty-one green park benches and three picnic tables border the edges of this space. It is sparsely populated by babysitters, stay-at-home parents, and older local residents, many of whom are Italian immigrants, and of course children, strollers, and pigeons waiting patiently for a child to drop a snack. Behind the benches are several large trees, which in the summer can look lush but in the winter stand strong and naked. On the south side of the park, and regardless of where you are sitting, you can see the neighborhood elementary school; on the north side are a newly opened chain drug store, several four-story brownstone homes, and the entrance to a subway station.

I continue my walk across the courtyard via a narrow ramp bordered by a cast-iron fence. This ramp leads downward toward a playground where a children's sprinkler separates two play areas, one for infants and toddlers and the other for older children. Both have swing sets and jungle gyms and are enclosed by iron gates. There is a public restroom area with a sink and two stalls (one for men and one for women) separated by a storage space with upkeep equipment such as brooms, rakes, leaf blowers, and cleaners. The city park employees (many of them African American) who use this equipment wear blue and green uniforms and have begun their duties for the day by the time I arrive. At this point I usually look out for some of the West Indian sitters that regularly enter the park area after ten o'clock. I always feel self-conscious as I prepare to absorb the daily events that may or may not arise in the West Indian childcare community, not knowing how these women actually perceive me, a neighborhood resident.

As I sit, a svelte woman walks toward me, well groomed from head to toe. Her jet black hair is tied up in a large ponytail—pin straight, and if I close my eyes and take a deep breath, the fresh smell of Dark and Lovely hair relaxer penetrates my nostrils. Her voluptuous lips, marking the beauty of her ancestors, are red like strawberries, her eyes deep black. She is pushing a one- or two-year-old white child in a stroller over to the swings. Other black women with white children can now be seen at every turn.

Previous researchers have argued that one reason domestic childcare providers' work is emotionally taxing is that it is isolating: they are left in the private household of their employer with few options for constructing an identity outside the work they do. In many cities across the United States domestic childcare workers need transportation such as a car or reliable bus service if they want to move about public spaces in order to break some of the isolation felt during the workday. In such cities, homes may be far apart, so providers are scattered and it is more difficult for them to create a community. Providers are usually working one on one with a child in the employer's home, which at every turn underscores the inequality of the relationship the provider has with her employer. Boundaries of the job's responsibilities become ill defined in such a private sphere and are almost reminiscent of past relationships between servants and their masters. The racial difference between employer and employee heightens the potential for exploitation in this relationship regardless of the geographic location. Sociological studies by Mary Romero on Chicana domestic workers in the Southwest and by Pierette Hondagneu-Sotelo in Los Angeles with Mexican undocumented immigrants employed in middle-class residential areas show how the private sphere can be isolating when domestic workers do not have access to the public spheres that other urban areas offer.[2] In contrast, this study examines gentrifying neighborhoods in Brooklyn, New York, where the public sphere is geographically close to dense residential housing. While access to the public sphere or spaces in these neighborhoods does not entirely dispel the isolation of domestic work, I show how childcare providers, through their use of public spaces, can create a collective space and collective definitions of what they are doing during the day. Providers can reach some form of consensus about how their work should be conducted, what they do, what constitutes a good parent, and what employers can and cannot ask of them. They find ways to preserve their autonomy in the public places where they gather and rely on new communications technologies (mobile phones, Internet) to do the same thing when they are physically apart in both private and public places. Community streets and public parks in Brooklyn became quasi-offices for several babysitters, rendering them visible to the rest of the community and ultimately their employers.

Given this form of control that providers have over their workday, parents are reduced to certain tactics in order to combat their feelings of losing ground: as I show in this book, they may, for instance, use various means of surveillance, develop new rules, or simply speak badly about childcare providers—not always without reason. I also show how parents can overcome their feelings of losing control by tapping into the social solidarity and autonomy of childcare providers, since it may improve not only their relationship with the provider but also the relationship between the provider and the child being cared for.

For several days each week, I spent time in the park with my daughter and eventually both my daughter and son. My purpose was twofold. My children benefited from playing and socializing with other children and adults, and I would participate in the conversations and daily activities of different types of people. Mainly I spent time with West Indian childcare providers because they could see I was not a potential employer and thus not a potential nuisance. After all, I was with two children who had a complexion like my own. Somehow my lighter but obviously black phenotype meant that I wasn't a typical (i.e., white) neighborhood member, and because I was using the parks on weekdays the sitters did not at first see me as a "working mother" (the issue of phenotype and my own West Indian identity among the sitters will be taken up in later chapters). In the beginning, I believed that park visits served to let out the energy of children and dispel some of the monotony of the workday at home, but I later found them to involve much more than that. For many babysitters, as well as stay-at-home parents, the public park was a venue for participating in sociability and cultural expression. Complex cultural expression and networking occurred on multiple levels for various parkgoers and partially determined the daily events in which children would be involved. For babysitters, the park became, among other things, a place where food was exchanged and talked about frequently, a central point for meeting before going about daily activities, and a place where solidarity was formed. The children being cared for in this public place became the benefactors of such solidarity and sociability, in part by forming relationships with other children and their caregivers in their neighborhoods, sometimes without their parents' knowledge.

In this book I provide a framework for understanding how social spaces are shaped by West Indian babysitters who move between public and private places in gentrified neighborhoods, how their identities are reconstructed through these spaces, and the meanings they create in their everyday interactions. I illustrate how a group of women who are traditionally viewed as one-dimensional in their work have multidimensional experiences influenced by cultural traditions: through these traditions, communities are formed and a communal life invigorates an otherwise mundane workday.

My position as a field researcher creates inevitable self-consciousness and biases in terms of the interpretations I offer. This is a given drawback in doing fieldwork. However, I can obtain access to certain information that has not yet been written about. The similarity between my heritage and that of my participants allowed me to move from location to location, both public and private, and to trace daily social space construction by looking beyond domestic work alone to define these women's lived experiences. This knowledge was augmented by the longitudinal approach of my participant observation, which allowed me to discriminate between routine behavior and onetime unique events. The longitudinal approach gave depth to my observations and allowed me to form relationships with my participants to a point where I could clearly make meaning out of their daily work lives. Although I cannot truly confirm my acceptance in the group I studied, I have throughout this process had experiences that gave me a unique vantage point on participants' collective life. Through the ethnic background that I shared with these women, I was able to gain insights into a world characterized by striking cultural juxtapositions (between employers and sitters, as well as among sitters) and solidarity within the sitters' shared West Indian culture.

Daily life in the park is filled with mundane activity—a caregiver feeding a child; a child playing on a slide, then on a swing, then going back to the slide; a caregiver providing another feeding. But the women presented in this research have somehow managed to develop a sense of community out of, or in spite of, these routines. The park is a public place, which I define as a physical and geographical structure with specific boundaries that is open to the public. Specifically, I look at public places as points of contact for purposes of socializing, as do other urban and community studies.[3]

Social Space and Public Place

Why are place and social space important? A city location alone cannot provide enough information about a group of people. The study of the way particular ethnic groups come to be associated with a community's image, what Graeme Evans has called the "symbolic association" of a group of people with a community, helps one to truly comprehend how places and social spaces are created.[4] The social spaces occupied by babysitters are considerably more intimate than any other kind of workspace,[5] just as the relationships with families for whom they provide care are more intimate than other kinds of employer-employee relationships, and babysitters are being paid to demonstrate care in a variety of ways and places. Yet for decades many studies of West Indian domestic workers have bypassed the importance of the interaction order within the public place of the park.[6] While it is known that public parks in Brooklyn act as an anchor to the larger community, how they ensure the face-to-face interactions of West Indian sitters has been relatively unresearched. Thus the formation of community and the meanings created by these women within public parks have been overlooked.

The Changing Face of Brooklyn

Understanding Brooklyn as a place is requisite for framing how people use its spaces. The places of Brooklyn have their roots in a history-rich past. The place-names and cultures that ultimately embellished this borough can be traced back to Native Americans, followed by European settlers including the Dutch and English in the 1600s.[7] During colonial times Brooklyn's economy heavily relied on slavery. As early as the mid-1800s Brooklyn was a rapidly developing metropolis that housed a variety of businesses and diverse newcomers, and the bridge built in 1883 would forever change the place by connecting it to Manhattan.

Brooklyn, as one of the most populated cities in America, conceded to its merger with New York by the end of the century and became one of the boroughs of New York. Popular landmarks continue to bring visitors from around the world as well as locals. By the mid-1950s, white flight to the suburbs brought blight to the borough in terms of education, housing, and race relations. It wasn't until the early 1990s that the rapid gentrification of Brooklyn by builders, small business owners, and residents began.

One of my four sites, like many of the gentrified places studied for this book, had a residential history of mainly European working-class migrants. Composed primarily of first-generation Latinos and Italians, it saw a change in population from 1995 to 2005.[8] It is now made up of mostly white upper-middle-class residents from a variety of backgrounds (both European and American), many of them former Manhattanites with young children. The community is currently regarded as an area where professional and college-educated young couples move in.[9] Many of these residents work both in and out of the home. With a higher median household income than in the 1980s, these families seek the comforts of a friendly neighborhood with the unique "Manhattan-style" conveniences.[10] Up until the 1990s Brooklyn was in the shadow of Manhattan as far as being a cultural hub or place that families would seek out for a higher standard of living. It has since developed its own identity as a borough that builders and businesses can invest in and that professionals with families move to, or, as urban sociologists would say, gentrify. The sociologist Sharon Zukin defines gentrification as "a process of spatial and social differentiation" that results from the influx of middle-class people into low-income areas.[11] Gentrification, then, always focuses on changes in the resident population.

Gentrification and Childcare in Brooklyn

Gentrification includes changes in commercial streets and services, but more importantly changes in population demographics and the lifestyle accommodations that are made on behalf of the incoming group. In gentrified areas in Brooklyn, the incoming group includes many two-income households in which both parents work in Manhattan, requiring the services of childcare providers for longer hours to accommodate parents' commuting. It also includes employers who are part of what Richard Florida calls the "creative class," or what the sociologist Julia Wrigley calls the "cultural specialists," working as freelancers from home (four out of ten parents in this research worked from home regularly) but requiring childcare while they work, and thus forcing childcare providers out of the home and into public places.[12] People today celebrate the breaking down of barriers between home and work space, but this can be problematic. Creative class employers have a flexible workday, and their employees must be similarly flexible, with the result that childcare is more difficult, not less. When Mom or Dad is home, providers have limited use of the house or apartment and do not necessarily feel comfortable using the home in the way that they normally would. Often, they must keep the noise level to a minimum so that the employer can work from home, a challenge when dealing with small children, and must repeatedly explain to the children why they cannot enter the area where the parent is working. Consequently childcare providers often spend more weekday hours out in their employers' neighborhood than inside their employers' home.

The sitters use public spaces for work on behalf of the upper middle class, mainly during the weekdays, and their presence as sitters in itself serves to indicate their employers' upper-middle-class status. My research looks at the contradictions that arise out of the obvious racial differences between sitters, their employers, their employers' children, and stay-at-home mothers and their children. These contradictions are continuously negotiated in both the public social spaces created in public parks and the private spaces of the employer's home. This book, therefore, also discusses the sitters' bodies as marked by class and race locations within the social order of public spaces and compares the extent of the sitters' authority in the private space of the employer's home versus the public social spaces of the "white" gentrified neighborhood.[13] It describes the design of the public places, particularly parks, that West Indian babysitters frequent as an influence on their interactions and explores the kinds of control that are exerted in these public places and social spaces.

I learned about the various ways in which West Indian babysitters create and maintain unique collective social spaces while dealing with the tensions and negotiating the power dynamics inherent in their work. Specifically, I observed their acute awareness and understanding of racial and ethnic identity, and of that identity's implications for their workdays. In the parks, I witnessed how special events organized by babysitters for babysitters, and typically centering on the sharing of food, solidified their relationships or sometimes disrupted them.

I also learned from sitters and domestic workers' advocates that some parents "graded" different racial/ethnic groups on their suitability for employment as childcare providers, whether on the Internet or in direct conversation, and that there was a prejudice against West Indians in particular. Some West Indian women I interviewed were cognizant of their disadvantage both in getting hired and in keeping their jobs and therefore went out of their way to accommodate their employers by submitting to requests that exceeded their perceived responsibilities.

Gentrification of an area also raises issues concerning who is entitled to frequent public places because of race and class and the surveillance tactics that employers use to monitor sitters who are working away from the employer's home. The gentrified neighborhood that I resided in and used as one of my research sites maintained a presence from the pregentrification population or "old-timers" who were predominantly Italian and to a lesser extent Latino. Some blacks lived in the neighborhood, but the majority resided in nearby housing projects that were considered hostile territory. Some housing project residents would shop on nearby commercial streets that bordered the gentrifying neighborhood, but that spillover was limited. This was important because it meant that participants in my study were marked racially and probably considered outsiders to many of the old-timers, thereby perhaps facilitating their surveillance in public places. In other gentrifying neighborhoods in Brooklyn with a predominantly black population, such as Fort Greene and Prospect-Lefferts Gardens, or with a substantial black minority among older working-class residents from a variety of backgrounds, such as Park Slope and Boerum Hill, my participants might not have been seen as outsiders in the same way.

While my research took place mainly in smaller public parks in Brooklyn, I also explored other neighborhood areas outside that public place. Public parks were sites that were markers of gentrification in terms of who used them and what type of events would be held throughout the day. Some parks had maintenance employees that parkgoers could call by name if there was a problem or if a toy was requested since some parks stock donated used toys for toddlers. Parents and other community members volunteered their time throughout the workweek to plant flowers, paint trash cans with child-friendly designs, and hold special events such as birthday parties or music shows.

I also studied the meanings created by West Indian babysitters in the public library, in other local play spaces, and even in my own home, where several sitters came to spend time with the children they cared for. Through this shadowing and extended place methods—which sociologist Mitchell Duneier explains as the extension of a study from one local site to other sites as a way of connecting local events and features to larger political, social, and economic events and forces (e.g., moving from a local gathering of homeless people to the city council or corporate offices that produced the policies that created the gathering)—I learned of the intimate relationships these women had with one another and how social spaces could be created in public and then dispersed (though to some degree maintained through cell phone contact) as providers entered the private space of their employer's home.[14]

My research enabled me to learn not only about the workday experiences of these women but also about the educational aspirations that many had, and thus to understand more about their private lives. Though some women expressed fears about going back to school, more often they expressed a desire to further educate themselves. In this aim, they had the moral support of the older babysitters. Often the younger West Indian babysitters viewed domestic work as a stepping-stone to living the American Dream, while older ones viewed it as a way of keeping up their hopes of one day achieving the American Dream.

Most of my time in public parks focused on West Indian women who were hired to care for white children. I slowly discovered that the structure of the workday had several components that led to a social order that embodied race, ethnicity, nationality, and gender. During this ordered workday, much of which was spent in public places, onlookers such as potential employers assessed babysitters and sometimes made reports to Web sites on their actions. Several studies have demonstrated how West Indian women migrate to the United States to find work that can improve their family's life chances and depend on the existing cultural networks to find domestic work.[15] My research is different because it focuses on the lived experiences of this work.

Sample and Methods

I first entered the social group of the childcare providers that I studied through frequent visits to the local park with my newborn daughter in 2004. Indeed, my child acted as an aide throughout my research.[16] In the park, I came to know Hazel, a soft-spoken Grenadian childcare provider in her mid-twenties, who later introduced me to others in her circle, including West Indian babysitters from Guyana, Trinidad, and St. Lucia.

After two months I became a fixture among this group of women: I was introduced to other sitters and participated in daily activities among a variety of social groups with overlapping membership. After two years in the field, I spent several hours each week with babysitters at the park and in other public places such as the local library and children's movement classes, and on playdates held in private homes. While I did not work as a babysitter for other people's children, from the fall of 2004 to the spring of 2007 I spent my days as someone who cared for children throughout the workdays and paid for some additional childcare. Thus I felt that I could somewhat relate to the monotony of the days these childcare providers endured. It is noteworthy that many of these women also had their own biological children to care for outside their duties to their employers, so that their job was far more difficult than my own privileged situation.

Over those three years, I spent time observing West Indian and other childcare providers. I conducted in-depth interviews with twenty-five West Indian childcare providers, ages twenty-five to sixty-one, whom I shadowed regularly as they moved from public parks to their employers' homes and from children's activities to other neighborhood locations. All the women were first-generation West Indian migrants. The majority of the interviewed providers (nine) came from Grenada; of the remainder, six were from Trinidad, three from Guyana, two from St. Lucia, two from Jamaica, two from St. Vincent, and one from Barbados. I also conducted interviews with ten employers whom I lived among.

As a member of the same racial and ethnic group these women belonged to, I found myself treated as a cultural "insider" after spending some time in the parks. This was displayed through the sitters' use of specific West Indian idioms and intentional accent dramatizations that only someone familiar with West Indian culture would understand. I was also seen as a student and college teacher who could help some of the younger babysitters navigate the higher educational system in New York City (see Appendix A for more information). However, my West Indian identity was constantly being challenged by the women in my study, since I am the daughter of Trinidadian parents who emigrated to Canada during the 1960s. Growing up in Canada, I identified as Canadian first and then West Indian and constructed a particular racial identity (black Trinidadian and Indian Trinidadian and others) that perhaps constrained my interactions, a dynamic I discuss later in the book. In negotiating my hours in the field, which included public parks and other places in an area where I resided, I had to consider and carefully time my work as a researcher and as a resident. While not all of my sites for observation were in my neighborhood, several were, and this raised issues.

At times I felt as though my social position was marked because of my ability to reside among several employers of West Indian childcare providers. Not only was I marked visibly by my children as I walked down the sidewalks in the neighborhood, but often, as was mentioned before, on my way to teach as an adjunct lecturer I wore clothes that were significantly different from those I wore in the parks. Often my hair would be styled in a way that showed its natural length (straightened with a hot iron), a characteristic that further exhibited my ethnic status, since many participants wore their hair in shorter styles or wore weaves to make their hair longer. When I encountered the women I studied, they always mentioned what I was wearing, how my hair was kept, or even the official nature of my walk with a bright red briefcase on my shoulder. It became an ongoing joke among us, and I found myself having to justify "the look." For the sake of my book, I wanted these women to feel comfortable with me and not necessarily associate me with their employer's status. I was earning less than what the sitters were making (I made $2,500 over a four-month semester as an adjunct teaching two hours a week while preparing and correcting work for six hours a week) and although I wasn't working as many hours as they did, I still felt that they associated me with the bourgeois residents they encountered on a daily basis while in the neighborhood since I had the "option" of staying home with my children and not having to worry about making an income.

My part-time babysitter was another indicator of my class status in the eyes of the providers I studied. Members of the community I lived in, which was predominantly white, usually hired West Indian providers (and women from other immigrant groups) to care for their children, but my family, considered a West Indian/Canadian/black professional family, hired a white woman (an Italian American who happened to live next to me when I had my first child) as our childcare provider. We chose her because we did not know anyone in the neighborhood and community members had recommended her as someone who had been raised in the neighborhood. This issue of having a white provider did not at first dawn on me as worthy of discussion, but I quickly found out that the providers noticed this white woman with black children at the park. I found myself explaining over and over again how she came to be our babysitter, but the providers never pressed any further in an effort to reserve explicit judgment (although I still felt it when they would comment on her dress or the amount of makeup on her face).

There was a seemingly inherent mistrust among the West Indian babysitters as well that didn't allow many of them to know each other's names, even after seeing one another at parks and other play spaces for over three years. Once I entered the field and babysitters began to understand, not only that I was participating in activities as a parent, but that I had an interest in what West Indian babysitters "did," some sitters chose not to "go on record" to tell me the details of their lives, though they did continue to interact with me and tell me specific information that they felt would be useful for my research. Sometimes it appeared as though having someone to listen to their story was better than having no one to listen at all. They needed a witness to their daily lived experiences, and I was their confidante.

I used my field participation to observe meanings as they were being constructed by participants as well to show patterns of action in their immediate context,[17] and to trace any inconsistencies inherent in the meanings that participants gave during the formal interview process. Semistructured interviews allowed participants to reflect on events while providing more in-depth narratives as constructed or remembered. Some of these semistructured interviews took place in my home, where some of the babysitters and I cooked West Indian food for lunch while the kids played in the house.

Seeing and talking with this group of women all working in the same gentrified neighborhoods at the same job with similar daily experiences, sharing similar cultural values and traditions, I often wondered whether they considered unionizing. Because of this, I wanted to understand the politics behind efforts to organize these women into a more cohesive group where wages were discussed openly and benefits negotiated with employers for a better standard of living. For this reason, I conducted additional interviews at the offices of volunteer organizations such as Domestic Workers United (DWU) and at the time what was called Immigrants Justice Solidarity Project (IJSP), where I also volunteered my time. Through participant observation at DWU and IJSP, I was able to experience the monthly efforts made in outreach work to domestic workers from all over New York City, but primarily to West Indian women from Brooklyn. The volunteer organizations addressed concerns on multiple levels, from training sessions in CPR to free legal services for those whose rights were violated in their workplace. I also questioned local residents, the employers of West Indian childcare providers, local storeowners, and park personnel. I conducted more than twenty-five interviews with the babysitters I shadowed in which I asked about their "immigrant story" and its connection to childcare work. These interviews, carried out on park benches, at private homes, and in coffee shops, lasted between one and four hours. I paid the babysitters fifty dollars when the interviews were complete. This was compensation for their time outside work.

After two years, it became clear which of the daily events, conversations, and activities were typical of everyday public place interaction. Over this period, I was able to fine-tune and expand my ethnographic methods with the use of a digital voice recorder. The recorder itself was usually attached to an outer pocket in my jacket or jeans, or sometimes on my diaper bag. It was used to pick up ambient noises along with some of the conversations I had with those babysitters whom I had met only a few times in the park. All sitters were made aware that the recorder was turned on. I have used pseudonyms because of the sensitive nature of the work these women do, the range of immigration statuses, and the confidentiality that I guaranteed them. For the voices of people who were not intending to be recorded in public places (e.g., a babysitter who came up to talk with a sitter that I was interviewing or with whom I was having a recorded conversation) I have also used pseudonyms after receiving their consent.

While several of the childcare providers who informed my research made clear what should be presented as an accurate portrait of their lives, I have selected only the narratives and other material that I feel illustrate their experiences as childcare providers in both public and private places. Interpretations of the research material presented in this book are based on my own working knowledge and the tools of ethnographic analysis, which I detail in Appendix A.

My goal has been to make the ideas, sentiments, and voices of the participants heard. To ensure this, I have included in quotation marks reasonably accurate transcriptions of conversations. In some cases, I have taken the liberty of slightly editing some of the dialect without risking changes in meaning in order to illustrate main ideas more clearly (e.g., when they said "deh" I would write it out as "they"). I have sometimes altered descriptors of the main participants in order to preserve confidentiality, since some babysitters could be easily identified. The terms *babysitter, sitter, nanny,* and *childcare provider* are used interchangeably, reflecting their interchangeable usage by participants themselves.

Terminology

Occupational Titles for Childcare

I was sitting at a table in a coffeehouse, reading for my oral exams in graduate school, when I overheard a customer talking on her cell phone as she was heading out the door with her child, whom she was pushing in a stroller. She was white and appeared to be upper middle class in that the stroller was a Bugaboo costing perhaps $800. The son was by my guess about a year old, since I had earlier seen him walking but still a little wobbly on his feet. The woman was saying, "I need someone just a few days a week. I just want to cry. It's not that Thomas's too much, it's that everything is too much."

But who is this "someone"? To construct a meaningful way of discussing childcare providers I wanted to have a concrete term that would be respectful to the people participating in this work, the people who are fighting for the labor rights of these workers, and the readers of this book. Judith Rollins's work on African American domestic workers and their dyadic relationship with their white female employers in Boston pointed out that domestic workers did not like the term *girl,* as did Shellee Colen in her domestic work research on West Indian women in New York when she said, "Many protest being referred to as 'the girl' or 'the maid.'"[18]

The term *nanny,* as popularized by shows such as *Supernanny* and *Nanny 911,* whose characters are all white and British, was used by West Indian childcare providers and throughout the mass media (as in "nanny-cams"). Only after I had immersed myself among West Indian childcare providers and their employers did I notice that terms such as *babysitter, sitter,* and *caregiver* were being used interchangeably with *nanny.* In an effort to understand this further, I asked some of my participants to explain how they defined their role in the work that they did. Perhaps, I imagined, the sitters, when speaking among themselves, would use different terms, and accord them different meanings, than employers would use among their peers or with their "own" child. I wanted to know if they used terms such as *servant,* as Julia Wrigley does when writing about domestic workers.[19] One November morning, while swinging my children on the swing set in the public park beside Hazel (who is from Grenada) and the child she cared for, I asked, "Do you call yourselves 'nannies'?" She told me that they called themselves sitters or babysitters but that the "parents call them nannies in order to make themselves seem important." Hazel was alluding to parents' attempts to claim upper-middle-class status by having private in-home childcare, a class marker among white women.[20]

By demonstrating the ability to hire an outside childcare provider, upper middle-class employers are publicly announcing their class status and thereby symbolically reconstituting it at the same time. It should be noted that no employer or West Indian worker ever used the term *servant.* However, not all babysitters felt the same way about specific terms.

During a conversation with Janet one afternoon, she used the term *nanny* to describe the other West Indian women in the neighborhood that she worked with. I stopped her right there to ask: "Why do you say *nanny* and not *babysitter*?" She said, "Nanny, babysitter, it's the same thing." Molly, Rachel, and Debbie, who were all close by, seemed to agree. Rachel, however, seemed more critical of my question and said, "Well, some people may think that 'nanny' is at the very bottom [of the social/employment hierarchy], and then some people may think that saying 'nanny' is something more than just a babysitter because maybe they cook and clean." Molly and Debbie began to explore this further by saying that they know women who "cook, clean, shop, wash clothes . . ." I asked: "Do these sitters get paid more than if they only care for the children?" and Molly said no, not necessarily. So while some of the childcare providers distinguished between terms on the basis of how they reflected the employer's status, others did so on the basis of the amount of responsibilities one had during a workday, and still others did not distinguish between the terms at all. In the end, it didn't matter which term I used in the field: all of the childcare providers encountered multiple terms and in the end understood what they denoted.

I asked the same questions of a worker at Domestic Workers United (DWU), an organization that is currently attempting to organize domestic workers in New York City. Which of the terms such as *nanny, housekeeper,* and *childcare worker* was most reflective of the work domestics did, or was most respected by employees? I wanted to understand how domestics perceived their position. Ai-jen, the director, responded, "I think that there's a range. I think that what we try to . . . do in terms of language . . . and recognizing that language is also very powerful in how people view this work . . . we try to really like talk about our identity and our role as workers. . . . And then I think we like to recognize that it's important to also reclaim . . . and bring dignity to some ways in which we are defined by society . . . but that terms like *help,* for example, aren't helpful . . . or *maid,* you know, we don't generally use those kind of terms. . . . But, anything like *worker* or *housekeeper,* or anything like that, we feel like yeah, that's the profession, and it should be respected."

I then asked Ai-jen more specifically about the terms *nanny* versus *babysitter,* since in my fieldwork sitters disagreed regarding them. Ai-jen responded that in her work contention did sometimes arise surrounding such terms but that "it's not usually that significant." She continued, "I mean, it definitely comes up, and some people prefer *babysitter* and some people prefer *nanny.* Like some people feel like *nanny* sounds more professional . . . and some people feel the other way around. . . . So, I think in general we tend to support the ways in which workers define it, or what they like to be called . . . unless it is in some way directly derogatory or something . . . unless, you know, people feel like we need to reclaim *maid,* which some workers may feel better reflects the work that is being done."

Recognizing that language does play a role in how society in general views domestic work and childcare work more specifically, Ai-jen offered more explanation about using a term such as *maid* to describe the work that domestic workers do: "You know, and they feel like that might make sense under some set of conditions. But in general it's about really talking about the fact that without this work, nothing else could happen. And that's always been true, and . . . it's part of how patriarchy has shaped our society and economy that like the whole system and society is built on taking for granted the work that women have done to raise families. . . . You know, there would be no working class without women raising the working class, you know?" Ai-jen's comment refers to a point that has been made by several scholars: the structure of the American labor market affects how housework and family work are constituted and who performs them.[21]

Childcare providers' willingness to accept a variety of titles to describe the work they did gave me the impression that what they considered important was really the work they did (although that work seemed to go unrecognized often by the employers), not how it might be categorized. A provider's use of one work title over another might also have had something to do with the social status of childcare and domestic work "back home": if in the home country certain terms used for domestic work referred to positions that were respected, the childcare providers in Brooklyn would use those terms.

I use *childcare provider* when speaking of my participants in general, but where the providers themselves used a specific title, I adhere to that specific term. In addition, I use other terms such as *sitter* or *babysitter* since these are the most common terms used in the field among West Indian childcare providers.

"My" Child

When employers talked with me about their childcare providers, they often used a metaphor of family, as in "Oh, we just love her, she is like family." Sometimes employers took advantage of this: for example, asking providers to work later than usual by making them feel as if all "family" members had to chip in. Providers attempted to push back on such requests by rationalizing the job situation and defining boundaries: setting hours, explicitly outlining responsibilities, and itemizing tasks that they refused to do. Employers might see this as laziness or inflexibility, but the control that providers were trying to gain could be seen as a way to make the hierarchical employer-employee relationship more equal.

Working in people's homes, a situation that fostered isolation and unclear boundaries, led childcare providers to slip into family metaphors as well: talking about the child as if the child were family and, at times, expressing pride and satisfaction when the children being cared for seemed closer to them than to the parent. And although West Indian babysitters did not encourage the children they cared for to call them anything but their first name, the amount of awake, hands-on caring time that children spent with providers, which included everything from feeding, to being tucked in for naps, to being taken out to play in the park, contributed to the tendency of children to refer to their sitters as "Mommy" or "Mama."

Often, these sitters took on the responsibility of treating the children they cared for as their own, as one sitter, Flora, explained to me. After commenting that the other nannies in the park were "mostly nice, but some are not so attentive with the children, but most of them are nice," she continued, "We all take care of these children as if they are our own because we wouldn't want someone not taking care of our children." An indicator of this attitude was the sitters' tendency to refer to the child they cared for as "my child," a phrase that sounded parental when said. I saw this occur when I was invited to come with my daughter to a "playdate" that Sara, from Grenada, hosted in her employer's home. During the many formula feedings that occurred in the hours that I was participating in this playdate, the nannies would all boast about which child could hold their bottle on his or her own. But it was more than boasting; the personal attachment that they felt towards these children quickly turned the boasting into a competition. Catherine could be heard saying, "Look at Sally, look at her, well, *my* child can already hold her bottle by herself." All the babysitters laughed. Soon after, Molly, one of the matriarchs of the childcare provider community—a black Guyanese childcare provider in her early sixties, mother to seven children who were now all adults—piped up with "Well, *my* child can almost stand up and she's only nine months old." This professional competition over who could do what continued, indicating a constructed norm that the childcare provider was doing her job well, but what was most striking was the phrase "my child," used consistently throughout the conversation and in a tone that emphasized possessiveness.

Another incident, which occurred at the public library at storytime, showed both a sitter and a child using the term *mama* to refer to a childcare provider. That day, I was with both of my children and a few of the providers and their charges. At one point during a storytime session, I had to deal with a problem with my daughter, so Molly took my son and held him. Immediately the two-year-old girl that Molly cared for came up to her as Debbie, another provider, said to the little girl from over my left shoulder, "You want your mama." Molly then stated that the little girl was jealous because she was holding my son, so I took my son back up in my arms. Then Taylor, Debbie's charge, came over to Debbie, calling "Mama" and again two more times, "Mama, Mama," and Debbie responded to her without hesitation. I would think the child's use of this name for the sitter would pierce the heart of any mother who heard it (or perhaps not, because it was at least an indication that the child felt secure). It was not the first time I had heard children call their sitter "Mama" or "Mommy." The sitters just responded to the children and didn't correct them. (The children were often not corrected for saying "Mommy" when out in the playground until they "should know better," according to a sitter I overheard one day in the park.) Perhaps this nonresponse should come as no surprise given the sitters' expressed indifference, for the most part, regarding what occupational titles they were given. It became increasingly obvious that these children were close to the sitters, who would eventually be replaced by other kinds of caregivers (teachers, other family members, family friends) who could not be mistaken for their "mama."

Providers' and Employers' Terms for Each Other

In my fieldwork, I never heard a childcare provider call her employer by his or her first name, but I did hear employers call a provider by hers. Providers would often refer to their employer as "the mother of the child." Calling one's employer by his or her first name would be considered disrespectful or else might suggest that the provider was "too close" to her employer (an issue taken up later in the book). Some employees couldn't even remember the names of their employers because they did not call them by name (much as providers did not necessarily know each other's names but could still recognize each other). Others, when asked the name of their employer, had to think about it for a while. Frequent turnover in childcare jobs, even within the span of a few years, and frequent work for more than one family at a time could be another reason for this.

Some employers were less comfortable with the term *babysitter* than the childcare providers, perhaps because they felt it devalued the work being done in the home or because it made them feel uncomfortable to admit that they needed childcare. Other employers, however, used the term freely, perhaps because it suggested casual, occasional work and thus downplayed the amount of time they spent apart from their children. Some simply used the term because the provider herself did.

The Term *Ladies*

Sitters used the term *ladies* to refer to other West Indian sitters. I would often hear one provider speak of other West Indian providers as "the ladies sitting over there" or say something like "The ladies will be coming to the park just now." It appeared that the term was used not to indicate a job-based identity but rather in some way to elevate the childcare providers' status. In addition, the sitters saw the term *ladies* as a call for respect when it was applied to other childcare providers, since in the Caribbean titles are often used for family members or even close friends of the family. For example, my children called all of the providers they met in the park "Auntie" because in Trinidad you must address the elders you visit regularly with respect. To call a person, especially an elder, by his or her first name is considered rude.

Plan of the Book

I begin the empirical portion of this book with a chapter addressing the history of domestic work in New York City and how West Indian women came to be one of the dominant groups that do this type of work. This first chapter also looks at the economic conditions in New York households, specifically those of the white middle class, that create the demand for low-wage workers. Through an analysis of national ethnic identities and a pan-ethnic identity that I am calling "West Indianness," this chapter shows how West Indian childcare providers saw their role in the Brooklyn communities where they worked, as well as the divisiveness that was sometimes expressed between childcare providers of different ethnic, national, and racial identities.

Chapters 2 and 3 concern childcare providers' use of public places and spaces during the workweek. In chapter 2 I look at how West Indian childcare providers used and interacted in Brooklyn public parks and how local residents, parents, and a park employee perceived them. Chapter 3 identifies the other places where West Indian childcare providers took the children they cared for, either on behalf of their employers or because they wanted to occupy their workdays with events: specifically public libraries and movement studios that offered classes for young children and their parents or caregivers.

Foodways were a key element in the preservation of West Indian culture among the childcare providers I studied. Chapter 4 takes a closer look at these foodways in a variety of public and private places to determine the meanings of West Indian food for this group of women in terms of culture and identity. Providers discussed how they shared food with each other, how they associated food preparation with good mothering, and how they judged their employers on the basis of food issues.

Providers frequently used cell phones to construct workday norms and patterns of interaction. Chapter 5 discusses cell phones as one of the tools that providers now need to do their job effectively. However, the question of who is responsible for ensuring that this "tool" is managed and paid for becomes important to understanding how domestic work has evolved. Providers viewed their personal cell phones as a means for reaching out to one another and to family back in the islands, but some employers felt that cell phone use should be work related, limited to such functions as keeping employers involved in what was going on at home or contacting help in an emergency. This chapter also discusses surveillance, through the use of both cell phones and the Internet, as a dimension of childcare employment that

West Indian providers had to contend with. Nanny-cams, parenting blogs, and frequent calls by employers have created a dynamic between employers and employees that often goes unacknowledged in studies of domestic work.

Chapter 6 looks at the informal economic savings accounts called "susus" among West Indian childcare providers. This chapter provides a small window into the world of providers that is rooted in the preservation of culture. The providers go into detail about the structure of susus, how the saved money is used, and why this institution works or doesn't work. Finally, chapter 7 looks specifically at how one organization, Domestic Workers United, is trying to formally organize West Indian domestic workers in and around New York City to obtain labor rights that would include a minimum hourly rate, a signed contract between employer and employee, severance pay, and other benefits.

This book draws on the varied perspectives of the many people I interviewed, including the providers, their employers, members of Domestic Workers United, park employees, and other people who worked in public spaces to describe how the West Indian childcare providers I studied used public places and found ways to live collectively during their workweek.[22] Understanding the networks between childcare providers can help employers not only to obtain the childcare they seek but also to gain a broader sense of the relationships that are building the social worlds of their children. This book shows how the complex networks of childcare providers benefit employers, providers, and children alike. It also promotes understanding of the tensions involved in childcare work in both the private and the public spheres and how these affect relationships between providers, between employers and employees, and between providers and the children under their care. The group of women who became the subject of this book helped me to connect personally and professionally with West Indian culture in the form of social groups that confront everyday experiences while giving depth to a world that is not widely written about. I hope to bring this to life and to provide a glimpse of the dynamic collectivity that these women share.

1
West Indians Raising New York

One day in 2007 I sat at my dining room table with Jennie, a thirty-four-year-old childcare provider from Grenada, while the girl she cared for and my two children played in the living room together. Jennie and I were engaging in one of our formal interviews after two years of observation. Although we interrupted the interview several times to make sure that the children weren't getting into trouble as they moved from the living area to the bedrooms, we were able to speak deeply about Jennie's work as a childcare provider and how it had affected her outlook on the field of domestic work in general. Jennie usually wore dreadlocks tied up with a scarf or in a bun. She cared for two siblings: one boy, who was six years old and in school during the weekdays, and Sam, a two-year-old girl. She had aspired to be a registered nurse back in Grenada, but because she needed more coursework than she could afford she ended up working instead at a day care center for a few months and then as a newspaper reporter in her homeland. She received a visitor's visa to come to the United States while still in her twenties and then stayed past her visa expiration. When I asked her why she had come to New York, she said she had cousins, an uncle, and her sister living here and wanted a fresh start in life. It had taken her a year to find work as a babysitter. One of the poignant remarks she made during our interview showed me that she viewed her work as a childcare provider in a broad historical context. She began, "After you know that we were once enslaved, and knowing how we were treated by white people and how our forefathers were treated by white people, how could you not treat us better after you know what it's like, I mean what it still is. . . . I think we have slavery now, it just happens differently." Jennie was expressing a politicized understanding of black childcare providers' shared history of subordination and exploitation. Her words may at first seem harsh, but they speak to the history that the people most profoundly affected by it have never forgotten.

To understand the complex work lives of the women I discuss in this book, it is important to first understand what that work entails and what its history is. Childcare providers fall under the rubric of domestic workers, a category that in recent years has come to include a variety of duties. The responsibilities of the group of domestic workers in this study involved primarily childcare, although there were some additional duties such as housecleaning, grocery shopping, and walking the dog. Childcare itself included such tasks as feeding the children, reading to them, bathing them, taking them to lessons or playdates, taking them on walks, arranging their birthday parties, and helping with schoolwork. The typical day extended anywhere from seven in the morning to seven in the evening, three to five days a week, although the majority of the women in my study worked from eight in the morning to five in the evening. Most of the women I observed and later interviewed interacted mainly with a female employer, and three interacted mainly with a male employer (the husband) who worked flexible hours during the day, although in almost every case the female employer took care of the payments to the provider and communicated the schedule that the provider would have to follow. In this chapter I discuss the historical trajectory of Caribbean-born immigrant women, the focus of this book, who have gained employment primarily as domestic workers.[1] An overview of the history of domestic work in the United States will set the stage for the discussion of domestic work as an occupational field for West Indian immigrant women, particularly in New York. I will trace the changing relationship between domestic workers and employees, especially in the context of racial relations, social constructions of race, and a changing labor market.

History of West Indian Immigration and Domestic Work

West Indian migration to New York began in the late nineteenth century and continued into the early twentieth century as a result of unemployment "push" factors from the Caribbean and opportunity "pull" factors from the United States.[2] Between 1900 and 1910, around thirty thousand West Indians immigrated to the United States, many of them highly literate and highly skilled as professionals or white-collar workers—more so even than the native-born white population in the United States or European immigrants.[3] This group laid the foundation for Afro-Caribbean life in New York City.[4] A steady increase in immigration, due to the economic hardships of the declining sugar industry between 1910 and 1924, had brought this number to one hundred thousand when immigration was halted by Congress. The Immigration Act of 1924, which restricted nonwhite and European immigration via a quota system, decreased but did not entirely stop Caribbean migration to the United States.

By the 1930s, one-half of black immigrants went to New York.[5] At that time, over 90 percent of these immigrants were of Caribbean descent, constituting a fifth to a quarter of New York's black population.[6]

Between 1940 and 1950, over four hundred thousand African American women left domestic employment to obtain work in factories, shipyards, and other war-related industries, where they could earn relatively decent wages. At the same time, Caribbean immigration began to increase because in the Caribbean many workers were being forced off the farms and had to find work elsewhere; these immigrants found low-skilled work in agriculture and soon in other sectors of the American economy, since the percentage of professionals among West Indian immigrants was beginning to decline.[7]

At the end of the war, many African Americans and women of other ethnic or racial groups were laid off and economically forced to return to domestic labor in private homes. But by 1945, and increasingly afterward, some African American women, resisting the return to domestic service, found jobs in manufacturing and in offices, and their upward mobility allowed Caribbean immigrants to establish themselves in the low-wage positions that African American women had vacated. Such positions proliferated after the mid-1970s.[8] Caribbean women could obtain American visas much more easily than Caribbean men and thus solidified their position in the domestic sphere.[9]

By 2001, West Indians ages twenty-five to fifty-four made up 58 percent of New York's black population.[10] West Indian women have played a crucial role in New York's economy by providing low-wage domestic services, thus supporting white middle-class (and in this case upper-middle-class) employment.[11] (Nonwhite employers have tended to depend mainly on familial or kinship networks or on paid day care centers as primary childcare.) In the 1960s West Indian women came to New York with the assurance of gaining a work visa for domestic work that would eventually allow for future mobility.[12] Other West Indian women who came to the United States later overstayed their tourist or education visas to remain in the United States, a practice that continues today.[13] They were also considered more likely to send money back home (compared to their male counterparts) in the form of remittances.[14] These women made substantial sacrifices, which sometimes included leaving more prestigious professional careers back in their native homelands, in the hopes of providing their families with the "American Dream."[15] That dream, however, has been limited for first-generation West Indian women, who have for the most part experienced downward mobility, housing segregation, and limited economic opportunities leading to their employment in the domestic services sector.[16]

In New York City, where, at various periods of history, the majority of non-Hispanic black immigrants in the United States have lived, white upper-middle-class working women, unlike their black counterparts, have often depended on this group for their domestic needs, specifically childcare.[17] In particular, West Indian domestic workers/childcare providers are hired for a variety of reasons, including that, for most, their native language is English, they have more education on average than their Latino immigrant counterparts, and they will accept lower wages than some other groups of childcare providers.[18]

White upper-middle-class households continue to maintain distinct divisions of labor along both gender and class lines.[19] Although over the last few decades men have participated more in housework and childcare, these tasks are still the primary responsibility of women, including employed women.[20] Women are forced into a balancing act of contributing to household income as wage-earning women while experiencing a crisis in terms of meeting in-home domestic responsibilities.[21] "The second shift," as Hochschild and Machung have called it—taking care of the home after working outside the home—leads to stress and guilt among working middle-class women, who feel that their children may suffer from their absence.[22] In the absence of publicly provided childcare or available assistance from family members, white working women who can afford it often cope with these feelings by looking for outside domestic help, specifically low-cost "off the books" immigrant domestic help.[23] This allows them to feel secure in their "commitments to personal ideologies of care," in which employing a private childcare worker in the home is considered preferable to using outside public day care.[24] Ruth Milkman, Ellen Reese, and Benita Roth show how the macroeconomic structure of New York influences this reliance on private childcare as well.[25] Urban centers have a higher maternal labor force rate and thus a greater demand for domestic care. As the economic disparity in urban centers increases, the rich hire the poor to do private domestic work, supporting further economic disparity. This dynamic, especially in a place like New York City, sets the conditions for West Indian and other immigrants who come to the United States looking for employment.

Recent West Indian Migration to New York

New York City census tract figures across the span of the three decades ending in 1980, 1990, and 2000 for place of birth and employment by gender show that the percentage of West Indian women in New York City who are employed has increased more than the comparable percentage for West

Indian men.[26] These numbers are not adjusted for the probable undercounting of undocumented people.

Census data also show an increase, over three decades (1980, 1990, 2000) in the percentage of those employed West Indian women who are in the childcare occupation. Again, numbers are not adjusted for the possible undercounting of undocumented people. For Brooklyn specifically we see increases, from 1980 to the latest 2006/2008 census, among West Indians (mostly women) aged sixteen and up who reported themselves to be "childcare workers." In 1980 such workers numbered 980, in 1990 they numbered 1,752, in 2000 they numbered 7,007, and in 2006/08 they numbered 9,232.[27] Numbers can at best only be estimated, since many West Indians are reluctant to say they are babysitters or childcare workers and perhaps say instead that they are cosmetologists or identify their occupation by whatever other training they may have received.[28] Also, many are working for cash and may be reluctant to say too much to the Census Bureau.

Many transnational families have changed in their patterns of migration. In the early 1900s, men typically settled overseas and gradually brought other family members to join them. West Indian women, however, have had a long history of migrating and leaving their families behind in the homeland, a phenomenon that has been termed "transnational motherhood."[29] Transnational mothers are Filipina and Latin American as well as West Indian, and together these groups make up the great majority of transnational mothers in the United States.[30] West Indian childcare providers have immigrated to the United States both with their families (including their children and/or husbands) and on their own.

Flora, an Indo-Trinidadian sitter in her mid-thirties who had two children (ages eight and eleven) and was married to a West Indian man, described to me the "push factors" that had influenced her decision to migrate.[31] She had moved to the United States with her husband fifteen years ago because occupational opportunities in Trinidad were so limited. She stated, "There is a lack of opportunity in Trinidad—if you are not highly educated and working for the government, there is little reason to remain there. Everyone here does an honest day's work. . . . You can do anything and work as anything here. . . . Crime rates in Trinidad have escalated in the past few years and it is because of the government. . . . All of the top executives are pocketing the international monies being made instead of giving it to the people through the creation of jobs."

Catherine, a sitter from Guyana in her mid-twenties, was single and had no children. She had moved to New York around five years earlier and now lived in Brooklyn. Back home in Guyana she had worked as a data entry analyst, but here she had found employment in childcare. When I asked her if this was her career, she replied, "No, this is just for now until I make enough money. . . . I want to go to school for nursing eventually, but haven't found the time to research how to go about doing it. . . . Many of the sitters feel the same way, but do actually enjoy what they are doing." When I asked why she chose New York, she said that she had family already living here. This was a recurring theme among sitters. Many of these women found the transition to New York easier when they had family already living there who could put them in contact with employers and who had an established residence that could serve as an interim place to stay.[32] In a sense, these women were fostered into the homes of their relatives. Specifically, West Indians found it easier to settle in Brooklyn (also in Queens and the Bronx) because these boroughs feature a distinct Caribbean ethnic enclave, including stores run by West Indians that sell many of the products, such as West Indian produce, other foods and spices, and hair care products, that they would get in their homelands, giving them a sense of comfort.

The large number of women immigrating from the Caribbean is reflected in New York's childcare industry and the presence in Brooklyn of one of the largest West Indian ethnic enclaves, many of whose residents work in a domestic capacity. Brooklyn is thus a prime area for the study of West Indian women and domestic work.

Concept of "West Indianness" and Group Ethnic Identity

The term *West Indian* as it is used throughout this book implies a uniform group identity used by all of the childcare providers I studied. While some providers came from Guyana, which is geographically part of South America, they all referred to themselves as West Indian or Caribbean and as such identified with other childcare providers from the Caribbean region.[33] This group identity differs from the racial identity of being black, although many of the childcare providers claimed that identity as well.[34] As noted by the sociologist Philip Kasinitz in his book *Caribbeans in New York*, the notion of "black" is problematic: it is a social construction whose meaning varies across space and time.[35]

The categories of race, then, differ from those of ethnicity, which "implies that a group shares a real or mythological common past and cultural focus, the central defining characteristic of ethnic groups is the belief in their own existence as groups."[36] The common features that make up group ethnic identity include shared "practices, languages, behaviors, or ancestral origins."[37] The West Indian women I encountered often referred to themselves as black, Caribbean, or West Indian. Their acceptance of a pan-ethnic label formed through the shared experience of an occupation in childcare allowed the women under study to construct certain norms that counteracted some of the injustices to which they found themselves subjected in the workplace. As I observed it over a three-year period, the acceptance of a pan-ethnic identity also facilitated the formation of everyday collective relationships in public spaces. This pan-ethnicity did have premigration antecedents: many who had worked previously in the Caribbean nations would have encountered others from various islands, and there are extensive occupationally driven migration patterns between countries such as Grenada and Trinidad or Guyana and Trinidad. Politically also there is a tradition of invoking an inclusive West Indian identity to demonstrate solidarity and power.

Consistent with sociologist Mary Waters's research on West Indians, I found identities among the childcare providers to be interchangeable, or what some might describe as fluid.[38] Sometimes the providers called themselves or others "island people," "immigrants," "Caribbean," or "West Indian"; at other times they would simply give a national identity, such as "Trinidadian" or "Guyanese." This flexibility in claiming ethnic identities was also found in the research by the sociologist Aubrey Bonnett on West Indians who participated in the informal economy by constructing a community "susu," or group in which people pooled money for savings purposes and redistributed it to the members at various times throughout the year.[39] Bonnett, as a West Indian himself, studied susus among the Caribbean community in New York to determine how they operated and under what conditions they were maintained, how community members benefited from them, and what type of identity was created by participating in one. One researcher quoted by Bonnett stated that there was a "tendency of West Indians—new immigrants and descendants of the old—to refer to other West Indians as 'one of us' or 'one of them,'" although they might have no accent or might have never visited the West Indies, and a corresponding tendency among most Americans to view black immigrants from the West Indies as a single, monolithic group.[40]

Jennie, whose voice we heard at the beginning of this chapter expressing her consciousness of the political implications of black people's domestic work, told me that working as a babysitter was different in the United States than back in Grenada: "In the islands, you don't do this as a way of life, you may do it once in a while, but not every day." She had left her homeland in pursuit of higher education. While she didn't use class-based terms, like *middle class,* to define her background, she did say she had lived a comfortable life while growing up in Grenada. Jennie and her siblings had finished high school, her mother owned their house, Jennie had never gone without food, and, in her words, "There were always people less fortunate than us." Jennie had grown up primarily under the care of her grandmother while her mother worked off and on in Trinidad as a secretary. Her mother had now settled in Grenada where she owned a "shop" (grocery store). Jennie did not have a relationship with her father, who now lived in Canada. In New York, Jennie started working with "older folks doing companion jobs as a live-in job." She was paid $120 each weekend, but she didn't like living with families and stated, "We're not used to that in the islands, we're not used to these kinds of jobs. We're in another man's land, life is different, whatever certificates you have, nobody takes it."

Because of Jennie's statement about the differences between Grenada and the United States and because of her use of the word *we,* I asked her what it felt like being in New York where there was a large population from the Caribbean and whether that had made her job transition any easier. She answered, "When you're here [in a white neighborhood] and you see someone [another black woman], you want to run outside [and say,] 'I just know she is from the islands.' . . . You feel more at home, because even if you don't know them or where they're from, you just know from a distance that 'hey, I know she's from the islands . . . although they may be [African] American."

I asked Jennie if having a West Indian identity was important to her. She said that it helped when sitters were out in public and saw other sitters from a West Indian background. At the park, she went on, "you just meet your own. . . . Even if you don't talk to every nanny you meet, you just feel comfortable, you're among your people. When you're at home [the employer's home], you know you're just working, you're not among your own people." Jennie felt that the comfort of being around Caribbean women in parks and other public spaces translated into a tolerable life for a childcare provider, unlike that of working in the suburbs, where sitters might not see others of their same ethnic group. I then asked if this West Indian group identity formed by childcare providers in public spaces, and the increasing diversity that Jennie had noted in gentrified neighborhoods, were enough to make her want to live in an area like that where her employers lived (at the time she lived in Crown Heights near Flatbush Avenue, which was known among the childcare providers as a West Indian shopping street). She replied, "It's a rich neighborhood, mainly white. Would I want to live here, no, because I'm not around my people. Even if I don't know them, I know they are from the islands and I know they are my people. I know they're from the islands and my food is there, I like my circle, that's where I feel comfortable. So even if I had a million dollars, I wouldn't live here."

Jennie knew that my husband (who is of Jamaican descent) and I lived across the street from her employer. So I was interested to understand her view of my West Indianness and the expectations a West Indian childcare provider would have of an employer from the same ethnic background. She told me, "Working for you would be different than working for a white person . . . because you could relate in so many ways. In terms of culture, even if you're not from the islands, because you're black I kind of expect that you would treat me better." Jennie was careful, though, to note that often black employers from Africa, the Caribbean, or America did not pay as much as white employers.

Intergroup Dynamics

To "outsiders" such as stay-at-home parents or sitters of European descent, all of the black babysitters in Brooklyn's public places might appear to be "West Indian." But sitters who "appeared" to be the same were not necessarily.[41] Not all black women in the public parks under study were of West Indian descent: a few were African American. On occasion, members of the two groups clashed, according to Marga, a park employee who worked in one of my sites.

Marga was a woman in her late fifties with a sixteen-year-old daughter. She had a full head of gray hair, deep wrinkles in her narrow face, and a cigarette that she felt comfortable smoking only if she went behind the washroom area so the park children couldn't see her, and in her words she was several generations "white American." She described to me an incident between an African American babysitter and a West Indian babysitter: "One time . . . an African American sitter who has been a sitter in the park for as long as I've been here . . . was jealous because these Caribbean sitters were coming in and watching kids full time and she was always part time, couldn't get a full time. And I know one day she was giving one of the Caribbean sitters a hard time because she said that the sitter wasn't taking care of the child properly. . . . I finally had to ask her to leave."

I clarified, "The African American sitter?"

"Yeah, yeah, because I knew her better than the others, so I said just go, because we don't need any fights here, you know. Somebody was saying they were going to call 911. . . . It got heated . . . you know, just yelling back and forth. . . . Well, some of the parents who were in the park, you know, trying to break it up because you do not want your children to see two grown women fighting. Right? . . . So I just did the best I could to get there to get her out of the park."

"And so have they confronted each other again?" I asked.

"I don't think so, I don't think so. I think she just kind of stays away from them [Caribbean sitters]. I know she sits around and talks about the Caribbean sitters all the time."

Carol, a West Indian childcare provider whom we'll hear more from in later chapters, also had a confrontation with an African American sitter in the public park once when she passed the African American woman and by accident brushed against her arm. The woman called out some derogatory phrase about 'immigrants . . . all you immigrants,' and Carol immediately yelled back, "You're not in your freakin' bedroom . . . I said bitch . . . I pay Uncle Sam to stay here, I have plenty money . . . and furthermore don't talk to me because Uncle Sam gives you dental free, so go fix your mouth."

Carol was even more upset because the woman was "a black woman just like me. . . . We [West Indian babysitters] always say these black Americans don't like us. . . . From the time they hear we're from the Caribbean, they want to treat you like shit. . . . From the time they hear you talk, they have a different attitude . . . but we don't come here and take nothing from them." The African American woman had responded, "All of all you come here and take all the jobs." Carol took this comment to heart, later exclaiming to me, "Them don't like to work, they hate to work." She justified this outburst by saying that when it had come time for her to apply for her green card, her sponsor and then employer had been required to post the job for a certain amount of time in which no African Americans applied for the position.[42] Unfortunately, the idea that African Americans don't like to work is a common stereotype that has been perpetuated historically through all forms of media and political propaganda both here in the United States and more recently in the Caribbean nations. This stereotype finds its way into the dynamics between two groups of people who could potentially fight common injustices if unified. The sociologist Mary Waters, in her research on West Indians in New York, has explored the complex relations between them and African Americans, who have faced similar oppression and discrimination. She shows how West Indians attempt to distance themselves from African Americans because of the risk of being seen as stereotypical "lazy" workers. Milton Vickerman, another sociologist who has written extensively about the complexities of race and ethnicity in America for West Indian immigrants, has also discussed this social distancing phenomenon and has shown how exposure to racism in the United States causes West Indian newcomers to shift from nonracial paradigms to racial ones.[43] Because of this shift West Indian childcare providers are able to construct themselves as the ideal choice for the subordinated carework that they do on a daily basis.

The "Other" Island People

Tensions and stereotyping were present not only between African American and West Indian babysitters but to some degree between babysitters who came from different islands in the Caribbean. A conversation I had with two West Indian childcare providers, Molly, who was Guyanese, and Rachel, who was from St. Lucia, showed how Jamaican babysitters could be stereotypically viewed as tough and "bad" because they came from a "bad island," referring to the well-publicized political controversies surrounding the Rastafarian drug-related image. Molly said, "This Jamaican babysitter I know has to cook, clean, wash clothes, and take care of the children. . . . She's one of the good Jamaicans." "And she's Jamaican," Rachel remarked. ". . . They don't usually do that stuff." In the same conversation, I asked Rachel, a provider in her late twenties who lived on her own in a rented apartment near Prospect Park, how Trinidadians were viewed in the playground and as part of the babysitter community. She replied, "They walk around like they're better than us sometimes. It's not that they're bad or anything, it's just a feeling you get." As soon as she said this, Janet pointed to me and said to Rachel, "You know she's from Trinidad, right?" Rachel, now looking slightly embarrassed, said, "Yes, but you know, she's different . . . she's more like one of us." Not understanding how I should take this because I knew Rachel had said before that she felt I was "a student, and a mother, and trying to get further just like one of us," I chuckled along with the other women at Rachel's comments and just left it alone. Rachel appeared to make distinctions about me as the researcher, me as a part of the West Indian babysitter community in the neighborhood, and me as the "other."

Most of the West Indian babysitters appreciated each other's work and the relationships that they had with each other. One warm afternoon, Rachel told me about her relationship to Molly, describing it as a mother-daughter relationship: "Molly is older than me and she's like my mom in a sense. She gives me advice and talks to me and says you can't do this forever, you are young, you need to go to college and get yourself a degree. . . . But sometimes Molly says some things . . . she doesn't understand how things work today." Some of the younger babysitters who were separated from their own mothers living in the islands accepted this generational difference, despite the differences of opinion that it created, because they felt as if they had a mother figure who was looking out for their best interests and wanted them to do something with their lives even if they hadn't come from the same island. This was where the West Indian identity as well as occupational identity overrode any cultural differences or generational anxieties that might be present.

The "Other" Sitters

From time to time West Indian sitters discussed other sitters in Brooklyn parks as a benchmark for how people should judge their own work. Through such discussions, they could further construct a work identity superior to that of others doing the same job. I observed a good example of such a conversation in November of 2004. Evelyn, who was from Grenada, said hello to the Trinidadian sitter Carol. They began speaking for a short spell, and not wanting to intrude on their conversation I sat silently, watching the kids play in the park. Carol asked if Evelyn had seen the news that morning about a New Jersey babysitter who had been caught abusing a child. Carol went on to describe the horror of how the woman had beaten the child and even pulled out some of the child's hair. Evelyn, in shock, responded, "No child could ever make me get to that point. What could that child have been doing?" Both Carol and Evelyn shook their heads in disbelief while kissing their teeth, the ultimate West Indian sound of disapproval.[44] Evelyn then stated, "This is what happens when they don't get paid well."

"What was she?" Evelyn quickly inquired, implicitly referring to the babysitter's nationality.

"Some Spanish girl," Carol said.

Evelyn continued, "Yes, it is they who don't get paid well and then lash out on the children."

I interjected, "Are some sitters not as nice as others?"

"Yes, it is those Latino and Filipino ladies who don't get paid well and then do things like that," Evelyn asserted.

The stereotypes of Latino and Filipino babysitters that Evelyn expressed almost appeared to be an attempt to deflect the negative stereotypes sometimes held regarding West Indian babysitters: that they used corporal punishment and were aggressive toward the children they cared for. Evelyn concluded that sitters' behavior toward children was a direct result of pay rates, not race or culture. Though she initially asked what ethnic group the woman being accused came from, she explicitly avoided a culture-of-poverty explanation and instead invoked one that was structural and wage based. I could not deduce from this conversation, or from follow-up conversations, whether this analysis came from Evelyn's own progressive politics, but there was some type of awareness on her part that the culture-of-poverty explanation would not be sufficient and therefore needed to be replaced by something more concrete, such as low pay. One might wish there would be solidarity among all babysitters on the basis of shared occupational or immigrant identities. But sometimes one group, in this case West Indian babysitters, instead gave allegiance to a ranking system that emphasized their own advantage, allowing them to see themselves as "the better group" of babysitters and boosting the image of their own ethnic identity. Employers tended to have different ranking systems that made other groups the preferred group.[45]

Constructing an Identity

> "That's Little Trinidad. The nanny hangout. The mothers usually sit on this side."
>
> *Momzillas*, by Jill Kargman

Throughout history, constructing identity has been a struggle for domestic workers. From slave, to in-house low-wage worker, to low-status immigrant worker, to subordinated childcare provider, black women in domestic work positions have had to reinvent how they see themselves in order to make the jobs that they do tolerable.

The epigraph above, while drawn from a fictional story about a mother's interaction with other mothers and childcare providers in Manhattan, New York, illustrates clearly how I observed West Indian women being judged in Brooklyn parks. The "nanny hangout" was a phrase I often overheard from local parents and workers in the park who sat on the periphery of "Little Trinidad." They used it to mention the phenomenon and, at the same time, to criticize it as problematic. The perception was that these "others" were making themselves comfortable at the expense of the neighborhood and its culture.

The childcare providers whom I interviewed and observed understood this stereotype and defended themselves by emphasizing that "I didn't come here on the boat," meaning they were not "fresh off the boat," as the typical saying goes. They sought to distinguish West Indians from other ethnic groups entering the United States by claiming they were savvier.[46] The ongoing process of identity construction and status claiming through comparison to other ethnic groups made it possible for West Indian providers to cope with the fact that perhaps they were not altogether happy with their subordinated positions in the households where they worked. Their identity was strengthened when they left the private spaces of their employers and entered the public spaces of Brooklyn. Public spaces offered a forum for identity construction and West Indian identity cohesion even as it left them open to having their actions and behaviors monitored by the employers' neighbors. The phenomenon of community among West Indian childcare providers is not new necessarily, but this community in gentrified Brooklyn is different from communities of childcare providers previously written about in terms of how they use public spaces and create public identities within those spaces. Between the 1930s and the 1960s, domestic workers were not frequently using public spaces. During the 1970s and the 1980s this began to change slightly as work demands changed, but it was not until the gentrification of neighborhoods in New York that a reduction of housework duties and a greater tendency for employers to work from home led to a greatly increased use of public spaces. The next chapter will examine how public spaces both hinder and foster community among West Indian childcare providers in gentrifying Brooklyn. Further, it explores changing relations between black domestic workers and their white employers. Gentrification is discussed as cultural change that affects childcare providers in various ways, both positive and negative.

2

Public Parks and Social Spaces

Surveillance and the Creation of Communities

Moving along the sidewalks of gentrified Brooklyn, I found myself wondering, Who is watching me? There I was, a black woman pushing two children in an unbranded stroller I had bought off Craigslist, unlike the Bugaboo and Phil and Teds overpriced strollers that had become a staple in the neighborhoods I frequented. Were people watching me in the same way that childcare providers were being watched each day? Further, the isolation I felt once my husband left our home, was this the same isolation felt by the women I had decided to study? I began this book with the intention of describing the inherent isolation among West Indian childcare providers, along with that of the transnational motherhood so frequently mentioned as part of the plight of immigrant female domestic workers employed in private households. Researchers have called isolation the one factor that uniquely distinguishes domestic childcare from other forms of paid childcare and work in general, with female employer-employee relations dominating the discussion. Objectively defined, isolation would be a social state of being alone or separated from a community. For this study, isolation for West Indian childcare providers could also include not having an opportunity to create community through everyday work experiences.

What makes domestic work intriguing with regard to this topic of isolation is the household structures that limit workers' ability to forge meaningful ties with their employers or other community members. And once workers are out in the public sphere, where I posit community can be created to counter the isolation within the employer's household, the structures of surveillance in which the community is involved interfere with workers' opportunities to connect with each other.

A study by the sociologist Judith Rollins on domestic work by African American housecleaners for white female employers in Boston reported that the employer-employee relationship was marked by forms of "maternalism" from the employer side and social distancing through displays of deference (linguistic, spatial, gestural) on the part of the domestic worker.[1] Rollins described this relationship as a modification of the kind of paternalistic relationship that the head of a patriarchal household, in centuries-old arrangements, would have to other family members and by extension to servants, in which he offered protection, guidance, and rewards in exchange for the loyalty and services of dependents who occupied a space that never wholly belonged to them. Though maternalism places more emphasis on an affective bond between employer and employee, it is still based on the employer's need to preserve a wide gap in perceived status (i.e., income, education, assets, abilities) and to require a high degree of deference from the employee.[2] In particular, requirements of spatial deference, or restrictions over the use of household space, isolate domestic workers. Public space can be used to negate some of this isolation through the creation of community anchored in social spaces, but it also leaves childcare providers open to surveillance by neighborhood residents. It is a place where caregivers socialize but are forced to go even when they do not feel like going. Available, abundant public space in gentrifying neighborhoods both enables and constrains the work of childcare providers, thus making the issue of isolation in both public and private spheres more complex.

The Relationship between the Employee and the Female Employer

As Rollins has argued, the relationship between female employer and employee in the private household is fundamentally a patriarchal one in which the mother of the children being cared for takes on the role of traditional father figure, though, as Bonnie Thornton Dill has noted as well, it is in some ways unique in that it is more likely than a relationship with a male employer to be personalized, in both positive and negative ways, and to be charged with ambivalent feelings; in consequence the occupation of domestic work is itself viewed with ambivalence.[3] Rollins and Dill describe ways in which an employer might treat the employee as childlike, but Dill describes as well a reverse dynamic, in which black domestic employees tended to mother their female employers because they were often young and inexperienced, thus creating an image of domestic workers as all-knowing matriarchs and of female employers as childlike and in need of care.[4] Sometimes an employer might use such a dynamic exploitatively to get more work out of the employee, and the domestic worker would justify her subordinate position by taking refuge in a false sense of empowerment.[5] Dill explores how domestic workers have tried to assert their agency in the private homes of the employers by shaping the personalized employer-employee relationship to meet their own needs and setting limits and standards for the work they did.[6] The lack of such standardization in domestic work in general is precisely what Domestic Workers United is addressing in its efforts to establish fair labor standards and explicit contracts for domestics nationally.

Among occupations, domestic work is particularly likely to be undervalued, as Dill has noted, because it is considered "women's work," which, when performed within the family, is uncompensated and barely recognized as work.[7] The women's work that the providers do not only goes unnoticed but is ill paid. The low wages and lack of appreciation for childcare providers in general lead to the conclusion that having private childcare involves both racial and class oppression.[8] Middle- and upper-middle-class families benefit from this social inequality and find themselves with ample opportunities to hire poorer women of color who are frequently first-generation immigrants. Hiring a childcare provider becomes a means of conspicuous consumption for the employer, and although the provider is described by those who hire her as ostensibly part of "one big happy family," she is at the same time marked and separated from them by her class and race.[9] Further, as Julia Wrigley has pointed out, childcare providers undergo the humiliating experience of being constantly supervised,[10] even, as my own research shows, when they are not in the private spaces of the employer's home.

Domestic Work and Isolation

Georg Simmel's definition of isolation as "a relation which is lodged within an individual but which exists between him and a certain group or group life in general" throws light on how a domestic worker can experience isolation even while she is interacting with employers or taking care of children in the employer's home.[11] Almost all authors on domestic work discuss how various ethnic groups feel isolated in this type of work, especially when they are living in the home of the employer.[12] Shellee Colen has stated that exploitation in the employer-employee relationship is expressed not only through forms of "abysmal pay and long hours" but also through "isolation from kin, friends, community, and anyone outside the work environment."[13] Rollins has noted that the isolation in the private space of the employer's home separates domestic workers from supportive co-workers and thus makes women in this line of work more vulnerable to exploitation.[14] Pierette Hondagneu-Sotelo has described the loneliness Latina domestics feel when their work requires them to be separated from their family and friends.[15] Phyllis Palmer has detailed the ways capitalism forces employers and employees alike to choose between home life and employment.[16] Mary Romero has described the isolation of both maid and mistress in middle-class homes, and Wrigley has emphasized the social isolation among domestics resulting both from the structure of domestic work itself and from the employer's rules.[17]

Many domestic service workers have combated these conditions by attempting to shift from live-in to live-out work and from hourly pay, in which employers solely decide what jobs are done each hour, to a pay-per-job wage.[18] As Hondagneu-Sotelo has shown for Mexican immigrant women, such shifts in domestic work allow them not only more autonomy but also fewer work hours and more time with their own families.[19] An additional benefit, as Dill has shown, is that live-out workers do not become closely linked to their employers.[20] This book focuses on women who live outside their employers' homes.

The family's place in capitalist production often blurs the line between what may be considered private versus public. Because the family is a key site of social reproduction, the "private" home is not simply private but also part of the public sphere.[21] Domestic workers underscore, by the nature of their work, the observation that the family is not a refuge from capitalism but a workspace and a site of capitalist class reproduction. Because of this overlap between private and public activities, we cannot simply assume that all domestic workers are isolated all of the time, especially if we are discussing childcare providers in an urban center such as Brooklyn, where there are ample opportunities to use public spaces during working hours. However, it should be noted that employees did not always use these public spaces willingly. Some employers required providers to use public spaces, especially those "creative class" employers who worked from home on weekdays.

Once in the field, I soon realized that isolation was not a theme invoked by the West Indian childcare providers I was observing to describe themselves or their daily routines. In fact, the opposite appeared to be true. I was surprised to find that this group of women created social spaces and community along West Indian cultural lines in public places. The renowned geographer David Harvey, who has written extensively on issues pertaining to social space, particularly on the city as a site where capitalists accumulate wealth and use the state to control the working class, describes how social space takes on meaning only in terms of an individual's perceptions of his environment and that it is consequently "made up of a complex of individual feelings and images about and reactions towards the spatial symbolism which surrounds that individual."[22] Social space, then, is different from the physical space in that it is "variable from individual to individual and from group to group; it is also variable over time."[23] Childcare providers may have experienced some isolation in their employers' homes, but they found ways to cope with that isolation by connecting with others by cell phone and by meeting with each other in public places whenever possible. Because of the frequency and duration of their contacts with each other in public places, I shifted the focus of this study to the topic of how West Indian childcare providers created community through the use of public places and spaces, not only by invoking shared language, race, and immigration status, as noted in previous studies, but also by participating in food sharing, cell phone use, informal economic systems, and even labor organizing.[24] By becoming a participant observer, I was able to trace the movements of West Indian childcare providers from public sphere locations to the private spheres of their employers. Public sphere locations included public parks, sidewalks, commercial establishments on public shopping streets, child lesson facilities, and public libraries. The use of "extended place methods" in the ethnographic research process, connecting events at one site to events at other sites and to larger trends, allowed for continuous observation of meaning making as it occurred from place to place and offered the opportunity to determine the methods by which these women did indeed preserve their cultural traditions and identities.[25]

Public Places and Social Spaces

> "And avoid the Islands," added Bee. "I had this one woman from Trinidad. So much 'tude. And lazy! She moved like a glacier, and was the size of one, too. I'd have to point out everything. Like, hello? This silver picture frame could not be more tarnished! And the South American nannies, they're all busy gossiping and speaking Spanish and meanwhile the kids are dangling from the highest rung on the jungle gym."
>
> *Momzillas*, by Jill Kargman

While *Momzillas* is a book of fiction, the excerpt above reflects my observations about how childcare by nannies is now perceived as something that takes place more in the public than in the private sphere. It is useful to look at public places and spaces and to understand childcare providers in this context to move beyond what has been already written about extensively—the isolation in the private household where employment is gendered and exploitative—although this is also still relevant. What follows is a description of an exclusive social world that unfolds in public places and spaces. For this study, public places such as parks are treated as examples of the built environment that physically express a way of life, "providing the physical milieu for the reproduction of social meaning and ideology."[26] In other words, a society's values and its conceptualizations of the social world can be expressed and passed on in public parks. Public places and spaces foster "physical connections . . . based on the degree to which the location, design, resources, and arrangement of a place are reflective of the surrounding areas."[27] The social networks that develop and are maintained in public places are influenced by the aesthetics of public places as expressions of the neighborhoods where they are situated. A public place's positive meanings include "meanings . . . created by positive connections to people, connections that create a sense of belonging, of safety, a feeling that personal rights will be protected,"[28] and these connections in turn support the formation and strengthening of identities based on group membership. The daily uses of the physical public place allow for the social construction of space.[29] This social construction of space gives the physical use of public places/spaces like public parks symbolic meanings that stem from social exchanges.[30]

As much of Lyn Lofland's work has shown, "life in the public realm is thoroughly social" and is a "distinct area or arena of human activity."[31] Even when public environments may seem impersonal and their interactions rule patterned, "the human inhabitants of the realm relate to one another."[32] For example, Lofland speaks of "unpersonal/bounded relationships," typically originating in and maintained through the regular use of public spaces, where persons may share little information about themselves (e.g., their names) yet experience their relationship as "friendly" or "sociable."[33] In my research I saw that often sitters would recognize each other or even have encountered one another for years at public parks, yet would not know each other's names. But Lofland's observations about an unwritten social rule for face-to-face exchanges with strangers that specifies civility toward diversity (in race, accent, appearance, and so forth) and produces a "sense of freedom from judgment which many people report as a major pleasure of being 'out in public,'" appear naive when set against the experience of the West Indian child-care providers I studied, who were hypervisible to others' surveillance and judgments when out in public spaces and who often said they felt especially vulnerable to others' judgments on account of their skin color.[34] In the realm of the park, they as well as other park users decipher cues that symbolically help them to monitor their own behaviors and their use of public space.[35]

These cues and the invisible boundaries between groups that partition public places create what sociologists have called "social space." I studied how West Indian childcare providers in Brooklyn public parks constructed their own social spaces over time by organizing events, creating community, and sharing cultural practices. I also investigated how providers reconstituted a social space for themselves when they left the public sphere of the park and entered other public locations, and how that social space differed from the private spheres of their employers, places where primary relationships between family and friends or acquaintances were fostered in shared cultures and histories.[36] My research also considered how other users of public places (such as employers, neighborhood residents, and park workers) exhibited competing social space formation.

Public Parks in Brooklyn

Many Brooklyn parks were initially designated as private community gardens in the 1840s, but by the mid-1800s the city of Brooklyn had acquired much of this land for use as public parks.[37] Within two decades, these parks included Olmsted-inspired playgrounds and incorporated public space designs. Fredrick Law Olmsted was the founder of landscape architecture and aimed to design New York public parks as democratic, open urban spaces for the average citizen that would bring people of all socioeconomic levels together.[38] By the early 1990s, several of these public parks had been redesigned and reconstructed and are now maintained by community volunteers and the City of New York Parks and Recreation Department, which receives both public and private funds for improvements. The park is promoted through leaflets as a place to share the joys and challenges of childrearing and to meet with friends and neighbors while sitting on park benches under the shade of trees. All of the parks used in this research anchor Brooklyn communities that have undergone recent gentrification. The population change over the past decade has benefited public parks. Newer residents volunteer to conduct maintenance in the parks, as older residents are physically less able to do so. In addition, newer residents and their businesses, which are sometimes located in the neighborhoods where they live, can offer private funding for public parks. However, some park employees I interviewed felt that the parks had become somewhat less family oriented and noticed that more babysitters were now occupying these public spaces.

I interviewed a sample of city parks employees to better understand how neighborhood gentrification had affected public parks. The annual workers, most of whom I later found out were African American and welfare-to-work employees, shied away from being formally interviewed.[39] I asked one of the playground associates who wore a green City Parks T-shirt instead of the blue ones the other workers were wearing, thinking there might be a difference in employment rank. I had seen this employee over the previous two years walking in one of Brooklyn's oldest parks with children following her. Only after I approached her did I realize she was in charge of children's activities there. Marga, as mentioned before, was an older white single mother. As a playground associate over the previous twelve years, she was responsible for playing games with the kids in the playground area of the park and providing them with toys, "mostly arts and crafts," she told me. "That's what this park is, an arts and crafts park." The job lasted six months of the year, beginning in April, five days a week. When I asked Marga if there had been any changes over the years at this Brooklyn park, she replied, "In the time that I've been here, there's been a major change in the people in the park. It used to be when I first came here it was mostly Italian families, very few babysitters. I mean, there were occasional babysitters here and there, but now it just seems to be a lot of nannies."[40]

I asked Marga why she thought there had been more families in the past. She answered, "The people who lived here sold because they're getting such good prices for their homes, and have moved on. It's better-educated people now. You know, back in the day, Mom never went to college, you know. She stayed home and raised the family. Now, you know, when you have a family, two people need to be working. . . . So I think that's what the difference is, you know? The two-family income."

I wanted to find out who exactly Marga was speaking of when she mentioned dual-income earners and asked her if she felt these new families could now afford a childcare provider. She responded, "Yeah, because there's a lot of professionals in the neighborhood now. Most of the women are professionals, I've met a lot of attorneys and a lot of artists."

I then asked: "How has your relationship with them changed from maybe back when there were a lot of Italian parents here?"

"When I first came, the Italian mothers would always send me lunch. . . . It would be the leftovers from dinner the night before, they'd give them to me for lunch . . . so I never really had to buy lunch. . . . They were always appreciative of what I did," she said.

I wondered if Marga felt that the "gentrifying" parents in the neighborhood were less appreciative of her efforts to organize children's events throughout the weekdays. Perhaps this offering of food had demonstrated appreciation in a way that was no longer commonplace among the newer residents of the area. When I had spoken with parents in this neighborhood, everyone had seemed quite happy with the fact that there was someone designated to organize events at the public park, but Marga appeared to be looking for more than a simple "thank-you." Food sharing conveyed gratitude to her more strongly than mere verbal appreciation.

Marga's acute awareness of who was using the park and how led to extended conversations about how she viewed the new "nanny-centered" park makeup. As she worked throughout the day with the children in the park, she ultimately came into contact with parents and childcare providers along with grandparents and others in the park. I began to realize that in addition to the activities of her park employment she helped to carry out the surveillance of sitters in public spaces on parents' behalf.

A Typical Day of a Childcare Provider

A typical day for a childcare provider varied with each household. Irene, who was from Trinidad and had raised three children of her own in New York, gave a snapshot of what a typical day for her looked like. On days when she had to be at work by noon, she would get up at 6:00 a.m. Her kids got dressed themselves, but she had to make sure everything was in order (meaning that the clothes were taken out and laid on the bed). She sometimes had to let her older daughter know what was appropriate to wear, since some of her skirts were too short. Her son wore a uniform, so she had to make sure that he had everything on correctly because the school was strict. Her son had to be at the bus stop by 6:50 a.m., so she walked him there while the older daughter stayed at the house with Irene's four-year-old. Both children usually had cereal and milk before leaving the house or had breakfast at school. Irene admitted that she was not a breakfast person herself. When Irene returned from dropping off her son, her four-year-old daughter was usually still asleep. Her older daughter then left for school, usually walking there with a friend, since she was old enough. At this point Irene woke the four-year-old. She got her dressed, cooked her breakfast, and sang and talked with her because she sometimes woke up in a bad mood. By this time Irene's husband either had left for work or was just leaving. He was in the pest control business, so his hours were unusually flexible. On the days when Irene went in to work later, her husband went in to work early and vice versa. Irene then got the four-year-old to school by 8:30 a.m. at an early childhood center that she attended five days a week. Finally Irene got herself ready for work and commuted there, first by bus and then by train.

On the days where Irene had to be at work at 8:00 a.m., she got up at 5:00 a.m. Her husband took the kids to their respective schools and bus stop, but Irene was still responsible for making sure the clothes were all laid out and that the cereal was in the bowl and the milk on the table. As soon as she arrived at her employer's house—fifteen minutes early, at 7:45 a.m., when she was working the 8:00 a.m. shift—she fed her charges their breakfast, made sure they were dressed appropriately for the weather, and then took them to school. On her way back to the house, she would stop by the public parks to see the other West Indian childcare providers who were in her community. She would discuss the daily park happenings and then she would maybe ask one of the other providers to accompany her to the grocery store with their charges to get whatever the employer's family needed in terms of groceries, since she was responsible for cooking the family their dinner (not a typical responsibility for many of the providers I interviewed). Because Irene was caring for older children who attended school for a few hours a day, she had the added responsibilities of cleaning the house and doing errands like filling the employers' prescriptions or taking in their dry cleaning. Such responsibilities were not directly related to her childcare duties but were at times asked of childcare providers even when they had not been explicitly mentioned as part of the job. The employer usually requested them after a childcare provider had worked with the same family for a while and the employer felt more comfortable with asking or the children had gotten old enough to begin attending school. Additional compensation was not always given for these tasks. After picking up the children from school by midday, Irene took them to the public park or library for a few hours, then to their respective lessons in art or music. Finally she fed them dinner and made sure they started their homework before the parents returned at 7:00 or 8:00 p.m.

If you ever saw Irene walking on the sidewalks of the neighborhood she worked in, you would see her wearing a Bluetooth earpiece that allowed her to constantly connect with other providers throughout the day. She would tell you that the only way she could get through the day was to have her "ladies" to speak to while she was working. Bluetooth also helped her to stay connected to her family members. When asked how she managed to do her own errands, she stated that she either did them early in the morning on the days when she worked later or waited until Saturday. Irene's mother, who lived across the hallway, and her husband helped as well.

Irene found it odd that families in these gentrified neighborhoods didn't have their families around to help them in the same way that her own people did back in Trinidad: "Back at home, you would have your aunts and uncles always around. Even if they don't live a stone's throw away they would call to see if you need help. Here, on the other hand, it's very rare that you will find family living close together, whereas in the Caribbean islands more family live close together. It's always easy for you to find someone, and that's why at home we never needed a babysitter. We could go to work and grandma could take them afterwards, or the kids could walk from school by themselves because the schools were never far away. They are right there. Kids are guarded by the community in the Caribbean, and neighbors will discipline your children to keep them from straying. . . . Here people are so busy that they don't have the time."

This difference in how Irene perceived the ability of community formation was the same difference I heard employers discuss. New York living was fast-paced, and the fact that their families lived far from them pressed on employers in Brooklyn in ways that it might not in smaller midwestern communities. So while Brooklyn's gentrified neighborhoods provided a sense of closeness at least in terms of urban density, it lacked the kind of familial community that Marga described as being present for the Italian mothers who had once lived in the neighborhood.

Get Out!

Childcare providers were expected to take the children they cared for to the parks during the day, especially if the parent worked from home as a freelancer. Arlene, who was from Guyana, knew this scenario all too well and told me of her difficulties in having to be out of the house all day long. One day when we met up in a local coffee shop to find shelter from the rain, she began telling me about her day. As soon as Arlene would come to work, the employers wanted her out of the house with Josie, the three-year-old she cared for. Especially when the husband was at home with the son (he worked the night shift a few days and therefore had some weekdays off), they wanted her to be out of the house all day long. Arlene was supposed to take the daughter to the bookstore, to the public play spaces in the area, or to the parks. She had to find somewhere to go all day every day, even when she was sick. She claimed that the father was home all day with the son and wondered, "Why doesn't he take the boy out during the day, so that I can stay home with Josie since I'm sick?" Even when she was sick and it was raining, her employers still insisted that she stay out all day with her charge.

Darlene, a West Indian provider, was five feet tall and stocky with short dreadlocks. She was from Barbados and worked as a "nanny" (the term she used) forty hours a week, finishing each day at 4:30 p.m. and then volunteering her time to Domestic Workers United outside those hours. I was surprised to hear that she was a nanny as well as a volunteer given the amount of hours she worked. I asked her if she had been raised in England after noticing that her accent was vaguely familiar (my mother-in law was from England as well). She told me that yes, she had been born in Barbados but raised in Reading, England. When asked where she was from, she said Barbados and identified as a West Indian.

In an interview, Darlene blamed the advent of new technology for the demands that providers go out: "Modern technology is wonderful and everything, but it's got its drawbacks. In this age everything is computers, and back in the old days, people had to go to the office to work, but now they have this technology in people's homes. So now what's happening is you've got these buggers [the employers], they're not going out to the office, so now they're working from the house. So some of these people, they're saying to you . . . when you're going in the morning . . . some nannies will say to you that the stroller is packed and they have to go out with the child, regardless of what the weather is like, they have to go out."

Denyse, a fifty-four-year-old provider from Trinidad, wearing dark sunglasses and a baseball cap, sat with me on a park bench to discuss the matter of having to go out with the children. She said she had no problem with the stroller already being packed for going out all day since she'd rather be outside than inside when the parents were at home working; she would prefer spending all of her days at the park. But she stated that when her employers "tell me that I have to go out with the child, I have a problem with that . . . because if it's cold and I don't want to go out or if I'm not feeling well, because I might come to work, I may not feel well to go out, but at least I can work, so I could stay in the house with the child, but you telling me I have to go out, I have a problem with that." I think Denyse may not have recognized that her "having to go out" was implied by the mere fact that the stroller was packed for the day. In any event, as long as the employers did not say explicitly that she had to go out, Denyse found this preparation acceptable.

Placing these heavy demands on babysitters didn't just anger the babysitters; it created conflicts and tension between the employer and employee that strained their relationship. Parents expected their employees to be out all day with the children and stay "off the bench" for an eight- to twelve-hour day.

My Time, My Money

It was not uncommon for employers to ask sitters to stay late, suddenly decide to "go out" and ask the sitter to cover for them, or offer excuses for not getting home on time. During one of the playdates held at my home with five West Indian babysitters, Janet said she didn't like it when the employers came home late and blamed it on the subways being "messed up." Molly responded, "They does all say that . . . it's the subway." All of the "ladies" (the term West Indian childcare providers use to reference one another) shook their heads in agreement about this "excuse making" by employers. Janet, the sitter from St. Vincent, asserted, "The point here is that if the sitter is required to be at work on time [and risks being fired if she shows up late], then the employer should respect these same rules and come home on time regardless of what the subways are doing." In the babysitters' minds, employers should not have been using public transit delays as an excuse, regardless of whether they were telling the truth, since they would never tolerate an employee's use of this excuse. Besides, the sitters often saw their employers' lateness as evidencing a lack of regard for the sitter's time that was being taken away from their own families or private pursuits.

While I was at another Brooklyn park in the early evening, around 5:30 p.m., I went over to the swing set by the infant playground and spoke with a sitter from Jamaica named Monica who stood two swings from me. I asked her what time she got off work, and she said, "I don't know." I asked, "Don't you have set hours?" She replied, "No, the parents come whenever. . . . They come at different times because they work in executive jobs in Manhattan, in the city. . . . They come home at any time of the night, usually between 6:30 or 7:30 p.m., and I work until somebody comes home." I asked if that was difficult for her and she said yes. Monica had been babysitting for a fourteen-month-old boy since he was three weeks old, and although she claimed that she didn't mind working those long hours because he was so good, she also said she had told her employers, "The way it works is that I'm supposed to have a set time." They never gave her a set time, so she just worked until the first person came home.

Arlene, from Guyana, told me one day in a coffee shop where she had brought Josie to play, as she often did because she was required to leave the house when she worked, that she too had unstructured work hours. Originally in her verbal contract Arlene was supposed to work only two days a week at a rate of $250. She said to the employer, "You know what, pay me an extra $50 and I'll come a third day to do some cleaning. I'll take care of the girl and I'll do some cleaning for $300." Basically, Arlene was now earning $100 each day for an eight-hour day. The employers had a second child, and by the time he was born they had her coming in on Mondays in addition to the other three days, but they paid only an extra $40 for that whole day, and she was now caring for both kids. By offering an additional $40 for the Mondays, the employers avoided paying Arlene an hourly rate. If she had to work overtime, she didn't get paid more because they were paying her a flat rate. Childcare providers do themselves a disservice by agreeing in this way to a flat rate instead of an hourly wage: employers can take advantage of the flat rate by adding duties, such as care of an additional child or housecleaning.

For Arlene, there was no amount attached to the worth of each hour's work. She said, "They're using me like a donkey." They didn't preschedule days for her, they just called her up on the days they wanted her to work. She worked random days and sometimes could not afford her rent. For example, one Monday she couldn't afford the rent, so her sister had to help her out and the employers knew this, but they still didn't pay her more for her hours worked. The frustration here, though, had more to do with the discomfort that Arlene felt about fighting for her rights as a worker and demanding higher pay. Arlene was part of the vulnerable group of childcare workers who desperately needed the employment in order to survive. As a documented immigrant Arlene could potentially find more mainstream work, but because she was in her fifties now and had not upgraded her education she remained positioned as an "unskilled worker" and had only been able to find work as a childcare provider.

Tensions around employers' unscheduled and uncompensated extensions of one's workload were not unique to West Indian childcare providers. Victoria, a white woman who owned a movement arts studio, which will be discussed at length later, told me that when she had worked as a nanny she had not been prepared for the long hours that would be unexpectedly extended at a moment's notice. "Usually it was like, 'I'm not gonna be home on time,' an hour before [the workday ended]. You know, 'I'll be home an hour late.' Sometimes they would even call fifteen minutes before, saying they were a half hour late. . . . I mean, there was also days that I was asked, 'Would you stay late tonight? I want to go out.' So there would be days that I'd be there from 8:00 in the morning until 11:00 at night. . . . I would say there was a general lack of respect for my time throughout the whole time . . . absolutely. You know, just the coming home late on a regular basis, calling and assuming that I was available to stay late. You know, I will admit that there were often mornings where I was ten or fifteen minutes late for sure, so it's not all on one side." Victoria's interactions with her employers around payment were also stressful. "There were a lot of issues with getting paid on time." She explained, "I mean I'm pretty up front, so I'd say, 'Where's my money?' on Friday afternoon. 'Oh, I forgot it,' the employer would say. So actually, by the time I left, she would leave her ATM card for me and I would go take out my money myself and leave her a receipt. . . . Because, you know, she'd say, 'Can I pay you next Monday?' and I'd be like, 'I need the money today.' You know, I was a student and I was making between probably $450 and $600 a week, and I needed it."

Salary came up routinely in my conversations not only with Arlene and Victoria but with other providers as well. One day Irene commented that babysitters ought to get a cost-of-living increase every year for both part-time and full-time work. She explained, "If you think of it this way, if you leave your babysitter's salary one way whether they're full time or part time every year, remember every year stuff goes up. Rent goes up, electricity goes up . . . everything goes up and I'm sure where you work your salary goes up and . . . some people get upset for that. . . . If you're getting an increase because stuff is getting more expensive for you, my stuff is not staying the same price, my stuff is increasing too. . . . Most West Indian people are not really [asking for] seven hundred dollars, or 'I want a thousand dollars,' but the thing that people have to realize is that we appreciate the little things . . . and we appreciate when we see that you appreciate what we're doing—that we feel better, that we do our jobs better because we see that they really appreciate our effort. But if you're mean . . . it makes us feel uncomfortable because, remember, we're with your kids most of the time, and you know, we'll end up loving those kids just like they're our own."

How babysitters were paid and how they were treated by their employers determined how sitters valued their worth as employees as well as the job that they did for their employers. An increase in salary was often cited by West Indian babysitters as one of the best ways for employers to show that they valued the work that childcare providers did.

Structuring Sitters' Time

Victoria, the white movement arts studio owner who had formerly been a nanny, recounted in detail the conflicts that had arisen between herself and her employers when the time came to determine how the days would be spent: "She wanted me to stroll the children during their naptime, always, and I told her no way, which I ended up winning that battle. I explained to her that from my perspective there were lots of reasons not to do that, the first being that the child doesn't get the best rest, and sleeping in their crib is really—you know, that's what I was taught is the best way for the child to sleep. I also explained that I need some downtime because I'm with these kids ten hours straight. It's a very intense job. It's a very emotionally intense job. And pushing around kids for three hours in all kinds of weather is more than I feel comfortable doing. But mostly because it's not in the best interest of the child."

I asked how this changed during the winter months and if they still required her to go outside. Victoria answered, "Oh yeah, because that's how they did it. I mean she did the stroller naps and putting the kid in the car seat and driving the kid around as her naptime. But with me, the kids always slept in their cribs. . . . I would tell them twenty minutes before nap, you know, 'It's gonna be naptime soon.' We read books or did some sort of quiet puzzles, or watch a little bit of Baby Einstein and then they'd go down for their nap. . . . I definitely didn't feel that I was doing something detrimental. . . . I mean we did resolve it, and she did know that this was what I was doing. So, you know, we spoke about it. I didn't just go against her wishes."

One reason I interviewed Victoria was to see if her relations with her employers were different from those of West Indian childcare providers. And in fact, Arlene, from Guyana, had a different response to her employer wanting her to be out of the house with the children. While both providers lived in the United States legally, Arlene chose to remain silent about the troubling situation of being forced out of the house on a daily basis, regardless of the weather, whereas Victoria chose to confront her employers and defend her rights as an employee who could make judgment calls about how to spend the days with the children. The differences here might have been generational: Arlene was from an older generation that was socialized not to speak up against one's employer, especially in their private home, and Victoria, at the time, was a college student who felt empowered by the knowledge that unfair employment treatment could be fought legally. But race could have also played a role: Arlene's discomfort in speaking up about how she was treated could be a direct result of her not wanting to confront the racial "other," while Victoria may have felt more comfortable taking an oppositional stance because, as a white woman, she felt more equal to her employers.

West Indian babysitters, perhaps like babysitters in general, tired of using public places and spaces to care for the children they were responsible for. Most sitters that I observed would keep an eye on the child and on other children while they sat socializing on the benches. If a situation arose that required the sitter's attention, the sitter usually jumped to her feet to attend to the child. Marga and I discussed this idea of "it takes a village to raise a child":

"You talked about there being more families in the beginning [of your work in the park], so you could probably leave your younger child out because all the parents were watching?"

Marga nodded.

I asked Marga, "Do you think that that exists with the West Indian babysitters . . . they're all looking after each other's kids?"

She replied, "If they know each other, you know they're friends, then they'll watch out for each other's kids, but if you're not friends with them, they don't know who the child is."

"So do you see communities of sitters?" I asked.

"Yep, yeah," she affirmed.

In the three years that I participated in the community of sitters that Marga spoke of, I often saw West Indian sitters asking other West Indian sitters to watch their charges while they got something from the local bakery or ran back to the employer's house for something that they had forgotten. There were several communities of sitters, and the communities often changed throughout the day depending on the age of the children under care and the daily routine of the sitters. For example, in the morning hours I would see Rachel heading over to Molly's employer's home, where they would get ready for their day's activities. As they left the home, they would meet up with Janet on the street as she strolled up with Cameron. The three women would then go to the home where Debbie worked, since Debbie now cared for twin babies, and help her down the stairs with the double stroller. They would all head over to the park or run errands in the nearby stores. After lunch, when most sitters had gone indoors so that their charges could nap, Molly might take another walk to visit with Lyla (a sitter from Jamaica) or to drop off some food for other sitters either at the park or at their employer's home. Rachel, who often stayed away from her employers' home during the day because they lived a little further away, would go to a variety of parks throughout the afternoon (sometimes up to three) and spend a couple of hours at each with different sitters.

The communities of sitters existed and moved across social spaces throughout the day. Because of this, they were exposed to the public view and more obvious to both neighborhood residents and park workers than if they had remained inside the employer's home.

Cultural Clashes in Perceptions of Childrearing

The public display of childcare allowed those occupying public spaces to view childcare providers closely, especially when the sitters were West Indian. Marga spoke about her own observations of this care several times throughout our conversations. Her attitude toward West Indian childcare providers was clear: "Mostly all I see is just the sitters sitting and not interacting with the kids. I've never seen them abuse them. I never saw them really engaged with them either, you know?"

"So you see them sitting mostly during the day?" I asked.

"Yeah, mostly sitting. Sitting and talking with each other."

Marga acknowledged that there were communities of West Indian babysitters who looked out for each other's children, but she still maintained that some of the sitters she encountered needed to "get off the bench" and "onto the floor."[41]

Babysitters occupied the benches for a variety of reasons. One reason was to claim a space, by placing their diaper bags on the bench beside them, that could later be used when they needed to feed the child so that they wouldn't have to run after the child in the playground. Another reason was to seek refuge from the heat under the shady trees that these parks boasted about in their brochures. Molly and Debbie told me that on some of the hotter days they sat in the shade to keep themselves "cool from the sun." Yet another reason, reflecting more their ideas of correct parenting, was that the West Indian sitters didn't feel any need to be like a "helicopter mom" (a mother who hovers over her child every second at the park); instead they allowed the children in their care to explore independently. They had no added expectations of developing relationships with other parents by interacting constantly with the child to demonstrate how they fit in the community as a "good parent."

West Indian childcare providers also stayed on the bench because they did not want to get down on the ground or, within the park buildings, to get down on the floor to interact with the children they cared for, out of a concern for cleanliness that showed up in their claims that their employers were "dirty," "filthy," and "disgusting." Carol once told me that her new employer had her baby on the rug when Carol first came indoors, so Carol went to take her shoes off, but the employer told her not to bother. Carol said the father then walked over and put his street shoes on the same rug that the baby was lying on and that the rug was covered in dog hair. She said they were "nasty" people and she hadn't wanted anything to do with that rug, so she picked the baby up. Similarly, Molly made several comments, as other West Indian babysitters did, about the dogs that they had seen inside the homes of employers. Molly explained that back in the West Indies people kept dogs outdoors, where they ate the food that was left over from the family meal. She didn't understand how families in the United States could have dogs indoors, especially when there were children around.

Judgments like these and the values they represented showed up in other opinions that sitters held about their employers' childrearing. It was a common sentiment among West Indian childcare providers that employers didn't enjoy spending time with their kids and that white middle-class working women simply "had children in order to say that they had children," as one participant told me.[42] Carla said of her employer, "She just does not like to be alone with the children," which was why she worked so many hours, even on the weekends. Carla's definition of what good motherhood meant stemmed from her background as a black woman from Grenada: "As a mom myself . . . sitting down and looking at people, I don't want to seem biased because I am black . . . but I don't know I think there is something about black women that they seem to be very connected to their children. . . . Not that there aren't bad black mamas . . . but they seem to be very in tune, very patient, I see parents who go off, but you know I'm a parent too and I go off on my daughter. . . . If it's a parent I know, then I say, maybe you should try this . . . and the baby settle down. . . . I think they're very in tune . . . especially in my country [Grenada], we have been taking care of kids since we were you know because once you're twelve . . . eleven . . . you take care of your younger brothers and sisters, you change Pampers, you climb up on the stove to warm bottles, so it's something that's really in us and in the Caribbean, women, girls, are trained at a very young age almost from the time they pop out, to be mothers. To be the nurturing . . . you know, that's part of our culture, you train your daughter to be a good wife . . . so I think it's something in our culture." Carla strongly believed, on the basis of her experience in taking care of younger siblings, that there was a cultural difference in how women were trained to mother their children. She seemed not to realize, though, that West Indian families were not the only ones in which older siblings took care of younger siblings. This led me to believe that Carla embraced the stereotype that West Indian women were better nurturers than white women.[43]

According to the childcare providers I studied, a "real mother" was someone who took care of the meals for her family regardless of work hours, someone who prided herself in personally caring for her children by bathing them, ensuring their good citizenship through discipline, and showing them love when it was the right time. Watching over a child constantly was not considered part of being a "real mother." As providers frequently said to me, "You can't always be looking after a child—they need freedom to run around." Through their work, West Indian childcare providers tried to "teach" these lessons of being a "real mother" to their employers, although many of them complained that these "lessons" went unnoticed or at least that their employers did not connect them to any concept of motherhood.

Some providers did express an awareness that work demands prevented many women, including themselves, from giving their children as much hands-on care as they might wish to do. Irene told me, "You know what. Everyone has in their mind, every culture is different. Let me tell you about how it is in West Indian countries. We know you are a mother, you have to cook, you have to clean, you have to wash, but some mothers don't have the opportunity to do that. That doesn't make them a bad mother. If they have to go out and work to take care of their kids, that doesn't make them a bad mother, because we're doing the same thing. Well, not the same thing . . . but almost the same thing. The difference with West Indian parents is that although we're babysitters for other people, when we come home we still have to do everything we did for your kids for our kids. Half the time we don't have anybody to do it. We have to do it. So we're doing the same thing twice."

What Irene is speaking about here is women's "double day," or the "second shift," as Arlie Hochschild terms it—when women take on a second shift of family responsibilities at home after working a first shift at work outside of the home.[44] As Hochschild and others point out, in dual-earning families women tend to do more of the household labor than men do,[45] as Irene acknowledged when she talked about working during the day for her employer's family and then going back to her house to work the "second shift," doing the same work over again for her own family.

"And it depends on how they were brought up. Some people were brought up always having somebody to do something for them, so if they were brought up like that, they don't see that as bad when they do it. When they come home, they try to spend time with their kids, you know they do stuff with their kids, and that's how they view being a good mother. You can't be upset with them for that. Not because you think cooking, cleaning, washing as a mother, does not mean that they view it as that."

"So you think it's a difference in culture?" I asked.

"Yeah, it is. And you know what, the kids love them the same way. They might be mad at them for being away, but they love them . . . the same way! Because it's their mom!"

"What makes an employer a bad mother, then, as so many West Indian babysitters have claimed?" I wondered aloud. Irene openly admitted that there were some bad mothers and offered her definition of one: "A bad mother to me is if you neglect your kids and not do anything at all, not financially, not physically, nothing. You abuse them and you leave them and go and you don't come back, that's a bad mother. But if you have to go out there and work to take care of your kids and you make that effort on the weekends or when you come home at night to do something with them, spend at least an hour with them, then I don't see anything wrong with that. . . . We all do what we have to do. Because if you don't have the money for them to survive, you're going to be a bad mother."

Babysitters had different views about disciplining the children under their care than employers did, although cultural, racial, and class differences from their employers might inhibit them from expressing these views directly to the employer. Evelyn explained as we looked at the children she cared for in the park, "These kids can't get under my skin. . . . I leave them to sit and cry and pay them no mind when they want to act up. The parents [are] the ones who go to them every time when they act up. Not me. I just leave them to settle down."

Evelyn pointed out the little girl that she cared for and how she was sulking over on the jungle gym. She said to me, "You see that. She wants me to go over to her, but I won't. I will just leave her there until she really needs me." From where I sat it looked to me like the girl was simply looking for attention while her twin was running around and eating some snacks between play. Evelyn continued to explain how the parents had told her that one day the girl sat down in the middle of the crosswalk pouting. She was laughing while telling the story and saying that the parents had just let her sit down in the middle of the street until they had to finally pick her up. Evelyn said she didn't understand parents today with their permissive disciplinary ways. The children respected Evelyn more than the mother when it came to discipline.

Victoria had similar experiences with her employer. She talked of an incident when the older boy she cared for spit on her in front of the employer. Victoria explained, "I was waiting for her to say something and she didn't say anything. I actually said to him, 'Please never do that to me again. That is very mean. You never spit on someone, especially somebody who cares for you.' I just turned to her and said, 'I have to leave for the rest of the day.'" And Victoria left forty five minutes earlier than usual, upset and distraught. "I left and I called her that night and I said, 'Look, if I'm ever put in that position again, I can't work for you anymore.' Because he's four years old, you know. . . . So definitely I would say from my experience, my sort of discipline style is much more similar to other caregivers' than parents that I've encountered." Having every right to be upset at the employer for allowing her child to go without discipline for spitting on her, Victoria was able to use communication and possibly her empowerment as another white woman to be frank with her employer regardless of the possible repercussions.

Public Park Surveillance

Surveillance in Brooklyn public parks was a form of control that could sometimes be obvious, as in the signs that read, "Adult with child only," "No dogs allowed in play area," and "Park will be closed at 10 p.m." or the presence of a handful of police in the public parks to monitor older (sometimes mischievous) middle-school children after 4:00 p.m. through the evening hours. As Jane Jacobs reminds us, the phenomenon of "eyes on the street" can be positive.[46] Many gain a sense of safety in crowded public places because in theory someone is always watching.[47] But surveillance at the parks could also be hidden, as when parents, other neighborhood residents, or public park workers verbally reported their observations about the behavior of other park users or posted these observations on the Internet. Such informal surveillance supported the enforcement of park rules and regulations and the perception of maintaining public park safety.

One example of hidden, informal surveillance is a Web site called "I Saw Your Nanny" (http://isawyournanny.com). The title alone piqued my curiosity. This is a blog where parents and childcare providers can write descriptions of what they witness throughout the day, using detailed descriptions to inform readers of the "bad doings" of providers.[48] One entry, which came from someone who lived near one of the main parks that I observed, reported how a man had been accused of luring a child away with him and his dog while the mother was not paying attention. Several responders to this entry asked if the original author meant that the "babysitter" wasn't paying attention, but the author clarified in a later blog by stating no, it was the mother. The story showed the type of confusion that could arise given the medium in which the story was being recounted. Eventually someone stated that the man (who had a dog) had been brought in for questioning at the precinct but that as it turned out he was actually the father of the child. This correction was made after the entries had already been posted to the blog, but it did not stop the man from being viewed in the neighborhood as a predator and criminal. While the story did not turn out to be about an actual babysitter, it is important to be critical of such avenues of surveillance because parents with good intentions can also become the bearers of misinformation, potentially costing people their jobs and their dignity.

Irene, as a Trinidadian babysitter and mother of four, described how she had been the target of such unwarranted surveillance when she was loudly scolding a child for misbehavior. She explained, "Some people see you in public and they see you talking to a child, they don't know the circumstances around it and they're like, 'I saw this babysitter yelling at a child or something.' You don't know what happened. Like one time I told this person, 'Mind your business, I'm not talking to you, you know I'm dealing with it. . . . I'm not hitting her, I'm not doing her anything out of the way. . . . I'm talking to her and she's crying. You don't know what happened, but that's none of your business.'"

Irene acknowledged that some babysitters were not always good with the children they cared for, but, like Marga, she felt that the good babysitters were not appreciated in the way they should be: "I know there are some really mean babysitters, I'm not saying that we're all good, but when you see you have a babysitter and you see progress in your kids, and you're seeing your kids are happy and healthy, you come home, you can't get complaints from them and you're seeing stuff . . . show appreciation."

Irene, like many of the women I observed and spoken with, indicated that a good childcare provider was someone who ensured a child's happiness and kept them fed. Many felt that it went beyond this. If a child wanted to be with the provider even when the employer was back home, this too was an indication, according to Irene, that you were a good childcare provider. A bad provider would be considered by providers to be someone who spoke too loudly in public places, such as the park, or who "bad-talked" other providers to those in the parks. Providers disagreed about the acceptability of various ways of disciplining children, but many agreed that a provider shouldn't hit a child because that would most certainly get you fired, especially if done in a public place.

Babysitters are essentially "open persons" who become "vulnerable targets for harassment that violates the rules of public courtesy."[49] By occupying public places and spaces, babysitters, especially West Indians, who can be picked out among other Latin American babysitters because of their darker skin color, "black" features, and accents, are particularly vulnerable to surveillance both formal and informal. Marga discussed with me some of the ways in which she acted as a monitor of the public parks. She knew "95 percent of the children by name" and also knew which parents the children belonged to because she sometimes saw them together in the park either after work hours or on the weekend if she was working. I asked Marga how she determined whether a babysitter was indeed a babysitter and how she could differentiate babysitters from grandmothers in the park (since sometimes the babysitters were older and could be mistaken for grandparents). She said, "Grandmothers are good. Grandmothers are on top of their kids. . . . Grandmothers know that they're not going to go home and say, 'Uh oh, you know something happened in the park.'"

"What about all the other ethnic groups that you see here?" I asked so I could understand better how Marga "saw" race in the park.

Marga replied, "Most of them here are the Caribbean sitters, you know, so that's what I notice more. But I've had a couple of Latino sitters that I've dealt with. They take their job very seriously. . . . It's the same though with the Caribbean sitters. . . . They're either great or they're not. But it's more the Latinos that I think that are with their own kids . . . than I think with the Caribbeans."

"Well, how do you know they are with their own kids?" I asked with interest, knowing that there were a few black women (all African American) in the parks with their "own" white-looking children through marriage.

"Well, I . . . I . . . no, they're usually babysitting, but I think that they're with their own kids until I get talking with them [Latinos], I chat with them and I find out that they're sitters. That's how you know you have a good one . . . when people observing you think you have your own child with you. . . . And there are a lot of them [Latinos] in this park that, that I mistakenly thought had their own child with them."

Curious about the way Marga used race to categorize babysitters versus mothers, I probed further: "Now do you think maybe it's easier to know that a child is not the babysitter's . . . because I mean obviously Caribbean babysitters are black and the children are white . . . so with Latino babysitters, maybe it's harder to tell because their shading might be similar?"

"Well, no, because the children in the park are pretty white and I think it would be hard to get that kind of—" She paused, and knowing what the words coming next were, I asked, "Mixed up?" Marga replied with the apparent relief that I had said it first, "Yeah, yeah."

While perhaps the surveillance of Caribbean-born babysitters is constructed through racial categories in public parks, as evidenced by Marga's statements, it is troubling to think that most babysitters of color must endure always being monitored once people know or think they are sitters—troubling because they become easy targets when people like Marga feel obligated to watch them on behalf of their anxious employers. White ethnics, at times, endure ethnic categorization that places them in a certain position in the eyes of West Indian childcare providers as well. Sometimes West Indian domestic workers who were doing outreach in public parks for Domestic Workers United pointed out a childcare provider to me, saying she was "not the parent, she's Irish." I suppose Irish women could "only" be babysitters in the eyes of some West Indians.

One St. Lucian sitter that I met, named Ava, told me after seeing my daughter trip on the jungle gym at one Brooklyn park, "Henry fell really badly the other day and then said how I threw him down. . . . I asked him, 'Why would you say that? Did I throw you down, Henry?' He said, 'No.' I asked him, 'Who threw you down?' He said, 'I threw myself down.' I said, 'Then don't say that I threw you down.'" She then said in a low voice something I had to ask her to repeat: "He said I threw him down in front of all the white people in the park." It became clear to me at that moment how some West Indian women might feel that their position within this community was subordinate to that of "white people" who could potentially tell their employer what they had overheard in the park; further discussion with Ava revealed that she considered white residents to have ownership over the parks.

Molly expressed a similar fear at the mere mention of an accident involving a child at the park. I explained how one weekend two employers who had been watching their four nieces had a scare when one of the girls fell off of the top of the jungle gym. Molly immediately said that if you were a sitter, "You always have to have your eye on them [kids] because if anything were to happen, that's it, you're fired. . . . You have to be very careful." This fear of being fired was real to childcare providers and I could understand how it might come about, yet none of the providers I interviewed or observed had been fired because of an injury to their charges.

Off the Bench

Rose, a Russian woman who stood solidly at five-foot-nine and had long blonde hair just reaching the middle of her back, had employed a Grenadian babysitter, Ingrid, part time for two years. One day when I met Rose at the stairs in front of her condo she began asking me about my babysitter's hours because she was unhappy with Ingrid. Her husband, Dave, had even mentioned a few days earlier that they had stopped saying Ingrid's name around their daughter Lola so that Lola wouldn't ask for her, since the two had become close over the years. Dave and Rose had been troubled by Ingrid's behavior on a few occasions. About ten minutes before Ingrid was due to arrive to care for Lola, she would call or have someone (usually her son) call on her behalf to say that she was feeling sick and could not make it to work (a common tactic that providers used when they were not happy with working conditions, along with that of saying they needed to go back to their homeland because of a family member's death).[50] Soon after Rose and I began to discuss the hours of Sharon, my children's babysitter, for the coming months, Dave showed up at the base of the stairs. The two agreed that they'd had enough of Ingrid's last-minute cancellations; Dave said the next time she called he would have to tell her, "Enough is enough," meaning she would be fired.

Rose said that she had a recommended sitter coming for an interview on Saturday. I told her that I knew of a couple of sitters who might become available in February since the children they cared for were starting school, although by this point I was afraid to recommend anyone to her because of her coldness when speaking of Ingrid and the potential that Rose was a "bad employer," as the sitters would say. Soon after I mentioned the other potential sitters, Rose said to me, "I don't want a bench sitter, though." She motioned to me while saying, "Someone who sits in the park and talks all day." I found this surprising, since I often saw both Dave and Rose sitting on the benches at the park, coffee in hand, chatting with neighbors while Lola played on a jungle gym by herself. Besides, I found it interesting that Rose thought sitters just sat all day on the bench without keeping a close eye on the children or interacting with them. My participant observations over three years did not support such a lack of interaction or the regularity of inattention, although on occasion I saw both parents and babysitters "lose" a child temporarily when the parks became overcrowded on summer days. For example, on any given day in my observations, parents of children at the park could often be seen sitting on the benches watching their kids from afar, and grandparents almost always sat on benches, perhaps because they found it more difficult to play at a child's level or to stand for long periods. I had lengthy conversations with grandparents of children at the park while they had their newspapers right in front of their noses, blocking any possible visual contact with their toddler grandchild. Marga, however, who worked in the public parks every day during those same overcrowded summer days, saw the matter differently. For instance, she told me a story of seeing one particular West Indian babysitter: "The other day I had an experience with one of them [a West Indian babysitter]. She was taking care of a three-year old and the other one I know is just months old. She left the three-year-old sitting at my art table, and I didn't realize that he was there because there were so many other people around. I thought he was with somebody else. When I'm cleaning up, he's just looking at me. I said, 'Who are you with?' and he pointed at the babysitter who's in the other area, with the kid in the stroller, and she's talking on the cell phone. I brought the child over. Apparently, you know, because she was looking for him at my table, she didn't notice I'm right there in front of her. You could see the look of shock on her face because he's gone."[51]

Marga informed the sitter that she could not simply leave a three-year-old child sitting at the art table while sitting in a different area of the park. She told me that she had seen this happen quite a bit: the babysitters could not always locate the child that they were caring for in the park. In her view, this was simply a result of neglect. Angrily, Marga stated, "No, where they [West Indian babysitters] are is in one part of the park and the child is someplace else. The child might be crying and I've got to find the sitter and then [imitating a babysitter], 'Oh, I was watching.' . . . No. . . . You're not watching, not if you're that far away from the child. You're not watching them. You're glancing at them once in a while to make sure they're still there. . . . If that were my child, I wouldn't want that."

I wondered if Marga, who was the mother of one child, knew that some of these sitters were hired to care for two or three children at once. Maybe this didn't matter to Marga since the sitters were paid to be watchful. I asked Marga if she had ever had the opportunity to tell parents about the West Indian sitters that she observed neglecting children at the park. She said, "Yes, and some parents are grateful for it and other parents are totally, 'Aw, just stay out of it.'" Marga then offered two examples of incidents when a babysitter left the child she cared for to fend for himself in the public park. One four-year-old boy, a preschooler, came over to Marga because he needed to go to the bathroom. After she asked him to find his sitter, he stated, "I don't know where she is." Marga saw that he desperately needed to use the facilities and took him into the bathroom, where he stayed for half an hour because he had to go so badly. Yet the sitter "didn't miss him at all," Marga recalled: "I had someone go over and ask for the child's babysitter, and nobody answered. So when he came out, I went over and I said, 'Who's taking care of him today?' She said, 'I am.' I explained to her what happened, you know, 'For half an hour he's been inside with me. I don't want to have these kids in that situation. . . . What I'm afraid of, too is they're gonna turn around and say, 'Oh, you're abusing the child,' you know, because people call that out a lot. . . . So I don't like to be in a situation where I'm alone with them."

When I asked how the babysitter had responded to her, she said that according to the babysitter the parents had told her that the boy could go to the park and that Marga would watch him.[52] Marga, who knew the parents of this boy, didn't think this was very likely and told the babysitter, "When I see the parents . . . I'll figure that one out." Marga did indeed speak to the parents about the incident and stated that they had been glad and had spoken to the babysitter about it. It was also the last time that she saw this babysitter sitting in a different location than the child (the sitter was not fired on account of this incident). The babysitter confronted Marga afterwards, saying Marga shouldn't have said anything, but Marga told her that it was not her job to take care of the kids while the childcare provider was sitting around.

Because Marga had a relationship with parents living in the neighborhood, she could enforce the rules of the public park and control the babysitters' behavior there. In the second incident, involving a different West Indian babysitter, Marga stopped a two-and-a-half-year-old from walking out of the playground while chasing after a ball. At the time the sitter was sleeping for an hour and a half in a corner in the park according to Marga. But when Marga told the parents, they said it was none of her business, "that it's hard to find a good sitter," and that she should "just not tell anybody when these things happen." This made Marga "sad and angry," and she reflected for a moment, then said, "How can you not care about your child? You know, I mean, if I had not stopped this kid he could have gone out and gotten in a guy's car." She spoke negatively about the newer residents, whom she described as white and middle class (although in Marga's area of employment it would be considered upper middle class), saying, "The ones who don't care, I wonder why do you have children? You know, why did you bother?"

Marga did not always tell the parents what was going on in the parks and how West Indian babysitters were treating the children they cared for. For example, she claimed to see West Indian babysitters that she "wouldn't want taking care of [her] cats" because they were so negligent. She also stated that she noticed that a lot of them didn't let the kids out of the strollers. "They're in the strollers all day long, just sitting." In one incident that she recounted from about two years earlier, "A bunch of us had put in our money and bought lunch. We were sitting inside eating. This sitter sat out on the bench and ate the little girl's—the one she was taking care of—ate her lunch and then sent her in to me for food. . . . I said no. I mean if there's any left over, she's welcome to it. She gave me a hard time because I would not feed her child. It's not my job, especially when I see you sitting there eating her lunch."

When I asked Marga if she felt that because the hours are long maybe the sitters are tired by the time they get to the park, she replied, "I imagine they're all very tired because a lot of them tell me that no matter what the weather is, the parents insist they be outside with the kids. That has to be very, very tiring to be out chasing a child all day long. . . . And rain or snow you're outside, you know? So I don't know if it's real tired or just boredom, just had enough of doing this. . . . But they need the money. Like everyone else, they need to have a job." Thus Marga did sympathize to some degree with the sitters in the park, but she emphasized that sitters still needed to do their jobs to care for the children, even when the children walked away from the bench.

Rose could sit with me, coffee in hand, and chat while our kids played in the playground and feel it was acceptable for her to talk with people of her status and be a "bench mom." But perhaps because of a class and racial difference she did not feel that those who were being paid to care for children should be allowed to participate in this same form of socializing. Just because childcare providers are "symbols of middle-class status" does not necessarily "provide some protection against discrimination in public places."[53]

Molly had also heard the term *bench sitter* during her tenure as a childcare provider. She recalled going on an interview with a potential employer who told Molly about the term and asked her if she had heard it before. Molly said, "No," and the employer went on to explain that many mothers did not want their sitters to just sit on the bench while the children were playing. Although Molly was a vibrant woman in her sixties, this comment alone left a sour taste in her mouth. Molly said that even if the woman had called her back, the fact that she used such a label for childcare providers and felt comfortable talking about it with her was enough to make her decline the offer. As a provider, Molly knew that an employer who would be so forthcoming about such an insulting term was not an employer who would necessarily treat her well. The childcare providers appeared to be demonized by those outside their social network for transforming these public parks from an ultimately public domain where childcare providers were supposed to work, to a relatively private sphere where they would feel comfortable enough to carry on a conversation while the children are playing, in what constituted one form of producing or "creating" social space. This creation of social space within a public place warrants further discussion.

Community Formation: Language and Religion

Language and religion were factors that helped form community among West Indian childcare providers. Providers used language and accents in different ways to emphasize community. They dealt with the foreignness of their working neighborhoods by socializing with each other in public places such as parks, and they intensified or lessened spoken patois to separate from or connect to other parkgoers who did or did not understand it. For example, when I first entered this social world, the West Indian babysitters would speak slowly to me in what most would consider "standard English." However, it only took a few phrases on my part to indicate that I came from a West Indian background, and soon afterward these same babysitters would speak faster, using colloquial language or patois to include me in their conversations.[54] Over the years on several occasions babysitters on the bench would use patois to talk about their employers while their potential neighbors were sitting near them. Once the sitters broke out into their native tongue, others who were not considered "part of the group" would get up and leave the bench area that these women occupied. In other words, a common language was used to connect to other West Indians and dispel the feelings of isolation that could arise from the experiences of immigration and domestic work. In addition, the socializing among West Indian babysitters in public places created a social space that supported the work these women did.

Public park events in Brooklyn are often organized by the city parks and recreation staff or are sponsored and organized by outside corporations. But during my fieldwork among groups of West Indian providers, I noticed that these women also planned elaborate events for themselves and for the children in their care. In May of 2006, I was invited by Molly to attend an event that she was planning for the child in her care. It was Michelle's second birthday party and it would be held at one of the smaller public parks in Brooklyn. I received a verbal invitation to join Molly, Debbie, Hazel, and some of the other babysitters that Molly knew from the parks. I wondered why she was throwing a birthday party for the child she cared for when I had already received a formal invitation from Michelle's parents through Molly for another party a few days later, so I later asked Molly in a quiet place at the birthday party that her employers held at another public park (offering bagels, some fruit, and coffee) why she had thrown a party of her own. She replied that she had wanted to share the birthday with the "other ladies and children," to have everyone together (meaning the childcare providers), and to do something special for Michelle. The party gave Molly the opportunity to cook for the other sitters, which she always enjoyed doing, and to demonstrate her care for and special relationship with the child she cared for.

On the day of the birthday party, I brought my children with me and entered the iron gates that led to a picnic area in the park. I noticed a group of West Indian babysitters congregated around five large aluminum foil containers holding large amounts of prepared food. I headed toward them and found Molly organizing plates, cups, and spoons. Molly introduced me to the rest of the group as "a mother whose parents are West Indian" that she had invited to join the party. Once my position as a guest had been justified to the other women, I sent my kids to play with the other children in the park. After Molly had spent ten minutes preparing to have all the food served, she asked everyone to gather around the picnic table area. Then she asked one of the sitters to say grace while all ten adults held hands in a circle with the children under their care (although some of the smaller babies were in strollers). The woman began to say the blessing: "Oh God, please bless the food we are about to share. Oh God, please bless us as babysitters and as mothers to care for these children that we love. Oh God, bless these children and all of us who have children at home and give us strength and peace. Oh God in your name we pray . . . Amen." After this prayer, Molly continued, "God, bless these children and these women who care for these children each and every day and bless their parents and our families to have healthy lives. God give us the strength to do our jobs and to love one another . . . Amen."

Religion was an integral part of the providers' lives. Most of the women I observed and interviewed belonged to United churches that brought together many Caribbean people from a variety of religions, including Catholic, Presbyterian, and Anglican. Some women were self-proclaimed Seventh Day Adventists and others Baptists. While religion did not come up often throughout my participation with providers because it would be considered rude to ask about others' beliefs, it was spoken about in context of how other providers should act toward the children under their care. I would often hear that sitters should be firm but kind. Other sitters used religion to correct the behavior of other sitters whom they had befriended in public venues by jokingly stating, "God wouldn't like what you just said to me." Great laughter in the immediate park areas would follow statements like these. The providers would banter with one another about who was closer to following God's will.

The two employers who spoke to me about childcare providers and religion mentioned Seventh Day Adventists specifically. One was a male freelance journalist who during the weekdays employed a West Indian sitter from St. Lucia for his two-year-old son Luca. In our interview, he said that his sitter mostly kept to herself and did not frequently socialize as he saw other sitters doing in the neighborhood; he concluded that this was because she was a Seventh Day Adventist who was focused on following her religion by showing restraint and kindness. Yet although he saw this sitter as "not social," I saw the same woman congregating with several sitters in the parks and walking on the sidewalks with other sitters and the children under their care. She did socialize with the other childcare providers, even though she was more reserved than others in that she did not tend to initiate conversations.

The community organizer Erynn Esposito was also an employer of a Trinidadian provider and two Puerto Rican providers. She discussed with me her frustration with the "degree to which religion plays a part in the way West Indian sitters deal with adversity," claiming that West Indian women tended to say, "Trust in God and it will be okay." She singled out as a prime example of this attitude Debbie, a West Indian sitter who had helped to organize sitters but who now "said that she would stop working on the organizing because it conflicted with her religion as a Seventh Day Adventist that states that she is supposed to suffer." Erynn stated firmly her impression that "religion silences them."[55]

It is possible that Erynn and Luca's father simply did not notice how religion served as a means of uniting those from Caribbean islands. In general, providers tended to be more religiously identified than employers, although this was not always the case. In fact, Molly had found her current employers through her church, and others met their prospective employers through similar religious settings. Employer-employee conflicts about religion were rarely observed, but that may have been because employers needed a childcare provider regardless of any slight strain religion might bring in. West Indian childcare providers drew on religion as a cultural identifier and a domain in which they could find solidarity as immigrants to the United States.[56] I was even invited to join Janet and her family in church because she felt that I "would enjoy taking my kids there." Although I did not attend, I felt that Janet was trying to reach out to me as someone who might be a willing participant in this type of outing because of my West Indian background, since church could be seen as a social space where community was created in a less public situation. Through religion and other cultural markers West Indian providers found a common appreciation for each other and the work they did.

Social Capital and Social Networks

Although I only occasionally saw other babysitters holding birthday parties for the children in their care, I did notice that babysitters were brought into the process of drawing up the guest list for the parties their employers organized for their children and that they handed out invitations on the children's behalf to other babysitters and children in the parks. Often the employers themselves did not know who would be attending the parties since they were not always aware of who their children's friends were at the public parks that they frequented with their childcare providers. I met Michelle's parents for the first time at the birthday party to which they had invited me through Molly. West Indian babysitters acted as social networking agents on behalf of the parents in this sense and in some ways were increasing their employer's social capital by helping them connect with other parents in the neighborhood who held similar class status.[57] Their active social role made them strikingly different from the isolated childcare providers discussed in other research, whether they were directly networking on behalf of their employers or whether the connections that benefited their employers were merely a by-product of the collective lives of the providers themselves.

West Indian babysitters arranged celebrations not only for parents but for their own community. During my field research I attended an annual event held by and for West Indian babysitters in one of the larger public parks. I was invited by Molly to attend and to make a small donation for the food that would be supplied. I showed up on the day of the event and noticed a sea of red T-shirts with a design of little bears stamped on the chest. These shirts, which indicated that the wearer had made a monetary donation to receive food, literally territorialized the larger open space of the park. Large tables had been organized along the bocce ball alley fence to accommodate the food being served, and balloons decorated various parts of the open space. It was funny to see one half of the park occupied entirely by people dressed in red and the other half occupied by regular patrons of the park who didn't dare cross the "red line." While several of the women were enjoying traditional West Indian foods, other babysitters set up relay races among themselves near the basketball courts. As Debbie took part in one of the races, I overheard one of the children exclaim, "That's the quickest I've ever seen Debbie move in my life." Once all of the races were completed, ribbons for first, second, and third place were distributed. There was laughter, food, camaraderie, and ongoing debate over who had won the races as I took pictures to capture the event on their behalf.

I did see Marga, the park employee, walking around with her city parks and recreation designated green T-shirt among the red T-shirts worn by the West Indian providers. Later, when I asked Marga how she became involved in this event, she replied, "You know, they asked me if they could have it. Every summer they have this potluck lunch. They were asking me if it would be okay to do it. I was planning on doing my end-of-the-year party that day anyway, so I said, 'We'll do it together. In the morning, I'll do my games and give out prizes. In the afternoon, we'll do your races and you do what you want to do . . . but basically all they told me I had to do was eat.'"

While Marga distributed toys and prizes in the morning for her part of the day's events, she said that most of the babysitters were helping with the races and that she didn't have to do anything but eat for two hours. This was a different experience for Marga. She said, "They were involved in them [the races], and that was the busiest I've seen most of them. . . . It was a very fun day . . . because then they all come together and they're actually doing something with the kids rather than just sitting with them."

It is no surprise that Marga passed judgment on the West Indian babysitters whom she saw during the workweek at the park, but I felt it was unjust for her to say that these women "only" sat with the children they cared for throughout the day. From what I saw, West Indian babysitters had hectic days that sometimes began at 5:30 a.m. and ended at 7:00 p.m. Throughout the day, though not necessarily at the park, they were physically involved with the children's daily routines—packing their diaper bags, bathing them, feeding them often three meals a day, and putting them down to sleep for naps or for the night. Moreover, many were responsible for taking the children to and from storytime at the library, doctor's appointments, school, and a variety of lessons. All of this was done in the time that was not designated for public park play. These women were constantly moving from place to place and, given the larger rhythm of their day, it was no surprise that they decided to take some time out to sit down in the park once they arrived there. Also, these babysitters ranged in age from the early twenties to the early sixties. I noticed that employers did not take this into account when I spoke with them about the physical demands of childcare work. I myself was often surprised at the amount of physical labor involved in this "labor of love."

So how did workers in other public play spaces perceive West Indian babysitters and their use of the space? The next chapter concerns sitters' use of two such spaces: a library and a movement arts studio.

3

Indoor Public Play Spaces

Public spaces are not only outdoors in parks and on sidewalks; they also include public libraries and smaller spaces where children's lessons take place. I soon discovered that many of Brooklyn's open-to-the-public lessons that were meant for, as stated in the title, "Mommy and Me" were actually being held for, and thus should have been titled, "Sitter and Me." These lessons were paid for by parents of the children who attended. Enrolling my daughter in a children's tumbling class seemed like the socially appropriate thing to do since it seemed as if everyone else in my circle of friends with a child under the age of three was doing it, although enrolling a one-and-a-half-year-old in a structured class setting could also be seen as a desperate attempt by me as a parent to gain some form of cultural capital.[1] And well, if you loved your child enough to pay for the lessons (about $250 for a twelve-week session, forty-five minutes per week), other neighborhood residents considered you a "good mother." The photographs in the advertising used to promote these classes, showing mother and baby nose to nose, smiling at one another, suggested that the experience was sure to enhance the bond between mother and child.

The tumbling class that at first sounded like a class for parents (mothers more specifically) and their toddlers was in fact made up of both mothers and childcare providers; most of the latter were first-generation West Indian women. All of the adults had to take direction from the instructors and were required to keep the children under control. What caught my attention was that the adults were required to participate physically in all of the events, meaning they had to sit on the floor for stretching exercises, walk around the tumbling course while holding onto the child, sing songs, and direct the children in all activities. Some days it seemed that the adults were doing more work than the children by doing all of the activities first to ease the anxiety of the children.

While observing some West Indian childcare providers, I noticed that they were not as physically motivated to participate as some of the parents in the classes. They would not go out of their way to demonstrate to the child how to do something. Instead, they pointed to the teacher, directing the child to observe the movement. Several mentioned that this type of physical activity was not what they were paid to do, although some also talked about being grateful for something different to do outside the house. Breaking up the workweek with a lesson or two in a confined space that protected you from the sun or rain was a relief for many sitters and parents alike. Still, some childcare providers felt it was an imposition on their time and demanded too much physical exertion.

After several months in the spring of 2006, I began noticing that the majority of participants in these types of lessons, which included tumbling, dance, music, language, and even art, were West Indian babysitters and their charges. Janet, a babysitter from St. Vincent, came up to me in one of the smaller parks in Brooklyn one day, telling me that Cameron's parents had asked her to get a flyer and check out the classes available for Cameron during the workweek. Janet, a mother of two and an early childhood education student at Borough of Manhattan Community College, was upset and couldn't understand why the parents themselves wouldn't obtain this information since it was for "their child." She said quietly, "I don't know why they are telling me to go get this flyer for them when they live right there. If they want their son to go to lessons, they should find out for themselves and see the place instead of telling me to do the research." There was a distinct conflict between Janet's and her employers' perceptions of which responsibilities fell to Janet as a provider and which were those of a good parent. While some babysitters expressed this same concern over "doing the research," others were grateful for the diversion from their daily routine and quickly realized that the classes might make their job slightly more pleasant.

As much as this participation in children's activities was for the child's development, it was also an explicit demonstration of the employers' social capital. The sociologist Alejandro Portes refers to social capital as the accumulation of resources in one type of currency that are paid for in another type of currency: in this case, the employer paid for activities that were seen as good for the child's development and was repaid in the form of admittance to the community network that supported those activities.[2] Childcare providers became part of this process of obtaining social capital when they were asked to research lessons or to take the children to these lessons. The relationships that were formed between caregivers also served as a network for the children so that on the weekends when the parents were in the neighborhood and two children recognized each other from the lessons, their parents began to talk and might organize a playdate for the children. The gain for the providers was being able to connect with other West Indian childcare providers who shared their situation and daily routine. The lessons could become an occasion for providers to meet and then go out together with their charges for lunch or to the public park.

Victoria co-owned a studio with a West Indian man from Barbados. I spoke with her to determine what she thought of all the West Indian babysitters who attended classes with their charges, considering that the classes had been promoted in the beginning as classes for the parents of these same children.[3] I felt that Victoria's role, like Marga's role in the public parks though in a somewhat different way, contributed to the surveillance of childcare providers. The studio was indoors and created a more intimate setting where people could be observed closely in their interactions with children.

Both owners had lived in surrounding gentrified neighborhoods for around five years, and they had owned the studio for the last two years. Victoria's responsibilities with the company were to oversee administration, finances, public relations, and marketing and to teach half of the classes; her partner taught the other half of the classes. Ninety-nine percent of the studio's clients came from nearby gentrified neighborhoods and a few from Manhattan. Victoria described her clientele (meaning the people who paid for the classes) as 75 percent "upper-middle-class Caucasian families" with some African American and Asian families and one or two West Indian families like my own. I later found out that to support her college career she had also worked as a nanny for four years in one of the gentrified neighborhoods under study in Brooklyn.

Interacting with West Indian Babysitters

Victoria opened the doors to the studio sometime between 9:00 and 10:00 a.m. At that point parents and mostly West Indian childcare providers with small children walked in. Some children went to the two tables set at the front of the studio to color in pictures while their caregivers were trying to take off coats and shoes. Another set of children shyly buried their heads in their caregivers' tummies as if to disappear from anyone who might speak to them directly. Victoria greeted almost every child by first name and after three to five minutes ushered the children into a line before going into the studio space itself. Activities were set up for the kids to enjoy. Most parents would enter the studio space and begin interacting immediately as if they themselves needed some playtime, while West Indian childcare providers would allow the children to explore more freely. West Indian childcare providers made up 70 percent of the adults who used the studio, according to Victoria. They participated in daytime classes with the children they cared for or used the space for what was called "nonregistered playtime" when parents and providers could play for up to three hours at a time with unstructured activities. From my observations, most sitters did not actively participate in these activities; instead they sat along the wall watching the children and socializing among themselves. Nonregistered playtime was generally paid for by the employer at ten dollars per child or seventeen dollars for two and was used mainly on days when it was too cold, hot, or rainy to use the public parks. The "Mommy or Caregiver and Me" classes, as Victoria called them, were held in the mornings, and Victoria said she saw the sitters in a mothering role for that specific class time: "I would say that they're in that role for the entire time that they're the caretaker of the child. I would say my experience with every caregiver that I know, that I would consider a good caregiver, definitely takes over that mothering role for the time that they're with the child."

Trying to get Victoria to pinpoint what she meant by "mothering role," I specifically asked how the children's behavior was different with the caregivers than with their parents. She had this to say: "The caregivers are stricter and have higher expectations of the children than the parents do [in classes]. . . . I can tell you this, it's all a result of the way that the caregiver or parent participates. The child's behavior is completely a result of the adult in a Parent or Caregiver and Me class. . . . So if the caregiver or parent is active and participates and follows our instructions, the children do very well. If they don't, the child still might do well because they might be a focused child that's able to follow our verbal instructions anyway and is interested, and they might continue to do well. But there are many instances where they don't do well because the adult coming with them isn't doing their job."

While Victoria felt that there was an equal standard for "mothering" that depended entirely on participation level, she observed that some West Indian babysitters "don't want to participate, and they don't want to stand up, and they don't want to sing songs." When I continued to ask if she thought this was acceptable, she quickly responded, saying no because when she had worked as a nanny she had been more involved in the classes. I asked her if she thought this had to do with her having been much younger that most of the West Indian providers she encountered and she said that sometimes it could be about age but then went on: "We definitely try and accommodate people who are not physically able to do what we ask. You know, maybe they can't sit on the floor. We bring them a piece of gymnastics equipment to sit on."

When asked if she found that West Indian sitters played on the floor with the kids Victoria said, "From my experience [as a nanny], the ones that won't tell you up front before they're hired. . . . I definitely have encountered a lot of caregivers that say, 'I don't do this, this, this or this. I don't cook. I don't clean. I don't do this.' . . . All the ones that I know that act that way are very clear about that."

Because of the intimate nature of the studio and her years of observing West Indian providers and her own personal experiences doing childcare work I asked Victoria if she felt that was within the rights of the childcare providers to tell employers up front what they would or would not accept as their work duties. She replied, "I think if the employer is comfortable with that and they communicate it, and the employer still wants to hire them, then yeah. I think that this is a very sort of—you know, there's no sort of requirements or specifics about doing this job. So I think that it really has to be decided between the employer and the employee, what the responsibilities are. . . . I think that if you're dealing with a young child, that yes, you should be on the floor interacting with them, personally."

She continued, though, with the caveat that if the caregivers did not want to be on the floor with the child then they should compensate for that in other ways, such as reading a lot of books and doing art activities. Again, then, I heard repeated this mantra of being "on the floor" as a key element to caring for children, though Victoria had a more acute awareness than Marga, the park playground employee, that West Indian sitters might not be physically able to get on the floor.

Victoria was unique among many of the people that I had interviewed in her awareness and sensitivity toward these women, so I asked her if her partnership with a West Indian had benefited their studio in any way. She replied, "I think that there are people that feel more comfortable coming here because of that. I mean, I've noticed that we have a lot of interracial families that come here now, and I think the fact that we are two different races encourages that, and I like that aspect of it. You know, I like that. I also like that there's kids that maybe would never interact with a black man that are getting to, and seeing that he's not scary and he's not bad, and he really is a great teacher. . . . So I think it's been a positive thing for our business, and I think it's also definitely increased the number of people that want to come here. You know, nannies meet him on the street. They tell their employers about the studio. So I think it's definitely expanded our clientele for sure, having the two of us here and that we do come from different backgrounds." Victoria also noted that her business partner, as an insider to West Indian culture, was especially adept in dealing with possible cultural conflicts in the studio: "I think there [are] times that Derek knows how to deal with things much better than I do. The way that he would deal with it would be less offensive than the way I would deal with it, even though that would never be my intention. I mean we have conflicts because of our cultural differences, and it's just they're cultural differences. I think that, yeah, there's definitely times when he's said to me . . . 'Deal with this in this way, because the way that you're dealing with it might seem offensive to this group of people.'"

Victoria felt that having Derek as her friend at first, then as her co-worker, and now as her business partner also helped. "You know, people know that you're spending time with someone from their country" and this made it easier to socialize among this group of West Indian babysitters.

In many ways, Derek contributed to the social and economic capital of the studio simply by being West Indian and building a rapport with the West Indian childcare providers. He was part of the community of providers on a cultural level and was able to leverage this when it came to business.

The Public Library

Another way of getting out of the house was to go to the public library. In the early fall of 2004, Hazel invited me to the library's "storytime" just a few blocks away from three of the public parks we would visit in the mornings. At least two mornings a week, a crowd of West Indian women (all babysitters) and other parents or childcare providers could be seen entering a side door just off the neighborhood's main street. It led to an elevator that took people to the basement of the public library. Once the elevator arrived at the basement level, women pushed strollers up a ramp, talking as they walked, until they came to a room with low ceilings, tiled floors, a worn-looking carpet located in the middle filled with toys, a television, and, of course, books.

When Hazel and I first arrived together at the library for storytime, she immediately introduced me and my daughter, who at the time was only a few months old, to several babysitters. A young white man (in his early thirties) came out of another door that joined the room to the main library and began handing all of the adults white sheets of paper with the words and lyrics to children's rhymes and songs. He immediately broke into a welcome song signaling that the adults should sit in the chairs provided and that the children should sit in a semicircle around the man. We all followed along with standard tunes such as "Itsy Bitsy Spider" and "Twinkle, Twinkle, Little Star." After a few minutes of this, the man took out a book from his bag behind his back and began reading children's books in a slow, deliberate manner, so that all of the children could follow along, while many of the sitters sat around chatting with one another or, it seemed to me, staring into space from boredom. Storytime generally ended with one last song and, on several mornings, a disbursement of brand-new children's books from the children's librarian.

Hazel and I, and soon after Debbie, Sharon, and Evelyn, would all get together twice a week at storytime for thirty minutes to take part in this ritual, which offered a break from the monotony of park play. It ran from September to May, with a break for the summer months to allow for program adjustments and development. By our second year of participation in the weekly storytime, the number of participants had grown to a point where it was no longer possible for some of us to attend. It was as if the neighborhood was having its own baby boom. The children's librarian had also changed to a Chinese woman in her fifties. Because her accent was thick and sometimes difficult to understand, some children strayed away from storytime and played in the back of the room with the toys made available to them. The West Indian childcare providers also seemed to lack interest in this new librarian, as demonstrated by their increased socializing among themselves while stories were being told. The sitters would constantly complain that they couldn't understand what the librarian was saying. "She's not as good as the other man," Debbie stated, adding that she "preferred it last year with the other man." But by this time, I was securely socialized into the storytime culture, feeling as if I had done something good for my child.

The West Indian babysitters were aggressively competitive when books were distributed at the end of storytime—Molly, Rachel, and Janet would get up only to ensure that their charges received "good" books. Many participants would dive in and grab two to three books, until one day the woman librarian began the distribution by announcing, "You can only take one book per child." I would overhear sitters telling each other that the "mother likes it when I can show them that I've done something." Admittedly, I also liked scrambling at the end of a session for a new book for my daughter and feeling as if I had just won the lottery.

For security reasons, adults were required to sign in to storytime on a sheet of paper with the child's name and some form of contact information. After two years of attending storytime sessions I realized that the library sign-in sheet could be inspected by parents who wanted to ensure that their childcare provider had indeed gone to the library. Further, parents could check to see whether the provider had brought home one of the distributed books. None of the parents I observed or interviewed ever commented on this fact, but the chaos at book distribution time suggested to me that providers were determined to get books to children as proof for their employers that they had indeed attended.

I interviewed the children's librarian to talk about her interactions with the West Indian babysitters she encountered during the workweek. Mei was a first-generation Chinese woman who had begun working in the United States as a seamstress in a factory in New York. She then went back to school in order to obtain her aesthetician's license. After some years of working as a domestic worker (housecleaner), she went back to school and took a position within the public library in Brooklyn, where she moved up the ranks to children's librarian. As a first-generation immigrant to New York City, she understood how difficult it could be to become part of the neighborhood. Because of this, she stated that she tried to accommodate everyone at the library. As a mother herself, she knew how difficult it could be to keep children occupied.

Winter months were the busiest for storytime since most babysitters wanted to be indoors. Mei noted that the West Indian childcare providers, who made up around 50 percent of her adult participants, mostly seemed to care for the children they brought into storytime. She mentioned to me that "the Caribbean babysitters are more strict than the parents I see with the children. . . . They [the sitters] don't let the children scream and tend to make sure that the kids behave." She did not typically see the babysitters interacting with parents in the library or during storytime, something that I had noticed as well. The close quarters of the small branch public library would lend itself to socializing between parents and babysitters, but in two years I never saw such interaction occur in any meaningful way.

In my interview with Mei, she mentioned that the West Indian babysitters did socialize among themselves within the public library and at times needed to be told to keep it down but that she rarely ever had "a problem with them." She said that she had observed on several occasions how the West Indian babysitters sat and talked with one another, "exchanging recipes with one another or sharing food with one another" and sometimes with her too. This socializing made her job easier when she was planning special events at the public library. She said that although she used the public library Web site, the local public parks, and storytime to distribute printed event calendars for promotion purposes, "I use event calendars because not everyone goes online. . . . They pass information on to each other, which is sometimes better than the paper." Through the sociability of the West Indian babysitters, the librarian could find enough participants for public events so that those events could be held. The community would be poorer without these networks, Mei said, and she would need to find new ways of serving the neighborhood's children and adults. In essence, West Indian babysitters were providing services to the parent community of the neighborhood by "passing on" information that parents could use themselves to interact with their children and the community on weekends, thus increasing once more the social capital of their employers.

Employers' social capital was reinforced by West Indian childcare providers' activities in public spaces in all of the neighborhoods that I studied. Whether these were activities that brought parents together outside the workweek or established friends for the children in the providers' care, employers were able to participate, to a certain degree, in the social networks maintained by their employees. By default, many employers benefited from the built-in networks of West Indian childcare providers and their ability to dispel the isolation of domestic work by meeting with each other. This, in turn, enabled employers to reconstitute their positions in the social hierarchy.

Providers' activities in public spaces placed them under the scrutiny of public employees and, in the parks, other park users (many of whom were friends, parents, or relatives from the gentrified neighborhoods under study). Surveillance in this form controlled socializing among West Indian childcare providers and kept them subordinate in ways that were further reinforced in the private spaces of the employers' homes. While providers might feel constrained by the surveillance of strangers and employers in both public and private spaces, they found ways of justifying their frustrations by commenting on their rights to regular hours or their ability to take care of children better than their employers, whom they deemed unfit or unclean. Their inversion of outsiders' assumptions as to who was "fit" and or "unfit" to take care of children was one way they combated isolation in the domestic sphere and was part of the collective life that gave West Indian providers the voice or language to do so.

4

A Taste of Home

How Food Creates Community

"*You have to listen to the Woman with the Pepper Sauce because she is Boss!*" This is the first thing I heard as I entered the park through the black iron gates leading to the infant playground. The woman making this statement was a childcare provider from St. Vincent in her mid-sixties who wore glasses and had long cascading braids tied at the back of her head with a blue-and-white-patterned headscarf. She was directing her statement to four other West Indian sitters who were comfortably situated at one of the park benches directly in front of the swing set where they could observe the children under their care. They were feeding the children some crackers as they ran back and forth between the bench and the playground. After the ladies laughed together at the statement, they bantered back and forth for about five minutes in a jokingly competitive way as to whose word should be taken as authoritative. Every now and then they would break out in laughter between verbal jabs. Food continued to be dispensed to the children while serving, simultaneously, as an indicator for who the providers should concede to as the most knowledgeable person in the group.

This chapter builds on previous chapters to suggest how childcare providers used food to create community among each other. Their West Indian food culture was a prominent part of their daily lives and bonded them as Caribbean women. Below, I explore how providers made food preparation a measure of mothering ability against which their employers were judged and found wanting, as well as a means of asserting control within the employer's household. I also show how providers shared food among themselves and how occasions of food sharing evoked cultural memories. In some ways providers had to relinquish or adapt West Indian foodways as they moved from their own home or from public spaces to the employer's home. Exploring such matters requires first some background about foodways and how the place of food in a culture is constructed.

Foodways, the practices and regulations that dictate the food experience in its sensory aspects and in the social context of communication, have long been of interest to many social scientists. But how we understand the "place" of foodways from a sociological standpoint has not been fully clarified. Until recently, the discussion of foodways has traditionally been steeped in anthropological and folkloric cultural analysis.[1] There has been little sociological analysis of food practices, thereby limiting dialogue on the role of these practices in creating and maintaining social groups.[2] Further, few have researched the relationship between food and care in private and public places.[3] This relationship is key not only to understanding food as a symbol but also to demonstrating how food sustains a shared understanding of culture and social life, as exercised through rituals of offering and eating food, and how such rituals produce a set of patterned meanings associated with *sociability*.[4]

This chapter examines how childcare providers used food as a symbol of power to resist the inequality of employer and employee relationship as it was manifested in control of household spaces and, sometimes, to assert a form of perceived control over their employers by giving West Indian food to the employers' children. I also show how providers used food to create certain social spaces while simultaneously bringing providers from different islands together in public places.

If "food indicates who we are, where we came from, and what we want to be," then social scientists must move beyond the typical culinary setting of the kitchen to explore public places (in a geographical or physical sense) as social food spaces in order to "understand how the experience of complexity might be gained in the urban environment."[5] It is partly through foodways that social differences become meaningful in an urban environment.

If a social space can be created by people's relationships and activities within physical boundaries, a social food space can be explained as a physical location where food is consumed, shared, and discussed (though not necessarily prepared) as part of the social relationships constructed in everyday life.[6] A social food space is created once complex individual and intergroup feelings, images, and attitudes are expressed symbolically through activities surrounding food in a physical place. Territorialization, with its creation of invisible boundaries, develops through the enacting of cultural codes such as language or dialect (in the case of West Indian culture, colloquial dialect or patois) and through the physical demarcation of spaces through special events that are organized by babysitters for babysitters. In this sense, as geographer David Harvey posits, the public urban environment has become "the primary level at which individuals now experience, live out, and react to the totality of social transformations and structures in the world around them."[7]

Looking at public parks in Brooklyn as social food spaces can provide insights into the foodways of West Indian/Caribbean babysitters who primarily occupy these urban public places during the weekdays. Since the populations that use the parks in the various routines of everyday life (e.g., parkgoers who live in the neighborhood versus users who perform their work in the park but do not live in the neighborhood) have different and sometimes conflicting purposes, the social food spaces constructed in the park are less predictable than private culinary spaces, where actions such as food preparation can be controlled and ordered in an established sequence of patterned events.[8] In this chapter, I look specifically at how childcare providers used parks as representational spaces—defined as spaces socially produced through practices that embody symbolic aspects of a community's life—while at the same time accommodating the uses of other parkgoers. I also consider how movement between public and private places (i.e., the employer's or sitter's home) constrains or alters West Indian foodways practices.

West Indian food as expressed through the foodways of the nations' peoples is arguably one of the key components to understanding transnationalism and globalization as it is experienced by West Indians in the United States.[9] Caribbean immigrants have a varied diet that differs culturally by territory,[10] so sensitivity to these differences is imperative.[11] It is therefore necessary to probe the ongoing relationship between U.S. and West Indian foodways and its effects on West Indians when they migrate to the United States.

In this research, I explore how West Indian childcare providers negotiated their movement from public places, where socializing was key to the creation of a daily collective life, to private places, such as the homes of their employers, where they occupied a subordinated position. In both of these places, as Hondagneu-Sotelo found for Latina domestic workers on the West Coast, food traditions became central to social interaction among sitters and between the sitters and the children they cared for.[12] West Indian providers' use of food and cooking as symbols of power seemed to challenge the private sphere inequalities found in other studies by asserting the role of the provider in the household.[13]

This chapter uses in-depth interviews and participant observation to illustrate the power of "food voice" in the life of West Indian babysitters.[14] Annie Hauck-Lawson defines food voice is "the voice of people as food makers and food consumers" that conveys the meanings of "food-related activities."[15]

Using as a model Jonathan Deutsch's work on communal food preparation in firehouse cooking among firemen, I was able to capture how childcare providers' practices and conversation around communal food preparation expressed sociability and their understanding of gender roles.[16] While sitters' communication and socializing involved other matters besides food, as discussed later in the book, their food voice was prominent in their everyday lives. The study of West Indian babysitters in public places shows how food voice is a means of maintaining social relationships based on shared culture in order to counteract the isolation that has typically plagued this group of working-class women.

As a participant observer in Brooklyn public parks, I listened to the many conversations sitters would engage in while they worked. I also noted their own food consumption and that of the children they cared for. I approached some participants while I played with my own children at the parks and asked general questions about food in the neighborhood that led to more detailed conversations about West Indian food. We discussed shopping for ingredients and spices, the differences in national foods between islands, the cooking process itself, the cultural meanings of food preparation and sharing, and the food interactions between sitters and the children they cared for. Through participant observations and interviews, specific themes emerged, and I was able to compare foodways as practiced across a variety of islands.

The Place of Food

Traditional medical remedies, recommended ways of dealing with a child who was "acting up," and most importantly food were common topics of discussion in the public parks I frequented. Food culture, its symbolic meaning and practices, was prominent at the park since many children and sitters ate snacks and, on occasion, had lunch there. Sitters who cared for infants bottle-fed them every few hours while participating in the social networking that went on at the park. The frequency of West Indian sitters' food activities thus made food culture an aspect of social food space worth analyzing.[17] Because the children that many of these women cared for were from white-middle class families, it was important to consider ethnicity and culture as contributors to differences in food consumption patterns between white employer families and West Indian providers. Cooking, as "the most ceremonial form of household work," is also key to understanding how food is considered to reflect on parenting.[18] It is ceremonial in the sense that it adheres to certain rituals carried out by a group of people. Different members in the group have clearly marked roles such as "the lead cook," "the assistant cook," and "the noncook." The rituals continue through the table setting and the order in which people eat. All of these practices together give a sense of group solidarity.

Black Food for White Children

I found that many of the sitters, though they had been living in New York for years, had not significantly changed their West Indian foodways. Many of them still shopped for West Indian spices and ingredients on a weekly basis and cooked West Indian foods for their own families' breakfast, lunch, and dinner. Most sitters with a family living in their own home got up at 5:30 or 6:30 a.m. to cook their family's breakfast. Those who were married prepared lunches for their husband to take to work and their children to take to school or day care. Others without a husband or children prepared their own lunches to bring to their employer's home. In the evenings when the sitters got home, sometimes as late as 7:00 p.m., they were expected to cook for their own family unless leftovers remained from the previous night (which was a rarity). Only on occasion and more typically among the younger babysitters would these women purchase food in a store while caring for children during the day, and the sitters made it explicit that they did not impose their West Indian foodways on the children they cared for.

For example, I asked two sitters, Sylma and Molly, whom I had met in the park one spring morning, if they cooked West Indian food for the kids they cared for. They both immediately shook their heads vigorously as if it were crazy for me to think so and said, "The parents leave food for them [the children]." Molly stated that she would need her employers' approval to bring food for the child in her care and that she did not want the additional work of cooking for a child. The child she cared for would come to her plate at lunch and want her West Indian food, which she had cooked the night before and taken with her for lunch at her employers' home. She added that when she saw what the parents had left for the child, she thought, "Yuck" (here she made a disgusted face while pretending to vomit). I asked both ladies what the parents left for the children to eat, and in unison they responded, "Pasta." Molly added that sometimes the parents of the child she cared for would leave spinach or peas—"lots of greens." Here Sylma jumped in to say that she didn't "understand about baby food": "We never used baby food. From four months you eat out of the pot" (meaning that you ate what the adults ate). Molly added that she didn't "understand why they use baby food." All of the babysitters that I interviewed claimed that baby food was unheard of in the Caribbean and that the babies simply ate whatever the rest of the family was eating, though mashed up in a smoother consistency. They did not understand why parents in the United States gave these restricted, flavorless foods to their children.

Sitters did tell some stories about giving West Indian food to the children they cared for, often at the children's request. Debbie, for example, told me that two-year-old Taylor loved the West Indian food that Debbie brought for herself for lunch: "She [Taylor] loves it, she got a taste one time and then she got addicted. . . . She will leave hers [food] and then she will eat all of Debbie's" (referring to herself in the third person). Arlene, a sitter from Guyana, threw more light on this topic when she told me a story about her West Indian niece, Samantha, who also sat for children: "Samantha used to make dumplings [a traditional West Indian addition to several dishes, made from flour, oil, and water mixed together, rolled up, and boiled] for the boy and girl she cared for, but they were only supposed to eat kosher food.[19] Samantha never did tell the parents that she fed it to them, and now that the children are older, they still ask Samantha to make the dumplings for them and ask her to bring it over."

Arlene went on, "If you start the kids early [eating different foods] they will like it." Her own employers' views on feeding the child she cared for, who was two years old, were very different from the views of Samantha's employers: "I don't bring my own food to work with me. The parents don't leave food for the girl. I buy food when I am there in the neighborhood for the two of us. We are a little team."

Though Arlene had done this without the parents' approval at first, she said she had later found out that the mother didn't care if Arlene fed the child different types of food as long as the child was eating. Arlene now regretted not having given her more of a selection when she was younger and said she "would have trained her to eat different foods."

Both Arlene and Samantha appeared to have felt especially close to the children they cared for because of the food they put into the mouths of these children, maybe even the act of feeding itself. In Samantha's case, the parents' food choices for the children obviously had a religious motivation, but the West Indian sitter had a countermotivation of her own—perhaps the aim of exposing the children to other foods in order to broaden their palate, but perhaps something that went even deeper. Arlene said of shopping with the child for West Indian food and cooking it for her, "We are a little team." And Samantha proudly recounted that the children she cared for still asked for dumplings, in an act against their parents' wishes and culture. The sitters were asserting their own claim on the physical bodies of these children and experiencing an emotional closeness to them through the food practice itself. History was essentially being fed to the children, as Gusfield would assert when he says the human body is a "perpetual source of meaning and an object of historical variation. It is an instrument of purpose and a goal of aesthetic perfection. . . . How the body is conceived and how human beings act toward it is as much a matter of culture and history as are the manners and morals of food habits."[20] The bodies of the children under care, then, were like vessels into which West Indian sitters could pour a culture different from that of their employers, with the goal of asserting some form of control through closeness.[21] Though the children had already acquired some ideas of culture imposed by their parents, they did recognize a difference in the culture that West Indian babysitters were asserting, as evidenced by their requesting specific foods from the sitters that were different from what their parents left them.

As mentioned earlier, some parents did not mind if childcare providers broadened the palate of their children by introducing them to West Indian foods. Carol, who cooked almost all of her own food and had worked in childcare jobs where she was responsible for the cooking, spoke about how good it made her feel to know that the children she cared for enjoyed her food: "Today I make okra and rice, cook it up together with chicken and coconut milk and stuff . . . and he [the child she cares for] tell me bring some rice for him because Monday I had rice . . . so I bring some today and what I cook in a little container. Would you believe when I bring him from school, if you see when he sit down . . . and them ladies does laugh in the park cause he does sit down and he chomp and chomp it down . . . Oh my God! His father calls him an Italian Trini [Trinidadian] because he eats fruit cake, he eats roti, everything!" Carol laughed and immediately continued with a story about a girl she cared for who couldn't pronounce her name correctly and therefore called her "Carrie." The little girl even wanted to have special playdates with Carol in the park on Saturdays and made food requests for the occasion such as macaroni pie, pelau (a rice and beans dish), and stewed chicken. The girl would ask, "Carrie, you take the order?" and she would reply laughingly, "Yes, I take the order." The girl would eat the food and tell Carol, "Oh Carrie, you make my day."

Again, Carol was amused that these children under her care enjoyed something that she had made for them herself. It was both a point of pride for Carol and a positive reflection on the children she cared for. In some way, she was putting on a performance that indicated her power over them and even the parents themselves, who were not, perhaps, able to make this type of food. Carol did not acknowledge, however, that she was now providing food purchased with her own money and additional unpaid services to the children in her care. The apparent loss of power through taking an "order" did not seem to bother her. After all, the work involved in meeting these special requests was something within her control since ultimately she could always decline the request. She also expressed a closeness to these children when she laughed at how much the children loved her cooking and her diligence in fulfilling their special requests.

Food Practices as Cultural Exploration and Preservation

Several West Indian sitters observed that traditional foods across the Caribbean, in spite of their sameness, might be named or prepared differently in the different countries. One of the greatest examples of such differences in preparation occurred with the "one-pot meal" that almost every participant in this study mentioned—callaloo.[22] This popular dish, which resembles a thick soup, is made with okra, ground dasheen leaves or spinach, butter, spices, and coconut milk. It was clearly the favorite among many of the sitters I observed and interviewed. Even younger sitters such as Hazel and Debbie who did not cook West Indian food on a daily basis claimed that callaloo was their favorite dish and would make it for themselves on occasion. However, descriptions of this dish's consistency varied. As Carol noted, "Trinidadians like their callaloo ground up and smooth. . . . I don't like the way Guyanese make it. . . . It's too thick with chunks of spinach. . . . They don't grind it up like we do." Because of the usually slight but sometimes significant differences in food across the Caribbean countries, sitters shared West Indian food at the park to introduce each other to types of food that were offered in one country but not in another, establishing what appeared to be a deeper cultural connection by affirming similarity through the exploration of differences. This food sharing also cemented a pan-Caribbean identity formed in public spaces by creating a solidarity with people "from the islands" without one's ever having to specify which island.

One cool fall morning, Carol came over to talk to Donna, another sitter from Grenada, as we were all sitting on a bench inside the infant playground near the slides and jungle gym. She immediately stated that she had "stopped cooking for the ladies because no one was coming around consistently." In a lengthier conversation two years later, Carol retracted that statement and explained in more detail that she did "still cook for the 'ladies,' but in the winter months it is too cold and they don't come around the park as much." She commented further that "all the women have been asking for [her] to bring food for them," a request she was accustomed to hearing from the children in her care. This park tradition was shared by Molly, who loved to cook and had regularly carried food for the other West Indian sitters at the park for years. When I asked her how the act of bringing food for others was prompted, Molly explained, "For example, Debbie don't know about saltfish cake, how we [Guyanese] make it. We make it a different way, so I always promising her to bring saltfish cake for her, but I don't tell her that I'm making it for tomorrow. I will give her a surprise tomorrow." And in response to being asked how sharing West Indian food with the other childcare providers in the park made her feel, she said, "It makes me feel good that I could make something and I could share it and they enjoy it. . . . I love to share. . . . I would like to think that they think of home." In a separate interview, Debbie said that every time she cooked or ate West Indian food she was reminded of Grenada: "It brings back memories. . . . These are the things we usually eat at home, so like when you eat it, you think about maybe your family because you always eat this together. You think about maybe your friends . . . the environment you used to be eating this food in and now you eat in a different environment."

Sharing food offered emotional solace to "homesick" immigrants who relished the memories of their homeland. The connectedness between providers deepened through this exchange of food and also helped to establish the power relations within the larger childcare provider community. For example, Debbie would sooner do a favor for Molly than for another provider with whom she did not share food. Food created bonds of reciprocity that helped sitters to create a collective protection against the isolation of their job duties.

Unlike Molly, Debbie had never cooked for her employers, nor did she cook for the other sitters in the park. She did say that if she were asked to cook for one of the other sitters she would do it, but she added that it "depends on the mood [she's] in and the type of food."[23]

Molly took pride in being able to cook for other sitters at the park, and when she promised to bring food for them she always followed through. I experienced this personally when Molly told me to meet her at 9:00 in the morning after our interview because she would make me some saltfish cakes. At exactly that time the next morning, Molly had my two saltfish cakes ready in a Ziploc bag. I told her that I would taste it and tell her what I thought.

A few days later, when I saw Molly waiting at the bus stop in the neighborhood, she stopped me to ask what I had thought of the cakes. I told her that "it tasted so good and had the right amount of pepper that I even let my daughter have some for lunch and she ate it all up," which was unusual for a twenty-one-month-old. Molly smiled and said that she was happy that I had shared it with my daughter. Perhaps it was her way of ensuring a form of West Indian cultural reproduction. As Elaine Kaplan notes, it is "through . . . her continual acts of food exchange, both as producer and as consumer, that [a] person is constituted as part of a community."[24] This food exchange between Molly, other sitters, and me reinforced the sense of community felt among us all while also offering a site for exchange and comparison.

Food Practices in Public versus Private Spaces

As sitters moved from public spaces, such as the public parks, to the private space of the employer's home, their expression of their West Indian foodways, which responded to the differing social orders that existed within these spaces, changed, typically in ways that constrained the sitter.

Molly talked extensively about bringing food to her employers, although it was not required as part of her primary job as a sitter. She explained to me that her employer would beg her, saying, "Oh, bring me food," when she became aware that Molly would be cooking that night back at her own home. Molly continued, "So I used to bring them [food]. . . . I used to bring to them nearly every week. . . . On the weekends I used to bring for them, but it's a couple weeks now that I haven't made for them. . . . Now they're telling me, 'Oh you're going home to cook a lot this weekend, Molly?' [since it was Easter weekend], and I said yes. They said 'Okay!' because they been looking for it."

While Molly's employers did not explicitly request that she bring food for them after the Easter weekend, by inquiring whether she would be cooking, and by communicating their enthusiasm at the prospect, they implied clearly their desire that she bring leftovers. This did not appear to bother her just then but did suggest that a power struggle could ensue because of the added obligation. Encroaching on Molly's time or expecting gifts of food apparently did not strike the employers as unfairly demanding of their employee. In other ways, however, it reversed the power relations between Molly and her employers: Molly could now determine whether and when to bring food, thereby leaving the employees guessing as to whether they needed to prepare their own food for the day, and that may have represented control to Molly.

Children's requests for West Indian food, discussed above, raised some similar issues of power relations between employer and employee.

I asked Debbie, who brought West Indian food with her for most of her lunches when working as a sitter for two-year-old Margaret, about the differences in eating West Indian foods at her own home versus her employers'. Debbie replied, "When you are eating in your own little environment you feel more comfortable than when you're eating out, you know, in somebody else's environment or among other people, maybe people you don't know that good or something like that. . . . You may tend to maybe do other things like . . . when you're eating home you play loud music, but when you're in someone else's place you may not be able to do that, so all of these things could change the way you feel."

Debbie's comment illustrates how the private space of the employee's own home could lend a sense of comfort that was not necessarily experienced within the home of the employer.[25] This sentiment was echoed by Arlene, who spoke to me about the difficulty she felt in eating at her employer's home. "It's too hard to warm up the food at work. . . . I wasn't raised with a microwave." She did claim that if there was a toaster-oven she would maybe use that but said that using the stove to heat up food at work made things too complicated. In addition, while I was walking home from a park with Arlene one sunny afternoon, she remarked that she had once gone to pour herself a glass of orange juice from the container in the fridge and had noticed that the mother must have drunk directly out of the carton although the container was quite full. Arlene was disgusted: "I saw this ring of lipstick around the nozzle of the container and it just made me sick to think that I almost poured a glass of juice from that container for myself . . . it was so nasty." Thus Arlene found that eating in the private residence of her employer was difficult on multiple levels, and she preferred to go out in the neighborhood and pick up something to eat.

Victoria, the white owner of the movement arts studio, told me that in her experiences as a nanny over a period of years she had also felt uncomfortable about eating in the employer's home. She said that she would sometimes be offered food but that she had generally brought her own lunch or had gone out with the two children to pick up something from a local store and eat it at the park rather than eating at the employer's home or, worse yet, asking for food from the employer's fridge. "There was never an open-refrigerator policy, you know, with 'Take whatever you like.' Every once in a while she [the mother] would say, 'Oh, I have takeout in there. If you want some for lunch go ahead.' But that was pretty much the only time that was discussed."

Comments like these illustrate further how spatial inequality was preserved in the private sphere of the employer's home and how public spaces were used to reduce such inequality.

One winter afternoon I observed five West Indian sitters, including Gail, a sitter from Grenada, as they hosted a "playdate" at the home of Gail's employers (presumably with their permission, as was usually the case). I had been invited to join in with my daughter. Gail was preparing to cook some West Indian stew chicken that another sitter, Natalie from Grenada, had bought, along with rice and beans. While Natalie and Gail were primarily in charge of cooking the meal, there was a sense of community at this playdate. On the bottom floor of the duplex in a brownstone close to the park where the sitters regularly met, many of the women were sitting on the carpet in front of the television playing with the children they cared for. It was a scene that contradicted previous literature as well as Marga's observations as a park employee, which had suggested that West Indian sitters did not play on the ground with the children they cared for.[26] The preparation of traditional foods at this event was for the women a starting point for social interaction, discussion, and cultural identification, perhaps more so since they were in the presence of the white children they cared for and may have more consciously wanted to reify their West Indianness.

The sitters proceeded with care in the preparation of the chicken, first cleaning it by rubbing it with lemon, then seasoning it with the "right spices" and debating with one another on the correct method of browning sugar for the chicken when stewing it. How much should the sugar should be browned when in the pan or pot? If it wasn't browned enough, the chicken could become too sweet, but if it became too black, as Arlene pointed out when I spoke with her in the park one day, the chicken would "have a bitter taste." The debate continued as an example of cultural variation in foodways, since at this particular playdate some sitters were Trinidadian and others Grenadian.

The food sharing and discussion that occurred during this playdate took various forms.[27] Some of the sitters ate their food on the floor while continuing to play with the children they cared for, while I and others sat on a couch or chair to eat the food. There were no formal arrangements for eating the food, but this might have had more to do with the casual setting of the playdate itself: since there weren't enough high chairs for all of the children to sit in, the children remained on the carpeted floor, and thus some of the sitters also remained seated on the floor with the children. Much of the discussion for the next half hour, as we ate the food, was about the taste of the food, how much of a particular ingredient (such as garlic, cumin, or coriander) had been used, and how the dish differed from another West Indian dish.

None of the children partook of the West Indian food, since most were still under the age of two at this playdate and/or were primarily being fed from a bottle. Since most employers were not present or had had their breastfeeding stopped so they could return to the workplace, providers were often prepared with powdered formula or cold bags of pumped breast milk for the children in their care. I should note here that breastfeeding never came up in my fieldwork as something a mother should or shouldn't do. Perhaps this had something to do with the fact that some of the providers knew I had breast-fed my children, as this was often the reason why I had to leave a site. But it could also be because they had grown up in the Caribbean, where both formula feeding with homemade formula (regular milk and some type of porridge-type cereal) and breastfeeding are common options. They never acknowledged any stigma to either feeding choice, in contrast to Blum's findings about African American women and breastfeeding, a difference that can be traced to the differing histories and cultures of the two groups.[28] While there was no stigma attached to the practice of breastfeeding among the providers whom I studied, they did express some annoyance when the employer's breastfeeding limited their outings to public places. If the employer was not pumping her milk and worked at home or was resting at home, the provider would sometimes have to go back there frequently throughout the day so that the baby could feed. Some providers saw this as a nuisance.

A playdate gathering of several sitters at an employer's home while the employer was not present offered a much greater comfort level than that experienced by Debbie and Arlene when they were alone in the homes of their employers with the children for whom they cared, even when the employer was not present. The private social food space of the playdate mimicked that of the public social food space at public parks where West Indian sitters could experience food sociability among each other—in groups. The potential isolation and inequality that enveloped the private household of the employer was for a time dispelled once the childcare providers were together sharing cultural food and what they called "old talk" (recalling memories from the homeland). The cultural background shared among these women gave them a feeling of ease that they did not necessarily experience when they were separated from other sitters and alone with their charges. When sitters had an opportunity to share their ethnic identities through the food they ate, food appeared to be given more meaning, as expressed through detailed conversations and banter about the preparation and taste of food and ultimately the food memories of "home."

Food and Mothering

Issues of control always seemed to come up when I heard West Indian women talk about food. I cannot count the number of discussions I had with Molly about various food dishes that ended up with her rolling her eyes because I had asked her to repeat a particular recipe ingredient that I should have remembered. Molly could rattle off any dish as if she were making it right in front of me in real time. This made me self-conscious because of my lack of interest in cooking, especially given the gender ideologies suggesting that as a mother I should know how to cook. I distinctly remember telling Annie, a Trinidadian sitter I met in Carroll Park who was in her mid-fifties and cared for a two-year-old girl part time, that "I always have to follow a recipe exactly in order to cook anything, especially West Indian food." Her reply was, "Nah man, if you taste it once, you know how to make it." At that moment, I began to question my mothering skills. What is it about food and mothering that pressures women into feeling that they should be able to whip up a meal within thirty minutes for a family of eight? As Deborah Lupton reminds us, the connection of food to maternal love has been marketed to audiences worldwide for decades and thus has been reproduced on all levels in society.[29] Often in conversation the sitters equated food practices with mothering skills.[30]

West Indian women, like the Latina domestic workers in Pierette Hondagneu-Sotelo's book, often commented that their employers didn't feed their children "proper food" and criticized employers for not physically feeding their children.[31] This sentiment was expressed in a variety of forms. For example, one early afternoon in June during the workweek I bumped into Deondra, a sitter from Trinidad in her late fifties, down the street from my home as I was heading out to the gym to exercise. The streets were quiet since it was just after the lunch hour, around 1:30 p.m. Deondra had only one of the three children she cared for with her in a stroller. She asked me, "Where are the children?" and I replied, "With Sharon," my sitter, whom I knew she had met in the park. I explained that I was heading to the gym (my clothing gave that away, as I was wearing spandex pants, running shoes, and a tank top and held in my right hand was a pair of headphones for listening to music while I worked out). I asked Deondra when she would be getting off work, and she said late. She told me that she had to put the kids down to nap. I told her that I tried to have the kids fed and napping before Sharon came over so that she had a couple of hours to relax before the chaos of two toddlers began. I added, "I try to always . . . have the food prepared in a bowl for them so she just has to heat it up in the microwave." Deondra surprised me by saying, "That's because you are a real mother and you care for your children." Intrigued by this statement, I asked, "What do you mean? Don't all mothers prepare the food for their children?" "No," Deondra answered, "these people [female employers] don't always prepare the food." She continued, "Motherhood means that you feed your children, you bathe your children, and you spend time with your children. . . . These mothers go to work and don't do anything for their children and then want the sitters or nannies to do everything, that's not motherhood. . . . See, you want to be with your children, feed them, give them a bath to be with them, that is a good mother."

While I was flattered by her validation of my mothering practices, I was also very concerned that perhaps Deondra didn't understand fully the life practices of the employers that she worked for. For example, Deondra seemed to be expressing the view of the sociologist Arlie Hochschild in her book *The Time Bind* that parents' long hours at work might be a tactic to avoid dealing with everyday hectic family life at home.[32] Modern companies offer food, flexible hours, and other benefits to make it seem as though they are "family friendly," yet Hochschild found that these "incentives" actually maintained the longer hours spent in the workplace and away from the family. Hochschild found that parents, given their work constraints, found it difficult to engage with their children during what she calls the "third shift," the time spent doing "emotional work . . . to repair the damage caused by time pressures at home."[33] Their guilt over not having the patience to deal with tantrums or emotional traumas led parents to work later hours or to buy their way out of the patience necessary to cope with their children through gift giving.

Everyone's economic position is different and everyone allocates her time differently, yet Deondra criticized the "choices" that her employer had made. I was privileged to have a husband whose salary could support a family of four and to have had flexible hours in graduate school, but childcare providers never considered this kind of privilege when they spoke of their employers' "good" versus "bad" mothering. Moreover, by making such broad claims, Deondra was expressing the inequality she felt as a domestic worker and demonstrating to me how power could be asserted through superior performance in the "job" of "mothering."

This topic came up again in a lecture I gave at Queens College. During the time for questions allotted at the end of my presentation on West Indian foodways, a woman of West Indian background exclaimed, "West Indian sitters bringing their home-cooked food to work with them and then allowing the children they care for to taste it makes it more difficult for working mothers who don't have the time to cook and can only give jar foods or pasta." It was bizarre enough that this woman seemed to be saying that it was unfair for kids to ever eat fresh foods and that they should live on jar foods and pasta, but what struck me most about this comment was this person's implication that babysitters were "nonworking mothers." How can this be? While we need to be careful about pitting employer against employee, let's consider a babysitter, who is a mother, waking up early enough to prepare breakfast for her family and take a half-hour to one-hour commute to work, caring for someone else's child for eight to twelve hours, and traveling back home to get food ready for her own family. How does this sitter find the time to cook? And how can it even be implied that she is a nonworking mother? Perhaps the answer to this question is that the work babysitters do is considered "mothering," which is unpaid when mothers do it and not visibly "real" work.

Food Fights

One late morning in fall 2006, I had Debbie, Molly, Rachel, and Janet over to my apartment with the children they cared for. They wanted to cook for my birthday. All of the ladies, with the exception of Molly, came at around noon. Once Molly arrived at 1:00 p.m., the cooking had already begun. Knowing how much Molly loved to cook, I was anxious to hear what she would have to say about the food that Janet and Debbie had already begun to prepare. No sooner had these thoughts run through my mind than Molly peered into the kitchen and asked, "What's going on? What are you making?" Janet and Debbie both blurted out, "Baked chicken."

Molly was obviously not happy with this answer and began to oversee the entire process. When Janet asked me for barbecue sauce to put over the chicken and I said, "Oh, I've never put that on my baked chicken before," Molly added, "Me neither." Janet resisted Molly's implicit criticism by saying, "Well, let's say it's barbecue chicken then." I asked her what to do with it and she said just to "pour it over the chicken" as it sat in the white casserole dish, so I did and asked if I was doing it right. Molly quickly jumped in with, "You have to put the chicken back in the bowl and mix it around to get the color all over." Janet didn't seem to think it made a difference, and Debbie said laughingly, "That's too much work," but I followed Molly's instructions and dumped the chicken back in the bowl while Debbie mixed it around to appease Molly. Molly, being the eldest and a mother who enjoyed cooking for her seven children, was assertive enough for the other babysitters and myself to fear her disapproval in the kitchen.

On another occasion, when I saw Molly sitting just outside the infant playground with one of the other West Indian sitters, she waved, and Jason, my husband, stayed to chat with her for a little while. I went into the playground to put my son in the swing, and Jason came over after a minute or so with my daughter to do the same. When Jason left, I went out to sit with Molly. After a few minutes I took out the photos of the sitters on their "Babysitter Appreciation Day," which Irene had organized at a local park, and started asking her who everyone was so that I could distribute the photos. Molly pointed to a photograph with Irene in it and asserted that "the lady in the striped shirt" was the "devil." When I asked her why, she said that Irene was argumentative and that if she tried to organize the event again next year, she (Molly) wouldn't come. She pointed to the picture of Carol and said, "If she organizes it, I would come, she is very organized." Molly then pointed back to the picture of Irene and said, "She is a warrior, she's the devil." I asked what that meant, and she said, "I heard that she gone cuss out Carol because she [Irene] didn't get any roti and was using foul language around all the white people." Molly continued, " I don't like when people get on like that because it makes it look like black people can't be organized."

Molly was evidently upset that Irene was speaking loudly and being argumentative in front of the white parkgoers. This was one of the only times I heard Molly speak of race as a marker of West Indian babysitters as "other" in the parks, but the food incident was enough of a trigger to bring out these feelings that Molly had of her place as an outsider in the park. Interestingly enough, this fight over food rights at the event was the only disagreement in the entire day where over fifty women gathered. The sitters set up West Indian food dishes that included rice and peas, pelau, baked chicken, curry chicken, roti, vegetables, and noodles, along with some other smaller side dishes such as macaroni. They created a social food space by designating an area of West Indian food that could be eaten only by those wearing the red T-shirt and by occupying an entire area of park benches by blocking them with strollers and diaper bags. The sitters also constructed this social food space by turning their backs to those not wearing the prerequisite shirts and using their (the sitters') bodies to cover their food. Even I had to be walked over to the food area with Molly so that she could explain that I was West Indian and was allowed to eat the food, even though I hadn't received a shirt, because I had donated money to the event.

How We Eat

From speaking and eating with the sitters on numerous occasions over the past few years, I could see that they took pride in the foods and eating practices of West Indian culture. Whether referring to the types of food purchased, the textures preferred, the cooking methods employed, or the finished meals themselves, sitters always commented on how West Indians did it differently from Americans. Much as Kaplan (2000) observed black students' pride in the foods they ate for lunch versus those of their white counterparts in high school, the babysitters were proud that "black mothers can cook better than white mothers."[34] Carol spoke of having to leave her sons at home while she took a live-in job in Long Island for eleven years. Her youngest of six sons would constantly call her in the evenings to request that she come back to Brooklyn to cook for him, although she would leave food for the older brother to defrost during the days so they could eat something in the evening. She talked about the youngest son pleading, "Ma, I wish you would come, I didn't eat no dinner." She told me, "Lord, and that used to freak me out. I used to stay downstairs in my room [in Long Island] and I crying long water, but me ain't tellin' she [the employer] nothing. It used to stress me when he would tell me he ain't eat. I never leave my children in Trinidad. . . . We eat more food than people in America here. We cook three times a day and heavy food. In the mornings, I didn't used to buy bread, I baked bread. When I baking bread, it's six and seven [loaves of] bread because it's like six children, me, and my husband, and boy children eat, I'm telling you. So in the morning before they go they're getting a slice of bread with sausage in it or cheese or whatever I have and a cup of tea. Never eating some cereal and going to school. In the Caribbean people . . . hardly buy cereal, that's a waste of time. Either they bake or they, you know, something heavy and eat and go to school. When a child goes to school down here [in the United States] they can't learn nothing, all they're looking to the clock to see is when to go and eat lunch. You always got to fill their belly before they go to school. So I used to do that."

This comment was frequently made by sitters. They all asserted that back in the Caribbean they had cooked their own meals throughout the day, making enough food for the entire family to eat. There were no discussions of Caribbean "fast food" when they talked about food, for they tended to see convenience food "as undermining cookery skills and traditions."[35] They might in fact use it sometimes, but the admission of doing so was enough to ensure constant teasing of being "not a real West Indian."

It was not only the preparation of food that sitters found different in the United States but also the method of eating. One day I overheard a conversation between a West Indian sitter and Derek, the West Indian instructor of a children's tumbling class in which my daughter and I were participating. Derek was saying something about "sucking the bones" when eating fish. He said to a sitter from Barbados, "I bet you suck the bones [of chicken and beef] too," and she replied, "Yes, that is the best part." I later asked the lady from Barbados if she meant "sucking the marrow," and she said, "Yes, that's where all the flavor is, it's the best part." Almost all of the West Indian babysitters I observed eating in Brooklyn parks ate their meat right down to the bone and began sucking on the ends to get the bone marrow out.

During one playdate that I organized at my own home with some of the sitters in the neighborhood, we prepared food (rice, beans, and chicken). When it was ready and most of the kids were getting hungry (as demonstrated by the frequent fights over toys), I put out plates and cutlery so that everyone could dish their food out in the kitchen. All of the adults got a plate of food and began eating while feeding the children from their plates or from their own little dishes that I provided. I asked if anyone needed a knife and Janet responded, "Yuh forget we are West Indian, we eat with our hands." I laughed as we continued to eat. It is true that several dishes in the West Indian culture can be eaten with one's hands, but it was the deliberate association of eating with the hands and "West Indianness" that struck me most in this brief dialogue.

West Indian babysitters have been able to create a social space within public parks that allows for cultural expression through the sharing and talk of food. Because of the daily interactions that occur in this negotiated space, which anchors the community in a unique way, West Indian ethnic solidarity is expressed through the symbol of food. I observed or heard about a few instances of interisland competitiveness regarding which national cuisine produced the best version of a dish, as with the example of callaloo, but this was relatively rare. The social food space was created by frequent food discussions, food sharing, and food rituals, used as mechanisms for social networking, in the public setting of a park and the nature of the intimate work being done in the park: childcare. Some childcare providers felt constrained with regard to their food practices in the private space of their employer's home. In public spaces that they shared, and sometimes in employers' homes as well, they sought to express their culture through West Indian foodways and to hold on to the "taste" of the homeland. Through the providers' voices, we see just how critical the symbol of food was to their interactions among themselves and the maintenance of West Indian cultural identities.

West Indian childcare providers were quick to point out differences among the food cultures of the West Indian islands as well as between West Indian and American food cultures. The providers saw American food culture as lacking not only flavor and texture but also love and a tie to cultural memories. Foodways in the United States did not reward home cooking or motherhood in the same way that they did in the Caribbean. In fact, the reverse was true: food preparation was a marker of subservience to the patriarchal hierarchy and a burden to parents, especially mothers. Even these differences, however, served to promote a group identity among West Indian childcare providers and at times allowed many of these women to feel that in the employer's household they held, not the subordinate position of a servant, but the more elevated status of a "real" mother. Further, providers' tendency to closely associate foodways with motherhood inadvertently showed their closeness to the children they cared for.

5

Mobility for the Nonmobile

Cell Phones, Technology, and Childcare

As we walked toward the park—Debbie with Taylor, the child she cared for, and I with my son, Matisse—Debbie stood still in front of the public library to check her cell phone. The phone's red light was flashing. There were three messages awaiting her. Debbie explained that Molly, who was working that day, was to meet her at the library before storytime to tell her what she was doing for the day, so she was expecting Molly's call. Debbie added just before listening to the messages that "if it was too cold, Molly said that we could go by her [employer's home], but that if it was nice, we could go to the park." Debbie listened to the messages: none from Molly, but one from Hazel and two from a friend who was looking into booking a flight to Atlanta for Debbie, Shamin (another sitter from Grenada), and a few others for the Caribbean Carnival weekend. We continued toward the park, but there were no signs of Molly or Hazel. The park was surprisingly empty for that time of the morning—perhaps the sixty-degree weather with cool winds didn't help. As soon as we entered the park, I sneezed several times in a row. Debbie was convinced that I was suffering from allergies. We stood on the ramp that led to the infant playground without entering once we noticed that no one we knew was inside the play area. With impatience and concern over my excessive sneezing, Debbie decided to find out where Hazel was instead of waiting for her and called her on the cell phone. Hazel answered and told Debbie that she was "now comin' to the park." We awaited her arrival.

Technology, Places, and Spaces

Relationships between people and the environment are continuously changing as we move from the industrial era to the technological era of the Internet, satellite radio, and mobile phones.[1] Our interactions in both public and private spheres have become more complicated as new communication technologies have developed around these inventions. Their use has become normative for people of most classes, all races, and both genders performing their daily routines of work and pleasure in a variety of spaces, though not necessarily in the same ways. Specifically, public places that are expansive geographically, such as parks and sidewalks, permit this language to become integrated into the environment because they allow for human mobility. This can be seen clearly in Brooklyn public parks, where phones become an appendage to people walking around, including childcare providers. Although people who do not necessarily know each other often populate urban public spaces such as parks, social activity can occur even when public social life appears to be disappearing on account of technological developments.[2] Gary Gumpert and Susan Drucker show how the home environment as a social space has been reorganized by new communication technologies that have multiplied the connections between the home and the public environment. As Gumpert and Drucker remind us, "Social rejection of technological innovation is a virtual impossibility because each of us is born into a preexisting web of communication and technology," so although some might question whether new communication technologies have facilitated sociability, our basic interactions are affected by them and expand how we move through time and place.[3]

A complication of these technologies is that they blur the boundaries between public and private places.[4] In the intimate social spaces created in the private home of the employers by the employers' shared cultural meanings, West Indian childcare providers could now find ways to somehow connect to their own cultural and familial norms during their workdays.[5] This "expanding nonphysical world of connection" that Gumpert and Drucker speak of changes the private home to a public space where conversations can occur with those not inhabiting the immediate environment.[6] West Indian childcare providers redefined their daily experiences by using cell phones in this way. They could arrange a meeting both from the private home and while on the move from private to public places, thereby keeping themselves continuously connected to their employers, peers, and family.[7]

This chapter examines how West Indian childcare providers used cell phones and the Internet to offset some of the isolation inherent in domestic work. I look specifically at how they patterned their interactions in public places through these forms of communication to create a social space. Sitters used their cell phones for many purposes: for example, to connect with other sitters while they were in transit or in parks in order to arrange where and when to meet during the workday or to make plans with other sitters for the weekend. Existing research on childcare workers in the United States has not looked in depth at the sociability that takes place through the use of cell phones or the limits that employers set on the use of cell phones that they themselves pay for (some providers in this study had two cell phones, one paid for by the employer and one paid for by themselves). Going beyond research that looks at how domestic workers use the mobile phone to establish a concealed "back stage" within the "front stage" of their working environment and how employers use it to insert a "front stage" into the backstage of workers' private lives on their days off, this study explores how cell phones, the Internet, and other technologies are used as mechanisms for surveillance while simultaneously fostering the creation of patterned social space in public and private places.[8]

Cell Phones

I first came to realize that West Indian childcare providers relied heavily on their cell phones when I gained entry into their social group.[9] I knew that I had achieved this status when Rachel, from St. Lucia, began calling me to arrange a meeting place with her and the rest of the sitters I had come to know either in the park or at storytime in the public library. They were no longer waiting to see if I was around at the park; instead they would seek me out by calling while en route to a particular location to see if I would be joining them. At this point, and after reading several field notes, I noticed that almost all childcare providers had a cell phone, something that our technological generation has now taken for granted as a symbol of middle-class and socially networked status.

Sitters used cell phones to combat isolation at work and maintain their personal social networks.[10] As Howard Rheingold has described for smart mobs, sitters were now able to interact "together in new ways and situations where collective action was not possible before."[11] Using cell phones, they could organize playdates, plan to meet at the public library for storytime, or simply arrange to meet and run errands together. Rachel told me that "all the babysitters carry cell phones," and Carla affirmed, "Oh yeah, all the time. That's what we use [it] for—playdates or you want to go to this park. Especially me and Jennie, we rack up some minutes."

The childcare providers used cell phones in other ways as well. Some were obvious: to call family members back in the islands or in New York, pay bills and transact other business, and stay in contact with employers. Some were not as obvious: the childcare providers were able to socially exclude others from their conversations even in their immediate presence as well as decide whom to interact with over the cell phone through caller identification. In a related vein, I also observed how cell phone users created more restricted social spaces in a public park through their language use and body position while on the phone. This, combined with the fact that many sitters called "back home" from a cell phone during the workday to stay in touch with family members and old friends, helped me explore how the providers might use cell phones to preserve West Indian culture and combat isolation in the workplace while at the same time excluding others.

Parallel Management of Work and Family

The cell phone was important not only to the West Indian providers whom I studied but also the employers of these women, especially the mothers. Mobile phone use is gendered in several ways. Researchers Louis Leung and Wei Ran found that women used cell phones for work longer than men did, and Lana Rakow and Vija Navarro found that women tended to use them more for managing household, family, and community tasks, in keeping with "women's subordinate social position" of bearing the main responsibility for these tasks.[12] Thus the cell phone is in a way similar to the washing machine in its pseudoliberatory effect. Just as the washing machine was seen as cutting down the amount of time needed to wash clothes when in fact it made it possible for women to do more washing and general housework, cell phones, by extending the ability to work from any location at any time, have subjected the mothers of babysitters' charges parallel shifts on which home and work duties can be carried out simultaneously.[13] West Indian childcare providers similarly carried out overlapping parallel shifts by using the cell phone to contact their own children, either in the United States or back in their homeland, while working in public places, where writing a note or calling on a land line might not be appropriate or possible.

For employers, the parallel management of work and family duties took a variety of forms. One provider, Brenda, told me, "She [the mother, who is a schoolteacher] only calls me if she wants me to do something for her. That's when she'll call me. Like Easter time, now last week, she called me to boil some eggs for her classroom . . ."

Unsure whether what I had just heard was correct, I asked, "You had to boil the eggs for her classroom work that she has to do?"

"Boil the eggs. She called me and asked me to boil the eggs for her classroom. And she came and picked it up and went back to school." Brenda made it clear from the roll of her eyes that she did not feel she should have to do a task that was part of her employer's teaching job and went beyond the childcare duties originally stipulated in Brenda's job description. The employer managed to provide services for her own job (in this case the Easter activity of decorating eggs) while exploiting Brenda in the process.

Mobile phones have redefined not only employers' workplaces but also the organization of domestic space.[14] Because of the parallel shift, which involves managing home and work responsibilities simultaneously, employers view the accessibility of their childcare provider as a crucial requirement of the job. Some employers go so far as making cell phone access mandatory and state that if need be they will get the provider a cell phone, with certain restrictions on its use. Brenda spoke candidly about these restrictions when I asked how often her employers called during the workday. "Sometimes, twice, three times, four times for the day," she said.

I asked her, "Was it more in the beginning?"

"First of all they gave me a cell phone when I just started to work. And then he said, the husband said to me, 'Oh, we're giving you that cell phone, but it's only for us to call you.'"

Since I knew that the employer was aware that Brenda had children of her own, I asked Brenda, "So no one else could be in touch with you?"

"I couldn't call my kids from off it," she replied.

For West Indian childcare providers, the possession of a cell phone that made them constantly accessible to their employers but that they could not use on their own behalf equated to a loss of control in their daily routine, but for female employers especially this arrangement was a means of existing "in their [employers'] domestic and work worlds simultaneously."[15] The employer was able to use what Rakow and Navarro have called "remote mothering" techniques, or parenting from a distance, often in public contexts where she would be perceived by other parents, her own family, and others (perhaps co-workers) as being constantly available, through the phone calls, to her children, family, and childcare provider.[16] Providers themselves used remote mothering with their own children. In the field, both employers and employees used cell phones to ensure that children had eaten their food, taken a nap, done their homework, had a successful music, dance, or art lesson, and more generally were behaving properly.

Carla's employer made checking in on the cell phone about her child's behavior a top priority. In a conversation with me about the reasons why her employer called on the cell phone, Carla explained how the employer attempted to pull information throughout the day to determine whether to come home: "She likes to ask what mood her son is in because her son . . . I'm not there, but from what I've heard from her and the other sitter, like he'll yell and run around on the floor and act the fool. You know, he thinks she [the mother] did something, you know or whatever. So she always calls every, like, every hour or so to see [imitating the mother] 'What mood is he in? Where is he? How is he doing?' And if I say good . . . I realize now that if I say, 'Oh yeah, he's in a great mood,' she comes in [meaning home] earlier. So he's always in a great mood." We both laughed. "Regardless of what he's doing?" I asked. Carla continued while pretending to speak to the employer over the cell phone: "Yeah, he's in a great mood, he's outside playing, he's having fun." She then resumed her regular speaking voice after her fooling performance to say, "Regardless of what mood he's in, come home and deal with him yourself . . . I'm gone." Fielding constant calls from employers who are "checking in" tends to be overlooked as one of the challenges that many childcare providers face.

Several of the sitters I studied had children and families of their own here in New York and in the islands from which they came, and they used the cell phones to handle family responsibilities as much as their employers did. Cell phones, by making it possible for users to be in contact at all times, do not require "nearness as a defining element" and allow for considerable flexibility in connecting with others even over great distances.[17] It is in this context that I place West Indian childcare providers' use of the mobile phone to call their family and friends in the Caribbean.

Calling Back Home

As Heather Horst points out in her study of how mobile phones have transformed transnational communication in Jamaica, the mobile phone provides continual ties to relatives in the United States. It has also become "an object of ambivalence, bringing unforeseen burdens and obligations."[18] Horst describes how transnational cell phone calls, by enabling people to connect and maintaining social relations without having to cross national borders, allow Jamaicans on the island to express their love and stay involved with relatives abroad in the United States, and even make requests for specific items they wish to receive in Jamaica. On the other hand, such plentiful communication has unintended consequences. Relatives in Jamaica sometimes become frustrated at family members' complaints about how hard their lives are in the United States and ask them why they left in the first place. Or they make excessive requests for money, leading relatives and friends in the United States to screen their calls via caller ID to avoid answering calls from

Jamaica, a situation that can lead to tensions in relationships. While the West Indian childcare providers in my study mentioned some of the disadvantages to having a cell phone that Horst reported, most enjoyed using cell phones to stay in constant touch with relatives and friends in the Caribbean.

When I asked Brenda how often she used her cell phone to call people back home in Grenada, she responded, "Oh Lord, sometimes it's bad. . . . Sometimes I run up my phone bill like two hundred, three hundred or something dollars. But this morning, I texted everybody."

Interested in how she used the text messaging function on the cell phone, I repeated, "You texted them?"

"Yes, I texted them to wish them Happy Easter. So I texted everybody, and everybody call me back saying, 'I don't know how to use the text.' I taught them how to do it, so they text me back most the time. I call often," Brenda replied.

"Like every day, would you say?"

"No, maybe twice a week."

"And whom do you talk to back home?"

"Talk to my cousins, my nieces, I have a friend and I talk to him all the time."

Speaking on the cell phone to family and friends was common among the providers, though some of them limited their phone use for this purpose. Rachel, for example, found comfort in knowing that she could keep in contact with her father in St. Lucia, who would give her the latest gossip on friends back home: "Did you hear that this one did this?" But she preferred not to call her dad on her cell phone because he liked so much to keep her up to date on events in St. Lucia that he would speak for too long and raise her phone bill. Likewise, some preferred to use their home land line because their employers paid for the cell phone and they did not feel comfortable using it to make personal calls when someone else was paying the bill. Jennie told me that when she called her friends and family in Grenada she used her home phone because "I want to feel comfortable and be able to talk for like an hour." She also said she didn't like other sitters to have her cell phone number: "I don't give too many sitters the phone [number], but the mother says, 'You can, you can,' so yes, I can give it to sitters who want to contact me for playdates." Carol owned her cell phone but commented, "I don't be on the cell like them other girls . . . my ears get tired." She even requested no long distance on it because she preferred to pay two dollars for a phone card for fifty-four minutes worth of time to call back home to Trinidad and speak with her husband twice a week.

Cell Phones and the Construction of Representational Space

West Indian childcare providers who used cell phones in public constructed representational space in a variety of ways. As Lee Humphreys has noted for cell phone users in general, they were able to "mark the boundaries of . . . an otherwise invisible place" while continuing to participate in a larger interaction group.[19] Humphreys' study found that when people use cell phones in public places their interactions with others in their immediate physical environment express both the society's newly developing codes of behavior in these circumstances and the power relations with the people who are physically accompanying or surrounding them.[20] As he explains, people "constantly negotiate their private and public sense of self when using and responding to cell phones in public spaces" and use specific markers to create a more limited social space for themselves when they are using the phone.[21] Some of the ways he lists are:

- Stood or sat away from others in an area, as if to avoid intrusion by other people or to avoid being rude to others in the area
- Paced as a way to demarcate their space within larger public space
- Used possessions such as bags to mark their territory where they did not want others to intrude
- Used "cell-yell" (speaking loudly to make their presence known)
- Maintained "minimal main involvement" in a larger group and its public space activity by staying present at the scene of the activity, even while talking on their mobile phone

West Indian childcare providers used all of these strategies to create representational spaces in the public park and on public sidewalks.

For instance, I saw West Indian childcare providers use cell phones while pacing back and forth with strollers to block off areas of the benches that surrounded the open park spaces from other public park users and, in addition, leave diaper bags on a nearby bench to indicate that they were using that space. Sometimes ten to fifteen such strollers and bags were placed along an entire side of the public park benches while the sitters were either using their cell phones or talking with one another while watching their charges.

I remember one morning seeing the strategy of physical self-isolation used by a West Indian babysitter who was sitting down at one of the picnic tables inside a large open park space. Her hair was shoulder length, black and relaxed straight, with a slim headband pulling the hair away from her face.

She wore dark denim pants, a blouse, and a heavy, knitted black sweater. I almost never saw this woman talk to others in the park, except for other West Indian childcare providers. She sat quietly as she did most mornings and used her cell phone to pay the bills that were stacked in her checkbook—the only time I had ever seen her use the cell phone. This routine of sitting by herself to make personal calls on her cell phone was her way of creating a private space within a public place. She indicated through her low tone, limited eye contact, and "bench-sitting" position that, like most individuals who are handling private financial matters, she did not want other people to intrude.

"Cell-yell" was not seen as commonly as the opposite, what I am tempted to call "cell-murmur." West Indian childcare providers typically did not want others to hear their private conversations with family or employers. They considered it insulting to other West Indians to boast about planned trips back to the homeland, since not everyone could afford to take such trips, or about other matters that would be seen to be of no concern to others. Often sitters did not want to fully disclose details about their relationships with their employers to other babysitters. Some tended to communicate to other babysitters that their working relationship was open, honest, and relaxed, though I actually overheard conversations in which the employer was dictating certain directions to the babysitter that would have made the babysitter feel disrespected in front of her peer group. Childcare providers would hide their true working relationships by speaking softly through their cell phones, although I was able to capture some discussions by sitting close enough during my observations. On the other hand, some childcare providers spoke quietly on their cell phones so as to not appear too "friendly" with employers whom they actually did like working for. There seemed to be an unwritten rule among some childcare providers that you shouldn't "like" your employer (when someone spoke positively about her employer, the providers became quiet and did not engage in further conversation, perhaps because of skepticism or denial that someone could possibly have a decent employer), so a provider would speak badly about her employer in public parks but then joke around with her employer on the cell phone. Other sitters spoke negatively about their employers in the parks and then said some of the most wonderful things about them to me in private. The ambivalence-charged social relations between employer and employee were evidenced through cell phone conversations.

Quiet cell phone use followed not only the West Indian cultural prescription that one should never boast about what one has or what one is doing and that one should maintain a good working relationship with the employers in private but also the belief, in many Caribbean cultures, that speaking in a low tone shows self-control and proper public conduct. Raising one's voice in public would be considered improper and a lack of "brought-upcy" (manners), so providers were careful to monitor their phone behavior in public places. This influenced childcare practices in that the self-control exercised by these women made them more successful as providers in the eyes of those observing their behavior (meaning other providers and possibly other people who used public spaces).

Who Pays the Cell Phone Bill?

All of the West Indian childcare providers I interviewed agreed that the employer should be responsible for paying some, if not all, of the cell phone bills, since a cell phone was now considered a crucial tool for the work of childcare providers. Moreover, cell phones that were used during the workday came with so many restrictions, such as limited free minutes, that some providers would refuse to answer their cell phones even when they knew it was the employer who was trying to contact them. Most providers agreed that the employer had every right to know what was going on during the day with their child, but not at the expense of the babysitter.

Brenda told me that the mother of the children in her care had told her not to use the home phone line anymore: "I used to answer their house phone, and she [the mother] stopped me from answering the house phone." When I asked why, she responded: "I think one day what happened was that I had the bigger one when he was a baby and somebody left a message on the phone and I forgot to tell her. So she was like, 'Don't answer the phone, let the answering machine pick up.' So what I do now—sometimes they would be calling and I know they're calling and I wouldn't answer the phone. I would run away from the phone, I wouldn't answer it. And then they would be calling me on my cell phone and I shut it off! And then when they come they say, 'I was trying to get you.' And I was like, well, I don't know . . . I didn't want to answer my phone, you know. I pay my cell phone bill, I pay all my bills."

Who paid the cell phone bill was a common concern among West Indian providers. They stated that they did not necessarily have enough money to pay for their cell phone bills, especially when the parents called frequently or, in the case of emergencies, when providers were out with their charges and needed to call the parents. The Trinidadian babysitter Irene was in this position after her youngest daughter dropped her personal cell phone in the fish tank. After going without a cell phone for some time, Irene finally told her employers that they needed to purchase her a cell phone for work. She said, "I'm always at doctor's appointments . . . somewhere with the kids [and] need to call car service in case of [an] emergency. In every job that I've had, they would get me a cell phone whether I had a cell phone or not. . . . Even if you have your own cell phone and they want to pay some of the bill, then that's fine. If you have your own cell phone, that doesn't have nothing to do with them [the employers] because if you're taking their kids out or anything, the cell phone is always good because of emergency."

Irene now had two cell phone plans and two phones, one that she shared with her husband and one that she shared with the employer.[22] She still called the latter phone "her phone," although the plan her employer had given her had limited minutes. Irene stated that she tried not to go over the minutes. She made some personal calls on the phone shared with the employer but did "try to use it just for them [the employers]. . . . I don't like to put personal stuff in work."

Darlene, on the other hand, did not "believe in" owning a cell phone unless the employer was paying for it, although she admitted she had been looking into it. She recognized with some amusement that if all cell phone plans actually offered the same features, such as free long distance or unlimited text messaging, the companies would all go bankrupt. She said she thought that cell phones were taking over the way babysitters did their work, but she made it clear who should be responsible for the purchase of cell phones for childcare providers: "I've never purchased a cell phone myself. . . . I've been in jobs where they give you a cell phone with the strictest understanding that it's only to be used for work purposes. . . . I see the way some people are with the cell phone, they've got the thing stuck to their ear every time you look at them. . . . People [employers] say, 'Do you have a cell phone?' and I say, 'No I don't.' 'Okay, we'll give you a cell phone.' And I've heard people went on the interview and the person asked if they had a cell phone, and she said, 'No,' and they said, 'Well, you've got to get a cell phone before you start this job.' They wanted the worker to pay for the cell phone. Now that to me is a job you don't want." As this story suggests, the cell phone has provoked a small social transformation in that ownership of one now determines, in some quarters, whether someone should or should not get a job.

The cell phone could also bring about another transformation: it could close the gap between public and private domains of communication in the employer-employee relationship, as when employers demanded access to employees' own personal cell phone numbers. Darlene became bothered when she talked about workers losing their jobs for refusing to go along with the employer on this, but she also admitted, "I blame the workers to a certain extent because if I [were to] have a cell phone, I don't see what business my cell phone has to do with my job, it's my cell phone." Darlene did not believe that a childcare provider should have to get a cell phone as a prerequisite for a job. Instead, she felt that the employer should provide it.

Concerned for that parent out there who desperately wanted to check in with his or her childcare provider, I asked, "What if the parents want to get in touch with you?" Darlene responded, "I have no problem with that, just give me a cell phone. If you want me to use my cell phone, you should be contributing to the costs. To me, you've got a nerve, I'm paying the bills, you probably aren't giving me enough money as it is anyway, and you've got the nerve demanding that I give you my cell phone number for you to use up my minutes? What am I, a Charlie [a dick]? Why would I agree to that? And if you're going to make those demands, then this isn't the job for me." Though I felt that Darlene was right to insist that she shouldn't have to pay for a cell phone to communicate with her employer, I was not fully convinced that childcare providers could be so selective about their employers that they could resist this demand.

Unlike Darlene, Grace, who also worked for Domestic Workers United, had recently become the owner of her own cell phone, a birthday gift from her cousin. But she didn't let her employers know this. "I had a lot of slack *[sic]* for not having a cell phone. . . . I didn't see the need for a cell phone . . . not to say that it's not a worthwhile tool. I'm just not one of those people. So I had one and I didn't even know the number . . . and I start giving out the number to a few people and stuff like that, but . . . the last job I had, I didn't get one. But when I got mine, I didn't tell them, I didn't give them the number. . . . If she [the mother] wants to be calling me on my number, she has to be paying me. She has to be contributing."

Very much like Darlene, Grace believed that an employer who wanted to "control" a babysitter's movements throughout the day via cell phone calls had to pay for the privilege. Both Darlene's and Grace's statements expressed not only some hostility or resentment but also a consciousness that a phone was a private and personal possession that should be respected as such throughout the workday. Grace continued, "She can get a phone and put me on her plan and it's just for her business. When I leave, I leave it at her house. . . . But if she wants it, she's going to have to pay. You can't let these people get the better of you . . . but if you feel you need to know every step I make, you give me a cell phone."

Victoria expressed the same view, that if the employer had access to her private cell phone she should contribute monetarily to its use, but she noted some advantages to having a cell phone as well: "It was my personal cell phone. So I definitely felt at times that maybe that they should be paying for it because the amount of time I spent talking on it during the day—which most people don't use their cell phones too much during the day—definitely it was substantial. It was definitely substantial. But, you know, I guess at other times it was positive to have a cell phone. You know, it's certainly good for making the playdates and all that kind of stuff, and finding out where mom is when she's not home on time and all of those things."

The advances in cell phone technology have made these phones accessible to almost everyone, with prices decreasing annually for the simplest phone and calling plans becoming more diverse. But it was still the consensus among West Indian providers that employers should pay for the cell phone if it was a requirement of the job position and that the person who was paying for the phone should allow the employer to have access to it only if the employer paid for the privilege—thereby defining the limits of the job and, in essence, the power relation.

Surveillance: Parent Blogs, Nanny-Cams, and Stroller License Plates

While many sitters gained primary employment through word-of-mouth networking, virtual technology had become a significant resource for many sitters. One day when some of the sitters came to my house for a playdate, Debbie asked me to submit a post for her on a babysitter Web site because she would be looking for a new job in spring 2007. Taylor, the two-year old Debbie cared for, would be staying home with her father, who was retiring and therefore wouldn't need hired childcare services any longer. There are several "parent blogs" on the Internet where parents and babysitters can post their needs for childcare or their employment availability. I asked several sitters if this was a regular means of getting a job as a sitter or nanny. They all said yes. They told me that sometimes the employers themselves helped sitters find new employment by posting an announcement of their availability accompanied by a reference. But a drawback to this new way of finding work was that several sitters did not have Internet access at home and therefore either did not know how to navigate the Internet or could not access it without paying a fee at an Internet café, which might charge up to a dollar a minute. Although the public library had computer access, sitters did not use it for this feature since they were watching small children when they were at the library. Moreover, providers reframed the library specifically as a play space; they did not view it as a place for books for their own use or Internet access.

The Internet is increasingly being used for surveillance of nannies, as are cell phones and other technological devices. A search of LexisNexis for articles in northeastern newspapers on this topic revealed that surveillance is one of employers' main uses of cell phones. Further, "nanny-cams," small cameras that can be creatively installed in various ornaments around the home, are being used to "keep an eye" on what the childcare provider is doing when the employer is not at home. The term *nanny-cam* alone is disturbing because it implies that among all the possible uses of spy cameras in the home, the surveillance of nannies is the most needed. Some companies even advertise themselves as "nanny surveillance companies" to play on the insecurities of parents with a new babysitter.[23] While these devices have indeed allowed some employers to monitor and ultimately "catch" their babysitters in some act of deviance, they are simultaneously a way to ensure that when the babysitter is in the private household she is continually under the employer's control. Childcare providers may feel that surveillance tactics diminish their self-esteem and autonomy—though sometimes they find ways to get around them. Darlene told me that her employer had recounted to her a conversation with a friend who had just had a nanny-cam for the sitter surreptitiously installed in an ornament. Darlene's employer told Darlene that she had simply laughed and said to the friend, "Darlene would never go for that, she'd figure it out in a second."

West Indian sitters, remaining a predominant choice for many Brooklyn families, still face some of the harshest criticism from the very people who employ them. This criticism is now posted on the Internet. Erynn Esposito, a community organizer and documentarian, informed me that Park Slope parents posting at sites on Yahoo Groups had gone to great lengths to "ensure the safety of their children" by reporting and discussing their observations about nannies online. One Yahoo Web site chat room even featured a comment thread in which parents graded "nannies" by race: "West Indian sitters were at the bottom and Tibetan women were rated #1." Apparently this "grading system" had begun when one parent told another that she had seen her West Indian sitter use physical means to discipline a child and wanted to get the sitter fired. Not all parents went along with the idea of grading sitters in this way. Some commenters stated that this type of discussion was completely racist, and one woman who employed a West Indian babysitter (not the sitter who had disciplined the child) remarked that it "makes me so upset that you are looking at my sitter with this racist eye while they are with my child."

When I asked Darlene about her take on such a grading system, she responded that West Indian women had been doing domestic work for many years in New York and had worked so many babysitting jobs that "they know what they're worth. . . . They know what they should or shouldn't do, and they have higher standards than someone who recently came in and are more placid . . . more agreeable . . . because you have some people that if they can take advantage of you they think you're wonderful, but if they cannot take advantage of you then you're not that wonderful." Darlene was saying here that newer immigrants to the city might not be as demanding as West Indians who had a history of work in New York and understood their value to employers. West Indian childcare providers might thus demand more in terms of their work's worth, and employers would see this as a generalizable trait—that West Indian providers were too demanding and not as "good" as the newcomers. Whether the newer immigrant Tibetan childcare providers were indeed more easily manipulated could not be confirmed. However, Darlene's conclusions were based on her experiences working for Domestic Workers United with a variety of ethnic and immigrant groups involved in domestic service.

A Grenadian provider, Tricia, whom I met at Carroll Park in June 2005 told me that some of the parents on this very Web site had reported that "the West Indian sitters are taking the white children to Jay Street [Fulton Mall, a mainly black ethnic enclave and shopping center] and they [the parents] disapprove." She was very upset by the comments made by these parents who were judging the responsibility level of babysitters in their everyday work. These comments also raise the question, Why was it so terrible for West Indian sitters to want to go to a shopping area that had mainly black clientele? No one ever questioned white parents' taking their children to white neighborhoods to shop. And why was the race of the neighborhood the first characteristic invoked to explain this disapproval? Maybe most parents saw certain gentrified neighborhoods as public spaces that were more "private," whereas they saw "ethnic" neighborhoods as "too public" and hence "unsafe." Some parents implied their greater comfort in "white" spaces in blog entries that expressed an unwarranted uneasiness with spaces such as Fulton Mall or the Flatbush area, which were inhabited predominantly by black Caribbeans. But what about the comfort level of babysitters who went out with the children in their care? Perhaps the babysitters were going there for even more rudimentary reasons than the comfort of contact with their own culture: the purchase prices of everyday items at the Fulton Mall were lower than those found in most of the neighborhoods where these babysitters worked.

Yet another means of doing surveillance on nannies through the Internet was reported in 2006 in a *New York Times* article called "Spying on Nanny." According to the article, a former New York City prosecutor had created a Web site offering parents a small license plate for their child's stroller for $50. I never came across anyone who used these license plates, but according to the article parents can "affix the plate to their child's stroller, [and] any 'concerned citizen' with access to the Internet can file an anonymous report on the nanny pushing the stroller so parents know where their children have been."[24]

Such new forms of surveillance through the Internet undermine the already strained relationship between employer and employee by playing up the fears that most parents already have when their children are under the care of another. They are becoming a concern for babysitters and parents alike because they show how easily individuals' privacy can be invaded by strangers.

Even the movement arts studio owner Victoria found that the surveillance of babysitters on the Internet could be damaging. Though she admittedly benefited from the advertising that she did online, she stated that the Internet was "probably more negative than positive" because it allowed information to spread "like wildfire" and because "I think that people are very willing to say things in that environment that they would never say to somebody in person." She noted that it was "easier," more comfortable, for employers to engage in surveillance through the various forms of technology than to confront an employee about what she might be doing incorrectly.

One of the more famous Web sites that supports Internet surveillance is "I Saw Your Nanny" (isawyournanny.com). Margaret Nelson and Anita Ilta Gary's book about the surveillance that contemporary families encounter has a chapter on this Web site based on a twenty-two-week analysis of over two hundred nanny sightings and over a thousand comments. Nelson and Gary found that 77 percent of the nannies identified on the Web site were marked either by race or ethnicity explicitly or by some other code of ethnicity, such as "speaks Spanish" or "attractive dark skinned, black hair nanny."[25] The children under care were far less likely to be identified by race or ethnic background, but when they were, 78 percent were identified as white. Indicators of class status were also used, such as descriptions of a bag that the nanny was carrying or descriptions of the nanny's clothing.[26] Class distinctions were also made in postings that suggested that if the nanny was shopping at a "nice" store she had to be shopping on behalf of her employer, whereas if she was shopping at a "lower-status" store she had to be making a purchase for herself. This became relevant in my research when the appropriateness of the nanny's location, such as the Fulton Mall, came up in a posting.

Though both parents and nannies could use this site, and though it was generally the nanny who was demonized in multiple ways, parents, particularly mothers (as the blog's founder and editor admitted), could also be "outed" as neglectful and thus publicly shamed.[27] If a neighbor was in the park and recognized a child in a nanny's care, he or she sometimes used the comments page to speak to the child's mother in patronizing tones, suggesting that the mother should be home with her child since children were vulnerable at such a young age. The mother would then become a public target for the community's criticism. She might feel obliged to explain the situation or defend the nanny on the Web site, or, even worse, to the neighbor if the neighbor identified him- or herself. This form of surveillance through blogs emphasized an "us-versus-them" dialogue (between employers and nannies, between other parents and nannies, and between parents themselves), thus stirring up conflicts and divisions between the parties engaged in the work of childcare and mothering that took place on everyone's behalf.

Most childcare providers do not search and comment on such Web sites, yet they learn about them through other providers or through other parents who tell them about recent comments. Gentrified Brooklyn is a prime site for postings, since its public spaces, bounded by residential neighborhoods and commercial streets, and its high population of "creative class" workers with flexible schedules who can be out and about in such spaces throughout the day just as the childcare providers are, offer many opportunities to closely observe the behaviors of others. The Web sites give posters the impression that they are part of a community that values this form of surveillance, and while this is true given the popularity of such sites and the many postings that come from the gentrified Brooklyn neighborhoods that I researched, it also demonstrates how the virtual community differs from the physical community. The like-mindedness of blog contributors encourages a kind of social identity different from that constructed in a physical community. In the physical space of a community people are as likely to say things to each other, but they are far less harsh than if they have an open and supposedly anonymous forum such as the Internet. In other words, in the physical community people will reflect on the consequences of their words more than if they are using an anonymous forum. The anonymous identity in the virtual world can be very different from the identity constructed in the physical world, and this needs to be taken into consideration as well.

The comfort that employers derive from Internet-facilitated surveillance and that employees derive from being able to connect with others by cell phone should not be overlooked. The frequent use of both cell phones and the Internet by providers and their employers has meaning for both parties. This meaning can be as simple as the ability to reach out to family members abroad and locally, or to other providers in the work communities, but the meaning can be deeper. Cell phones and the Internet make it easier to avoid confrontations with family members or with employees. They can also be tools of subordination through the various surveillance tactics that are being used to control public behavior. For all these reasons, the use of such new technologies is an ongoing topic of study. The more features become available—the iPhone's new video recording option, Skype's free video conferencing feature—the more complicated the issues of surveillance and networking become.

Digital technologies are a necessary part of how people do their work in the twenty-first century. As both employees' and employers' use of these technologies makes evident, they have become uniquely interwoven into the family dynamic: while making it easier for employees to contact their family members and friends, including those outside the country, they have also increased control over employees' public behavior through surveillance. Whether or not people want to believe that technology should play such a large role in everyday life, the Internet and cell phones have become integrated into our daily experiences. Therefore, it is important for both childcare providers and their employers to understand how people adapt to such technologies and to reach some form of consensus as to how they should be used throughout the workday. The flexible nature of childcare requires continual dialogue between employers and employees to negotiate ever-changing boundaries while respecting the autonomy of workers and the needs of employers.

6

Where's My Money?

How Susus Bridge the Financial Gap

One late morning in the summer of 2006, as I was walking from the park back to my home with Molly, who in her sixties walks briskly and with authority, and Michelle (who was in her stroller), Molly asked me if I knew anything about a "susu" (pronounced "sousou"). Not having a clue as to what she could be talking about, and not recognizing the term in my West Indian colloquial vocabulary, I immediately admitted that I did not. She began to explain that it was something that she and the other babysitters did together as an informal way of saving money. "Some island people call it a 'pot,' 'meeting,' 'partner,' or 'box,'" all terms that she appeared to think should ring a bell with me because of my West Indian background. She then told me that one of the sitters, Lyla, was the one who "organized" her susu (meaning that Lyla collected the money, distributed it, and was in charge of deciding who could be a member). Molly described the susu as a type of collective savings account among the babysitters, stemming from a West Indian tradition. All members of a group decided on the amount of money (a "hand," as they called it) to "throw" into the "pot" each week; then each member made a weekly contribution and in turn received the full amount that had accrued during her assigned week. The amount varied according to which susu you belonged to. As one babysitter described the susu, "You can do it as big as you want or as small as you want. You can do twenty-five dollars a week or a hundred dollars a week, it depends on how, you know, you want to run it. Most of the time it's a hundred dollars a week, usually. It runs for eighteen weeks. Each week eighteen people put in their hundred dollars [throw a hand in the pot], and one person gets $1,800 until each person gets their own [pot], and then you start it again."[1]

The use of words such as *pot* and *hand* evokes the language of card games. After investigating academic scholarship related to this issue, I came to realize that several groups of first-generation immigrants to the United States have had these forms of rotating credit organizations.[2] For the purposes of this book, rotating credit associations will be defined as "associations formed by a core of participants who agree to make regular contributions to a fund which is given in whole, or in part, to each contributor in rotation."[3] Molly said that it was through this kind of association that many childcare providers paid to go visit their homeland, demonstrated financial status to institutions in order to obtain formal loans or lines of credit, or saved up for some other goal. Susus are similar to Saskia Sassen-Koob's description of "sans," the rotating credit associations that people in the Dominican Republic use as a form of savings for social rituals such as weddings and funerals, and even for immigration documents or travel.[4]

The susu was not something that many of the babysitters talked about in public, yet it was organized in public places such as libraries, churches, and even hospitals.[5] None of the employers I interviewed or observed mentioned or knew about their babysitter's involvement with susus or knew that susus were being organized in public places, such as the parks their sitter occupied. When I eventually asked my mother if she knew anything about susus, I was surprised to find out that she had in fact organized one among her fellow librarians in 1965 at the University of the West Indies in Jamaica. It had been made up of eight people—all from West Indian backgrounds, including Trinidadians and Jamaicans. My mother recalled how one white British woman who worked in the library was approached to join the susu but refused because she felt it was better to deposit the money in the bank. Not until I began speaking more with West Indian childcare providers did I realize that the susu, though a traditional practice brought from the homeland, was something in which almost all of them, not just recent immigrants, had participated at some point, though participation lessened over the generations.

Background

The anthropologist Clifford Geertz analyzed rotating credit associations in Indonesia, China, Japan, Vietnam, and Africa as economic strategies occupying an intermediate position between those of traditional agrarian and nontraditional commercial economies, in that they were "device[s] by means of which traditionalistic forms of social relationships are mobilized so as to fulfill non-traditionalistic economic functions."[6] He stated that learning how to participate in such associations was an important part of children's socialization, although, as Aubrey Bonnett has since noted, this is less true for the children of first-generation immigrants in the United States, who have tended to culturally distance themselves from this practice.[7] Geertz's analysis compares across countries the practices regarding rotation order and the rules of obligation that are understood by members. For example, in Indonesia's version, called *arisan,* the person who draws from the monetary fund is responsible for preparing a small feast for the following meeting. The version of the Yoruba in Africa, called *esusu* (which is where the West Indian term *susu* is said to have originated), is more bureaucratic in that the organizer may not have any personal social relationship with the association's members.[8]

According to Nicole Biggart and Richard Castanias, social relations, far from being "impediments" to and "irrational" influences on economic exchange, have numerous useful functions in economic activity: in particular they can act as a kind of collateral to manage the risks of economic transactions.[9] This would apply to susus, in which one's close associations with other members act as a motivator to keep payments coming in. The authors' claim that "economic actors use their knowledge of their social relations and the relations of others to advance their interests" is also pertinent to susus, particularly susu organizers, as explored further below.[10]

Beyond the social aspects of rotating credit associations, there is a more concrete and practical use for these informal savings: they represent capital.[11] As the historian David Gerber has noted, rotating credit associations have been especially useful to ethnic groups that are discriminated against at banks or other formal institutions.[12] The sociologist Ivan Light was one of the first to explore the economic strategies that ethnic minorities in the United States used to establish small capitalist ventures. Noting that in Harlem in the early 1900s West Indian immigrants were far more likely than their African American counterparts to start small businesses, particularly businesses that risked competing with whites who were doing business in the ghetto, he posited that this was partly because the West Indians, unlike the African Americans, had acquired the habit of accumulating savings through rotating credit associations and thus had a strategy of accumulation to fall back on if they were initially turned down by banks.[13] But the sociologist Nancy Foner has pointed out that West Indians' ability to use these forms of mutual savings only partially explains how they gained capital for business opportunities in the United States: sometimes they brought family wealth with them, and sometimes they participated in certain economies that allowed them to gain business capital and from which they were not excluded in ways that African Americans were.[14] The sociologists Aubrey Bonnett and Philip Kasinitz both found that West Indian immigrants have relied primarily on means other than rotating credit associations to support business ventures.[15] For example, those who came to the United States with their families (as opposed to leaving family behind in their homeland) had the advantage, given cultural "norms stressing collective achievement," of drawing on pooled resources of family members and relying on kinship networks for purposes of capital investment.[16] My own research similarly shows susu money being used primarily for small consumption needs and not for larger capital investments in businesses.

West Indian Susus

According to Bonnett, who wrote a comprehensive book on how West Indian immigrants have used rotating credit associations, this form of savings has been "a generational adaptive mechanism to cope with the urban complexities of New York."[17] In essence, susus are more important to the first generation of West Indians than to their second-generation children, who have assimilated to Western culture and therefore use formal banking institutions. In my interviews, none of the childcare providers talked about their own children participating in such associations. However, several of the childcare providers' mothers were participants. It seemed that with each generation the susu was becoming less important as a means of saving money.

For susus to work among these women (all susu participants in this research were women childcare providers), the organizer of the susu had to be trustworthy and reliable. While there were no official rules that participants had to be of a particular race or ethnicity, West Indians made up the entire membership among this group of babysitters. The susus did not keep or give out receipts or invoices.[18] Only simple records, such as a list of names with dollar amounts next to them, were kept to determine who was in line for receiving the money from the pot or who owed money to the pot, and all transactions were made in cash. This made tracking such associations and determining the exact number of susus in operation difficult, as Bonnett found in his research. Default on payments (since each member was required to contribute every week) was rare in susus, but it did happen. Susus in the United States were legally run but were considered part of the informal economy, meaning they were not regulated by the state or private financial institutions that otherwise would regulate monetary circulation.[19] Bonnett states that friendships were used as collateral and this was why "some organizers try to limit membership to people whom they know very well, mainly those who are members of their social network."[20] Social relations were used essentially to "assure economic relations . . . to reduce risk and to sustain predictable economic outcomes."[21]

The responsibility for ensuring that susu money was paid was diffused among the women I studied.[22] Irene, one of the susu organizers among babysitters whom I interviewed, said, "You are responsible for any friend that you bring into the susu and doesn't pay their hand." A member who did not pay her hand would be excluded from future community relationships—in this case the West Indian babysitter community—although I never personally met anyone who had experienced this. Perhaps because of the possible embarrassment of not paying, providers always made sure they did pay. This social pressure to comply, then, was crucial to the reproduction of the susu. Some countries have integrated these credit association systems formally into their development strategy plans and commercial banking endeavors, but as Bonnett has reported, many first-generation West Indian immigrants to the United States continue to participate in the informal system in order to remain accountable and under the radar of authorities, since some are undocumented.[23]

A West Indian Thing

> Look, this susu is not a Trinidad thing, for Guyanese and Bajans [Barbadians], Jamaicans and small islanders have it, too. Of course, they call it by a different name. This is more a West Indian thing that cuts across the island groups. In my susu I have had members from all the islands. I only have to mention I'm starting one and people from all the islands ask me to join up. You would be amazed to know how it has helped us to get ourselves together. Yes, this is really a West Indian thing.
>
> Susu participant, quoted in Aubrey Bonnett's *Institutional Adaptation of West Indian Immigrants to America: An Analysis of Rotating Credit Associations*

The idea that susus were a "West Indian thing" was commonly heard among the providers. Though some features of susus had changed since Bonnett did his study of susus in the 1980s in Brooklyn (for example, the amount of money that was paid out to the organizer of the susu), the real story was how many of the susu traditions had remained the same.

Most childcare providers in my research had participated in susus at one time or another, yet they did not all agree with the unwritten rules that were followed, nor were they all participating at the time of my research. But those that did actively participate in the susu had strong feelings about its function within the West Indian community.

As Denyse and I sat in Washington Park in Manhattan with Darlene and another Trinidadian babysitter, who were there to hand out flyers for the town hall meeting for Domestic Workers United and the Bill of Rights, Denyse explained that "whoever gets the last 'hand' (payout) can now take the first hand in the following round, meaning that she has doubled her take." So if you wanted to double the money in the same month, you took the last hand of one ten-week cycle and the first hand of the next ten-week cycle. People used that money for whatever they wished: a downpayment on a house (after several rotations had been collected), a car, their kids' college tuition in the United States or in their homeland, trips back to the islands, trips to other destinations in Canada or the United States, or, of course, less expensive consumer goods, depending on the amount given each week or month.

I asked Darlene how she thought susus became so prevalent among West Indian babysitters in Brooklyn. She answered, "I think that probably came about many, many years ago where black people back in the islands didn't open up bank accounts and yet they needed money to do certain things with, and I think that's how it came back [in fashion here in the United States]." Bonnett sums this up by suggesting that this informal credit system "is the only way they can narrow the gap between their small incomes and consumption needs."[24]

I asked both Darlene and Denyse, "Why not simply put the money in an account to accrue interest? What is the benefit?"

Darlene, who was from Barbados and did not participate in a susu, responded, "What you say is true, is that there is no interest on it." She continued, "I guess the difference is also like you can say, 'Well, why not go to the bank and borrow the money?' but if you go to the bank, there's procedure."

"I guess they could be afraid too if they're undocumented," I said taking my cue from Darlene's term *procedure.*

"Actually, some places you can open up a bank account even if you're undocumented."

"But aren't they afraid of the transactions?" I asked, thinking that there had to be some concrete answer to why West Indian babysitters didn't exclusively rely on bank accounts for savings. Darlene matter-of-factly stated, "They could be, but if they are, they wouldn't try to open up a bank account." As she saw that I was still not convinced, Darlene went on, "If she [pointing to Denyse—another provider] wanted money, and say if something happened to her family back in Trinidad, and she wanted money immediately, she could call up whoever is running the susu" to get an early hand.

Another explanation for the continued validity of the susu has been advanced by Bonnett, who found that susus allowed "low minimum investments," whereas formal financial institutions often demanded higher minimum investments.[25] Finally, there was the social pressure to participate in a susu.

In a later conversation, Carol reaffirmed the advantage of the susu in paying out large sums of money. When asked why she did not simply put the money into a savings account at the bank, she replied, "You just figure you're getting the money in a bulk that's why most people do that." Carol, who had used her susu money primarily for green card fees (totaling $1,500), was a supporter of the system: "I makin' sure I throw that susu. . . . That's how Trini people does pay their bills, they buy their house and everything with the susu. . . . That's what helped me pay immigration, for the lawyer" (and any other penalties for staying beyond the period of her permit). She finally exclaimed, "They don't give anything free in immigration."

In a different discussion, Irene told me why participants preferred saving money through susus to saving it through a formal bank: "Not a lot of people understand it if they're not West Indian. If you're not West Indian, you won't understand it. In the sense that . . . It's easier, it's like a savings. It's like you're saving money. Because if you were to say, 'Okay, I'm going to put aside a hundred dollars every week,' sometimes that never happens. You end up spending it. But when you know you're committed to giving to somebody, you're committed to something, you're going to give it. So sometimes people do it for vacations, people do it to pay a bill, people do it for kids' graduations that are coming up, they do it for that. . . . People do it just to have money for the summer to go vacation, stuff that you can't usually save money for. This is a good way of saving money, so that's why I say people do it as big as they want, or as little as they want."

When I pressed her further about the fact that it was not possible to accrue interest on the susu money, she replied, "I don't know if your mom . . . but if you ask your mom, she'll be like—no. You know why? Because a bank, for me, a bank you can always go and take it out. . . . Somehow we feel like if it's in a bank and not in my hand—it has to be somewhere where I know I could do like this [as she slaps her hand with the other to show the money is tangible] and get it. But if you put it . . . because you know you're committed. You know if you don't get that person that money, when it's time to get your hand, you're not going to get it, or they gonna take out whatever you owe. So it's . . . this is something that started—please, how many years ago. I knew it growing up as a kid, my mom knew it growing up as a kid, so this was a way for us to save, like West Indian people of poorer class to save. And somehow we felt safer doing it like that . . . rather than putting it into a bank. . . . You have to face that person every time, because it's usually somebody in your area, or in your job, or somebody that you're going to see all the time."

"So they know where you live or where you work," I stated.

"And I can come get you," Irene said with a smirk. We both laughed.

So although susus were not being used to start small businesses in the West Indian childcare provider community, they were clearly being used to uphold traditions and maintain social bonds that created an enforceable trust among the "ladies." This social pressure between providers created a security that banks did not offer even if they provided small amounts of interest. The limited interest offered on a savings account was not enough to hold anyone accountable for the money that was to be "deposited" each month. Other investments with higher interest rates, such as CDs (certificate of deposits) at a bank, were still not enough for providers, since they did not allow for the flexibility of withdrawing money early, as Darlene explained.

Tips

Once a few people decided to form or participate in a susu together, a leader either was nominated by the group or volunteered herself to be the keeper of the money collected and responsible for the distribution of funds at each payout. This meant the leader would usually keep a paper record of who had contributed money and when, who had received the last payout of money, and what the order of future payouts would be. The leader could change for one reason or another, but typically all members designated one person as leader by verbal consent. While this person was not expected to get paid for her duties as leader, she might be offered or expecting to receive what was called a "tip" or an extra "hand" (payout).

In my conversations with Darlene and Denyse about susus and why they worked among West Indian babysitters, Darlene brought up an integral part of the susu economy that has been overlooked in most of the scholarly research. When describing interactions between the susu organizer and the other participants or "lenders," Darlene spoke specifically of the financial exchange that occurred ritually as someone was getting their "hand."[26] She explained, "Whoever is running (I mean, for me, we call it 'meetings'), whoever is running it, whoever takes their hand usually gives them [the person running the meeting] something." Confused, I asked, "Like a tip?" "All right, call it a tip," Darlene said.

Denyse interjected, "Well, we call it the pot . . . but it all depends on who runs it and where it is run. Because we do it in a church setting, so nobody takes any money. If you take $1,000, and it's ten people, you get your $1,000, but if it's a village setting [meaning more casual, in the park or with people you know], the person who is doing it [organizing the susu or keeping the money] receives $5 from every person . . . in a village setting. . . . Because I remember at home [in Trinidad] when I used to do it, the person who is holding that money gets the 'pot,' they get five dollars . . . so actually, the person who is holding the money gets something in return."

While some of the providers acknowledged that there was a difference between church and village settings, not all were convinced that one was any better than the other, especially regarding honorary donations that members might be expected to make to the organizer of the susu. For example, Jennie, who was from Grenada and was fully aware of susus among childcare providers and other groups, told me that she had once belonged to a susu organized in a church setting among both male and female West Indians but that she would never join one again. Jennie had originally joined the susu in order to save $2,000 for her wedding expenses in 1999. The couple in charge of the susu wanted her and her husband (they participated jointly since the money was for their wedding) to give them money as compensation for handling the susu money and activities. When Jennie's husband went to pick up their "hand," he gave the male organizer in the church forty dollars for his time and effort, but the organizer told him, "People usually give me a lot more than that." At this moment Jennie realized that the susu was being held "in order to take money out of poor people's hands." She said, "West Indians are poor people, and why must someone take money out of our hands and for what—to get rich themselves? It's not fair to the people who are trying to save what little money they have to buy the things they need. . . . I don't believe in that susu business, you just need to do the math . . . and realize that it's not worth it. How is it that I'm putting in my $1,000 and then have to pay someone a hundred dollars? Just do the math and it doesn't make sense. People are so stupid to get involved in that."

Irene told a very different story about how she ran her "village" susu among babysitters in Brooklyn: "Well, what happens is usually when people collect their hand they give you a $10 or a $20, you know, but you don't really do it for that. Some people do. Some people are crazy with it. But, for me, since I know myself, I don't ever do it to gain anything. It's something that I think we're all average people, we don't have a lot of money. . . . Why would I try to take from you? Why would I take from you when we're all trying to make something, so usually I don't take. When they draw their hand they would say, you know, 'I'll take you to lunch,' or they give me $20 or whatever, instead of demanding, 'Okay, when you get it you have to give me a hundred dollars'—no, that's not how I do it."

Irene empathized with her susu members as immigrants who were earning low wages in New York, but there appeared to be some socioeconomic advantages to being an organizer that she was not acknowledging. Those organizers, like Irene, who claimed to not want anything in return still did in fact receive something, whether a free lunch or money (which she did not refuse), so organizers received benefits that were different from those of other susu members. Some organizers took $100 out of each payout and thus received an additional "hand" without even contributing to the "pot." There was an advantage to having power over people's money in this informal setting that made susu participants feel obligated to pay out an extra amount from their hand, similar to a bank's exorbitant fees. Probably even more significant was the fact that an individual could secure a higher social status by organizing a susu, much like that of a banker in a mainstream community. Therefore, even if an organizer did not take a "tip," she would have a social status among the other childcare providers that could benefit her beyond the susu.

Trust

The issue of "trust" among susu members, especially trust of new members if the susu had been long-standing, was another much-discussed topic among the childcare providers.[27] Carol belonged to a susu organized by a Trinidadian friend who lived near her. Their children went to the same secondary school in Trinidad, and someone introduced them to each other in Brooklyn. They had been friends ever since. She had been in the friend's susu for around eleven years. Carol explained how susus worked both in Trinidad and here in Brooklyn when it came to trusting someone new: "When you get your hand, you have to make sure that you pay for someone else to get their hand. If it's not a fair person, you can't be in susu because you have to pay for someone else to get [their hand]. . . . When somebody just joins a susu, you mustn't give them no early hand, you have to wait. . . . If you want to throw a hundred, you could throw the hundred, but I throw fifty because I can't throw the hundred." She also stated that "you have to be honest with your susu. . . . If I can't make, I tell her that I can't make." As she made clear to me, susus had a protocol that members needed to be on time with, and forthcoming about, payments. Without these two things, a susu could not function properly because the bonds of trust would diminish over time.

Irene, like Carol, expressed the need for caution when dealing with new members in the susu that she organized among childcare providers in Brooklyn. Although she claimed that she had never had problems running her susu, she still did not take people she didn't know: "I don't take strange people, I don't take, you know, it's people that I know, that I trust, because if you're in it and you don't give it [the money] to me, there's nothing I can do to you. I will stand the losses because if I'm running it I have to make sure that when the time comes, the next person gets their money. So usually it's people that you know." Irene added, "My mom and I did it [organized a susu] between me, her, and a friend for years before it got bigger. You know, and usually it gets bigger with people that you know because they see you running it, they see you running it decent, and you're getting all your money, and you're fair, and they join. And it's up to me to say yes or no. And if I don't trust you, 'no.' And if you go into it the first time and I have problems getting to you to get the money, you're not in it again."

I asked whether people approached her about participating in the susu or she approached them. She responded, "Well, I never really had to approach anybody. It's usually like, if you're in it with me and you know a friend who says, 'Well, I need to save some money because next year I want to go on vacation or next year I want to pay down on a house' or whatever, then you can bring that person and say, 'Well, I know someone who is in a susu.' And I ask you, okay, if you bring this person in, you're responsible. If I don't know that person, you are responsible, so you better make sure that that person brings it [the money], otherwise you are going to have to give it [money] to me. If I know the person, then it's my responsibility. But no matter how it runs, at the end of the day, even if you don't get that person to give the money, I still have to find it [money] when it's the time to give that person the money because I'm the one who's running it."

Newer members to the West Indian susu were not always trustworthy, according to Jennie. While she acknowledged that some people benefited from susu money, she told a frightening story she had heard from a friend to illustrate that "the susu is getting out of hand." The friend's husband had been robbed at gun and knife point because the thieves knew that he was holding the susu money. Jennie's friend, who ran the susu, had taken someone new that year and believed it was that person who had robbed her husband. The thieves had to have known that the susu money was going to be paid out that day, for they waited for the wife to leave the house and then came in and robbed the husband. They even cut his long dreadlocks as a sign that they were not afraid. This type of story was not typical of susu tales among childcare providers, but it does show how violence could penetrate the informal system that had been set up among susu participants. Participants would have little recourse when such crimes occurred.

Community

Although susus might occasionally be mismanaged or dismantled for reasons not anticipated, in general they strengthened the bonds of community among childcare providers. Even someone like Jennie, who didn't believe in the value of participating in a susu herself, could not weaken these bonds, for she still understood the tradition, had participated in a susu, and could carry on a conversation about it. The cultural tradition of the susu was common to all of the women I spoke with (regardless of generation—not one childcare provider failed to recognize what I was speaking of when I mentioned it to them), and everyone spoke of the trust participants had to have in the leader and the other members. The economic function of the susu combined with the social connectedness that it fostered, both from the trust in the susu leader and participants that it required and the sense of participation in a long-held cultural tradition, contributed to a sense of community enmeshed with West Indian identity. The bonds between the women in this book went beyond their shared daily work of childcare and deepened as they entered into shared economic obligations—obligations that they did not trust standard American institutions to meet. In some ways, this repudiation of American capitalist institutions also bonded these women as West Indians.

Susus, then, have emotional and social elements that give them roles beyond their economic function, such as affirming trust among participants, using social pressure as a motivation to save money, and cementing friendships and kin relationships financially. The susu appears less informal to participants than to outsiders. Because susu participants have a built-in safety net if they need it through the possibility of getting an early payout, the tradition of such networks has continued to endure. Further, the community ties that are gained and the cultural tradition that is upheld make susus something of a staple among West Indian childcare providers. Susu participation grounds them in a collective memory of their homeland traditions—it is something their friends and family members did back home that they can continue in an effort to bond with their homeland and each other.

7

Organizing Resistance

The Case of Domestic Workers United

My initial interaction with the nonprofit group Domestic Workers United (DWU) was a telephone interview with Darlene, the childcare provider from Barbados mentioned at the beginning of this book, who was in her mid-fifties and had been raised in England with a high school-equivalent education. I had connected with Darlene through an employer of two domestic workers. Darlene was at first skeptical of my intentions as a researcher since DWU received requests for interviews on a regular basis. She made clear to me that in return for information I would have to volunteer some time phone banking for the organization (calling DWU members to remind them of upcoming events). My year of volunteer work, which required me to go in once a month, was enlightening. It took the effort of many existing members to recruit new members and maintain them. DWU workers and volunteers also attended multiple meetings in Albany to further their plans to organize domestic workers since they did not currently have regulated benefits such as health care, vacation time, sick days, or termination procedures.

Darlene proved to be a passionate advocate for domestic workers, especially black domestics. Her intensity was revealed in our introductory conversation when she expressed frustration about the public's ignorance or indifference about how domestic workers were treated in the United States. Referring to a current headline in the news, which reported that a man had lost his cat in the hollow wall of his house, she said, "They're making a big stink about a cat, a kitten that disappeared." I followed with "And there are people living in poor conditions, and who are not making enough money, and no one is helping them or putting it on television." She responded, "Exactly . . . makes me so mad." In the same conversation, drawing on group stereotypes, she boldly stated, "Us black people are not as determined as the Jews. The Jews have been talking about Holocaust for years. People say that you can compare slavery to the Holocaust, but what they forget is that the

Holocaust didn't happen here in America, but slavery did. You can't compare the Holocaust to slavery, it's apples and oranges."

This conversation, which would be the first of several interactions with Darlene, connected contemporary domestic work with the discrimination and exploitation that black women had been dealing with since the days of slavery; further, though she dismissed comparisons of slavery to the Holocaust, the very fact that she brought up both in the context of domestic work suggests the scale of the injustice that she felt contemporary domestic workers were facing.

My expanded understanding of the goals of DWU after volunteering with them led me to ask the childcare providers I was interacting with on a daily basis about DWU and to ask those who worked for DWU about the childcare providers specifically. I tried to connect the goals of the organization to the perceived realities of West Indian childcare providers, who were one of the targeted groups for this organization, and to understand their reactions to DWU workers who approached them in public spaces. A brief history of efforts to organize domestic workers, an overview of how DWU operates, and a discussion of the resistance to organizing that was common among West Indian childcare providers will show how the old union model of organizing—involving street demonstrations and other forms of public agitation—was largely ineffective with these workers given their tendency to avoid public exposure because of immigration status and other factors.

History of Organizing Domestic Workers

The struggle to organize domestic workers in the United States began in the early twentieth century when the National Labor Relations Act (NLRA) was passed as part of the New Deal, allowing workers, excluding domestic and farm workers, to organize and bargain collectively.[1] The exclusion of these two groups was intriguing: both were dominated by people of color, and both experienced "working conditions [that] resembled institutionalized slavery." The exclusion of domestic work specifically reflected "a system that explicitly disregards and renders invisible what is regarded as 'women's labor.'"[2] This "women's labor" has been predominantly immigrant women's labor, a fact that has further exempted domestic work from the ordinary protections afforded to workers by law.[3] According to Ai-jen Poo, DWU's director, "The overall nature of immigration policies and practices in the United States . . . [has] created a climate of pervasive fear among immigrant workers," and this climate has "created de facto immunity for all employers of domestics and undocumented workers generally."[4] Since the 1970s, a large immigrant influx of workers has resulted in competitive markets and "the disappearance of jobs at adequate wages."[5] This hostile environment to labor is even more pervasive in New York City, where "the horizontal structure of the . . . economy" accommodates "deregulation and declining industry standards, and weakens the ability of unions to organize workers."[6] As Ruth Needleman explains, "Labor has been most successful at organizing during periods when the economy and job market were expanding," not during periods of stabilization or decline.[7] (It would be interesting to know to what extent economic expansion itself might be an effect of good labor organizing.) In 2000, the AFL-CIO declared support for a general amnesty for undocumented immigrants, and the struggle for the rights of domestic workers and farm workers became a mainstream issue of the labor movement.

In the United States, and New York more specifically, immigrant women of color have ended up in traditionally female jobs at the low end of the "service, clerical, and manufacturing sectors," additionally marginalized in the contingent (freelance) workforce of U.S. labor markets,[8] and the use of coethnic networks by employers for hiring and by employees for finding work helps to keep them in their marginal position.[9] The competition for these lower-wage positions creates difficulty in organizing workers.[10] But my own research on West Indian childcare providers made apparent the need for organizing workers in the domestic sector: many of these women cannot afford childcare for their own biological children and are placed in a position where they have to leave their children without adult supervision in an apartment while they go to work to put food on the table.[11] Some West Indian babysitters have resisted the exploitation that has flourished in the domestic sector by participating in more formal labor organizations.[12]

Domestic Workers United

History, Funding, Membership, and Goals

DWU is an example of this kind of formal organization. To understand how DWU has been able to recruit over 1,300 members (of whom about 300 are active as of 2007) to fight for domestic workers' rights and to gain exposure in both worker communities and the state legislature, I interviewed five of the fifteen DWU organizers, some of whom were babysitters themselves, from West Indian backgrounds. I also spoke with twenty-five nonmember West Indian babysitters about DWU's work to understand the effectiveness of DWU's outreach efforts and why some outreach tactics did not succeed among West Indian childcare providers.

DWU was founded in 2000 through the efforts of two organizations in New York: the Women Workers Project of the Committee Against Anti-Asian Violence (CAAAV) and the Andolan Organizing South Asian Workers (AOSAW). The director of DWU, Ai-jen Poo, a thirty-three-old Chinese woman who had been born in Pittsburgh and had lived in New York since 1992, explained that CAAAV, founded in 1998, had been the first organization in New York to organize Filipina domestic workers, particularly those in Manhattan's Chinatown community, as well as Asian women who worked in low-wage service industries such as nail and beauty salons or restaurants, while the AOSAW was a Pan-Asian grassroots membership organization that focused on building power among low-income immigrant workers in the Asian community, especially the Southeast Asian refugee community in the Bronx. As Ai-jen explained, "After two years of kind of meeting, organizing themselves, supporting each other to fight their employers for better conditions and things like that, they were really like, 'We really need to work with all the workers in this industry, particularly the Caribbean workers and the Latina workers who are even larger populations of the workforce than we are, and we need to build the power of the workforce together. We need to build a movement in this industry,' and that's where the idea for Domestic Workers United came about. So, it was meant to be a vehicle to basically build the power of the entire industry, but also directly organize those populations of workers that were not being organized by either CAAAV or Andolan."

When I asked if any other organizations specifically organized West Indian domestic workers, or Latina domestic workers, Ai-jen replied, "No, there aren't any such organizations." "None at all?" I asked, surprised. She responded that CAAAV and Andolan were trying to build an alliance among the three ethnic groups.[13] Then she added, "And what we started to realize was that it really is no accident that it's all women of color doing this work, and it's no accident that it's migrants in this period [i.e., today] . . . or immigrant women. And it's no accident that the work to this day still isn't recognized, respected, or valued, that when you do the historical research you can see like a deliberate pattern of exclusion. . . . That the work and exploitation that the workforce was subjected to, and that the state actually condoned and supported [exclusion]." This is the pattern that Maxine Baca Zinn and Bonnie Thornton Dill illuminate in *Women of Color in U.S. Society,* a collection of essays that explore, among other topics, the long history of black women's restriction to a narrow range of occupations, primarily in domestic service, and their deliberate exclusion from other, better-compensated forms of employment.[14]

How Domestic Workers United Works

DWU is funded by five foundations and individual private donations. It is composed primarily of childcare providers, an estimated 70 percent of the membership according to Ai-jen. Around 20 percent are housekeepers and 10 percent are elder caregivers. The childcare provider industry breaks down into approximately 50 percent Caribbean born, 20 percent Latina, 10 percent Asian, and the rest African immigrant or other. The DWU membership as a whole is 80 percent Caribbean born, 15 percent Latina, and 5 percent African immigrant, Ai-jen told me.

DWU has four goals in organizing workers, according to Ai-jen—acquiring sufficient power to change the domestic industry, garnering respect for domestic work among both the public and domestic workers themselves, establishing parity for domestic workers under the Fair Labor Standards Act, and building a workers' movement. Ai-jen stated that the first goal had to be achieved, not by elected officials or expert professionals, but by the workers themselves, organizing and developing their own leadership. She said of the second goal that domestic work was generally seen as "unskilled, natural help. . . . The work is made invisible, it's not protected, the wages are low, their time is flexible, flexible to the advantage of the employers, not to the workers. . . . So, we really [need to] see education around respect for the work itself, not just as a form of wage labor, but as a form of work that traditionally women have done in the home for generations and continue to do, that isn't compensated."

Regarding the third goal of DWU, Ai-jen stated: "And so the third goal is about Fair Labor Standards, and that's really important to us, not because we feel like once we have standards in place all the problems are going to be solved at all. In fact, it's pretty clear to domestic workers the ways in which the legal system really isn't set up in their interest. . . . But that it is really important that these standards exist, because the exclusion of this workforce from legal recognition and protection has been such a huge part of how this workforce has been oppressed over time, and stayed denigrated over time. . . . We feel like fighting for standards is a really critical part of how we're then going to build towards more freedom and more protection and more recognition, you know? So, fighting for laws for us is really specific."

As of 2010, the National Labor Relations Act, which guarantees employees the right to organize, the Occupational Safety and Health Act, which governs working conditions, and civil rights laws, which protect against employment discrimination, all exclude domestic workers from their provisions. In addition, the Fair Labor Standards Act excludes live-in domestic workers from its overtime-pay provisions, and although its minimum-wage provisions do cover childcare as a regular occupation, they exempt workers who perform it on a "casual" basis (i.e., irregularly and intermittently).

To establish equal protection under labor laws, DWU had been gathering and publicizing information on domestic workers' current working conditions. Darlene told me, for example, about "a documentary based on domestic workers" that the DWU was working on, as well as a DWU survey "conducted with over five hundred respondents of all different ethnic domestic workers that ask questions about age, length of work, status in the U.S., employer treatment, benefits, pay scale, benefits, etc. This data is written up in what the UN will receive next month, and which I'm currently reviewing, called 'The Shadow Report,' by the University of North Carolina, prepared for the Human Rights Committee."

Most important, DWU had been campaigning for over six years to pass the Domestic Workers Bill of Rights in New York State and hoped to eventually pass such a bill on the national level.[15] The bill would establish a living wage; would give structure to termination procedures; would establish severance pay, overtime pay (currently not extended to live-in domestic workers), and pay for sick days, holidays, and vacations, as well as at least one day off a week; and would protect domestic workers from discrimination. The Bill of Rights would be the first piece of national legislation for domestic work. As Darlene explained to me, the bill "addresses the fact that domestic workers have been excluded from protections. . . . Farmworkers are getting further than us and they only started in 1999."

Because many West Indian domestic workers do not have legal immigration status, I was interested in knowing how such legislation would affect them. Darlene told me that the Domestic Workers Bill of Rights neither explicitly covered undocumented workers nor explicitly excluded them. This was because lawyers and lawmakers "told us [DWU] specifically to not add 'covers undocumented immigrants' to the bill we are currently trying to get passed because that just draws attention and the bill won't get passed." But "as of right now, undocumented workers have rights under two laws that cover domestic workers, and those are minimum wage rights and overtime rights" (though live-in workers are exempted from the overtime rights, and although the minimum wage for domestic workers who are considered "casual" workers is not enforced). Workers have the right to be paid what they are supposed to receive or to sue if they do not receive their proper wages (something that DWU helps its members to do). When I asked Ai-jen, "Are the Fair Labor Standards . . . something that . . . can [serve only] those that are documented versus those who are undocumented?" she answered, "Historically, in the United States, labor standards have been such that even though . . . the laws are really contradictory in different areas of law, so with immigration law, it is technically illegal for undocumented workers to work. But the way that the law works is that once you're in a job, you're protected by the same laws as any other worker. So, that's why undocumented workers can sue for unpaid wages. Everybody's protected under the Fair Labor Standards Act . . . once they've worked. . . . Otherwise it would be slavery . . . which is a criminal offense."

I wanted to know if undocumented workers fighting for standard employment rights could possible invoke such protections: "Now the government could still deport you, technically . . . but you could still get paid for the wages. . . . So, could an employer say, 'Oh, this person never worked for me,' if there's no documentation that they did?"

Ai-jen explained, "They could. And then the worker could say, "I did, and it was for this number of hours . . ."

". . . The worker would have to prove then that they actually did work?" I asked.

Ai-jen answered, "She would, but there are ways of doing that. She could basically like actually just write out every day what hours she did. And that's why we always encourage workers to keep good records, because if anything were to happen, those records, even if they're written on like napkins and things like that, can be submitted to court. Yeah, as evidence . . . testimonies from neighbors, doormen."

The last goal of the DWU, building a workers' movement, involves addressing the root causes (racial, gendered, and systemic) of oppression for all communities and thereby truly changing the day-to-day workings of this occupational system, which includes economic and political institutions. Coalition work with other organizations, such as those fighting for the rights of Haitian, Filipina, South Asian, and Nepalese immigrants, contributes to this goal.

Organizing and Outreach Strategies

DWU organizes domestic workers in a variety of ways. It privately and publicly negotiates with employers on behalf of its members. When DWU is approached by a worker who has not been paid for the work completed, one of the organizers makes a private phone call to the employer on the worker's behalf, which can sometimes lead to an argument, both verbal and legal. On occasion, the organization has sent letters to the employers demanding pay for DWU members or has publicly picketed their place of business or private home. Some employers will settle with the worker and pay the wages owed after such a public demonstration. One woman who came to DWU for support showed one of the representatives and free legal counsel the handwritten schedule she had obtained from her employer, yet when it came time for this worker to get paid, nothing was given to her and her living conditions were abysmal (she slept on a mattress on a leaky basement floor). After DWU members protested in front of the employer's place of business and handed out flyers describing how he treated his hired laborer, he became so frustrated with losing potential business that he finally settled the case for the money owed to her. Some employers risk DWU filing a lawsuit or finding allies within the communities of the employers. DWU will even go so far as to get local legislators to contact employers privately or inquire about the issue at hand and apply pressure if direct action doesn't work. Workers who find themselves in the position of having to seek out an organization such as DWU to fight for their rights (mostly live-in workers) are often separated from their families and made to live in isolation at their employer's home with no access to transportation.

DWU organizers spoke of outreach to domestic workers as an important way of overcoming the isolation that these workers experienced and providing them with more experiences of solidarity, though sometimes the isolating conditions themselves made these workers harder to reach. Ai-jen told me, "People [domestic workers] are generally isolated. . . . They find ways of resisting and surviving and supporting each other and stuff as a response to that isolation. . . . But in general I would say that people do still feel pretty isolated."

I asked whether their isolation differed from that of a stay-at-home mother.

"I think so," Ai-jen explained, "because they're employees, and they have—that it's about their livelihood and so the isolation doesn't have to do with just being alone in the home, but also the fact that you have so little control over your working conditions. . . . And the environment around you . . ."

Elena, who had stepped into the room a few moments earlier to prepare for a DWU meeting and whom I saw out of the corner of my eye scribbling notes for the upcoming meeting, overheard the discussion that Ai-jen and I were having and wanted to add something to it: "[DWU allows domestic workers to] come together to support one another, to be in a space where you can share experiences and be able to identify those patterns so that then, in our particular case, it's allowed us to be able to launch this campaign to fight for a Bill of Rights in New York State. . . . And what makes this that much more powerful is that it really came from the women—domestic workers coming together to say, 'These are all the experiences that we're having.' . . . And ourselves identifying those patterns so that we could then be able to craft together with, you know, people who know how to write legislation . . . and be able to craft a bill that really responded to the specific needs and conditions that people were facing. I wish there were more groups in, you know, around the country, because I'm sure that there's just thousands and thousands more who are working and living in isolation . . . and may not have other avenues of support."

Yet outreach has been problematic in the past for DWU and continues to be a major factor in their inability to organize in a way that would effect significant change in terms of getting the Bill of Rights passed, recruiting a critical mass, or potentially unionizing in the future. Ai-jen addressed this: "Outreach is really hard. It's the most important aspect of the work, but it's also the hardest part of organizing because when you do the outreach in the parks, no matter how much you believe in the organization, you're always going to run up with a variety of responses from workers. And it's definitely hard, you know? So, it's [DWU] a space for people . . . it's a process . . . [to] get support from each other. . . . But then for us to also strategize, like, how do we do this better, how do we reach more workers, what areas are we not reaching, and how can we improve our outreach materials?"

So how did DWU attract members when those targeted were resisting? Ai-jen described what Friedman would call "the use of selective incentives."[16] For example, DWU offers "nanny training programs" administered by certified professionals over four consecutive weekends. These programs, paid for at a reduced rate of $100 by the members, have graduated over four hundred workers with a CPR certificate through the American Heart Association, along with child psychology and pediatrics courses. As an organizing strategy, these programs boost the credentials of members when approaching potential or existing employers for increased wages. In addition, members receive a certificate for the leadership training program for workers to understand the history and development of their industry. It is hoped that by learning the history of the domestic work industry, workers will be able to "see how and why they have the potential to change the conditions they endure" and consider the historical context of their struggle.[17]

DWU started a girls' night out, on Friday nights after work, where people came who might not be drawn to a meeting but might be drawn to having a drink after work. They also did member outreach picnics and play groups outside when the weather was nice, as well as outreach at the commuter train stations where workers left for work in the suburbs. And when the weather was good, generally workers went outside to public parks and talked with sitters.

In charge of this membership recruitment were Ai-jen, who committed 75 percent of her time to DWU (approximately thirty hours a week), and Elena Perez, the Latina member coordinator and translator-interpreter at monthly member meetings or special events, who worked eight to fifteen hours per week. In addition, there were four West Indian workers and one Mexican worker who were nannies or housekeepers and put in time when they could (usually around eight hours per week), since their day work offered little flexibility. The women ranged in age from their late twenties to sixties. When I asked whether DWU had found certain West Indian workers to be strong leaders, Ai-jen responded, "What I have noticed is that a lot of members of DWU who really organically step into leadership [roles] were heavily involved in the trade union movements in their home countries. . . . So, like Barbara was a shop steward and on a national kind of steering committee for representing transport workers in the Barbados trade union." Ai-jen reflected aloud for a moment: "But it is about the members, really, like are we speaking to members, are we speaking to workers, their needs—are we connecting with them, are they feeling like this is their organization?"

Providers' Responses to DWU Outreach

When I asked Darlene about her participation in the 2006 marches for immigrant rights in New York, she said that she hadn't been able to attend the May 1 march because of a reception that she had to attend on behalf of the DWU, but that she had been able to go to the one on April 29. She told me that "the Latin American people were representing with flags, and it was a very warm feeling, but at the same time it was an embarrassment. . . . It is embarrassing to me to see so many Latin American representatives and so few West Indians at the march. . . . There was so much energy on that bridge."

"Do you think it is fear that keeps the West Indian workers away from protests?" I asked.

"What do you think it is?" she asked me in return. "I have been doing this since 1999. It's laziness."

"You think they are just lazy?" I asked her.

Darlene responded, "You know as black people, we talk a lot, but no action. . . . I want them to get off the benches and do something. . . . Our people want it [change in worker rights] but want everyone else to do it [protest]. They want you to plant the food, cook the food, put the plate out, and you might as well put the knife and fork there beside it too. . . . It's a lot of excuses: 'I can't be bothered because I don't have personal days or sick days.' One person can't win. . . . One woman said to me that 'I only have two days off a week and I have groceries to get and I want to spend time with my family.' They're lucky to have two days off. Most workers don't."

What Darlene was discussing here was the concept of "free riders," defined by J. Scott Lewis as "those self interested individuals who receive the benefits of group membership without a corresponding contribution to the group."[18] The free-rider problem is a classic problem that occurs across institutions. As Debra Friedman and Doug McAdam explain it, "Collective actions nearly always seek collective goods for their members, ends that, once achieved, all will benefit from. The problem is that if all will benefit, regardless of whether they have participated or not, no rational actor would ever choose to contribute his or her scarce resources to help achieve such ends."[19] "To the extent that the group's success depends on the wide adoption of its position, it suffers this problem more deeply."[20] The free-rider problem, then, is one that DWU must contend with in its quest for membership and domestic worker involvement.

Darlene asked me where my study participants were coming from and I told her that I was looking at areas of Brooklyn that were predominantly white, upper middle class, and gentrified. She proceeded to tell me that she had spent a lot of time in Brooklyn Heights, Park Slope, and Atlantic Avenue, distributing flyers to other workers. "More than one time that I have approached a West Indian babysitter [a black woman pushing a stroller] to give a flyer and as soon as they see the name of the organization they say 'I'm not interested' and they shake their heads. I ask them if I can explain what the organization does so that they know what they are saying no to. . . . They take off like their tail is on fire or they say, 'I know about it already.' . . . They have been given misinformation by those who haven't come to a meeting."

Darlene's frustration with the West Indian childcare community was not entirely misplaced, since she was working every spare moment to better the life of domestic workers, often without much involvement from them. But my interviews with these childcare providers left me with the impression that "laziness" was less of an obstacle to involvement than political pessimism, personal fears, and overwhelming family responsibilities. Further, although both Ai-jen and Elena spoke about how DWU's outreach could offer providers a way out of isolation, the West Indian childcare providers I studied, who did not live in their employer's home, never once mentioned isolation as part of their jobs, even when asked specifically; isolation did not seem to either motivate or inhibit their limited inclination to organize formally.

Some West Indian childcare providers were not motivated to fight for their rights simply because they felt helpless in a country where "whites rule" and "blacks are not heard." Jennie, a sitter from Grenada, exemplified this pessimistic attitude when she told me, "Things aren't going to get better unless sitters get out of this position. . . . Well, I mean it will never get better even if they get out because another generation is going to do it. . . . But I'm just saying on an individual basis, you don't want to be in this forever, this, there's nothing in this, there are no benefits in this."

"Now, what about things like Domestic Workers United? Have you heard of that group?" I asked.

"Yeah, I haven't been to any meetings."

"Why not?" I asked.

Jennie responded, "I've just never bothered, but it's a good thing."

"You think it's a good thing?"

Jennie affirmed, "It's a good thing because . . . we need that because the parents wouldn't do it for us because they want to be able to not pay you enough money. . . . They want to . . . have you work twelve hours a day."

Perplexed by Jennie's acknowledgment of DWU's contributions but reluctance to participate, I asked again,

"Do you know what Domestic Workers United is?"

"No, not really, I don't know much about it. I just think it's trying to get our rights, get like rights for nannies and get the salaries and the conditions people endure, but I've never been to the meetings. I've seen a lot of flyers about it."

Jennie said that whites, specifically white employers, would need to be the majority in any movement standing up for domestic workers because black domestic workers fighting for their rights would not be taken as seriously. She elaborated, "No, I'm saying if we get . . . we have one thousand blacks. If we get one hundred, five hundred whites to say, 'Hey, we need that,' people will think it will be more effective. Yes, because in America, you're black. Who's going to listen to *you* anyway? So if you get five thousand [white] parents who say, 'Hey, I want that too,' we guarantee that's going to change in the morning. But [white] people just think, Hey, it's just a bunch of [black] people who have nothing, who people think have no brain. It's going to happen, but when. I think if we see a shift in it [domestic work policy], if you see the majority who was [white] parents. . . . This is why I've never really bothered."

I asked if she felt that the employer parents needed to get more involved. Jennie responded that the employers needed to speak up more and say that what sitters were going through was wrong. She saw the only solution as coming from the employers, since they were "white" and therefore had more power to get people to listen. However, she added that "it wouldn't happen that way because they like that cheap labor. . . . They like that cheap labor, so this is why it just wouldn't [happen]. . . . I'm not saying that it would never, nothing's impossible, but when?"

Eventually I asked, "Do you think they [DWU] should stop doing what they're doing?"

"No, it's a good cause," Jennie stated.

I asked, "So you think it's good for those who want to join?"

"It's good, yeah, it's very good, um, it's a right step in a right direction. They should never stop because if you give up then nothing happens. . . . Um, I mean, today they have one thousand . . . by tomorrow they may have three thousand, you know, so . . . I'm not saying that they should give up. . . . Maybe see if they can get some of the other people [white parents] to sign. . . . I can't see that happening. You'll get a few parents, you won't get the majority who go to Congress and say, 'Yes,' because we need the majority, you know. People already see us as nothing once you're in that job."

I realized through this and other discussions that many childcare providers, though they understood what DWU was about, lacked any faith that the group would protect workers or improve working conditions and doubted that it was worth workers' time to participate in organizing.

Some of the reluctance of childcare providers to engage with DWU may also have been due to fear. Darlene herself alluded to providers' possible fears when she explained that "when people used to be on the picket lines [i.e., in the history of the labor movement], fewer people stuck with it because of fear of losing their jobs. . . . They [sitters] only want to be a part of it when the battle is won. . . . I see more Caucasians go out to protest [i.e., more white liberal organizers or employers than West Indian workers]." Here the free-rider problem is framed not just in terms of unwillingness to contribute effort to the cause but in terms of fears about taking the risks that it would involve.

Many childcare providers spoke to me about fears that they and others like them had about participation in organizing. Though I understood Darlene's frustrations, I did not think it was enough for her to dismiss the fears that were so real to other childcare providers: that going against one's employer could lead to loss of one's job and, for those without green cards, ultimately deportation. Three women I spoke with had seen their peers sent back to the islands and treated disrespectfully on their return, so the fear of being forcibly returned to the islands was real to them, as was the fear of being isolated back in their homeland with limited options for work.[21] Many women felt that deportation would leave them with the stigma of not being able to make it America because of their arrogance in leaving the homeland in the first place.

When I asked Jennie, "Why has it been so difficult to get more sitters to organize? You would think that if your rights aren't being met you would want to organize with a group," she replied, "It comes back to [immigration] status again. A lot of girls don't have their green cards, and people are afraid of this public, you know what I'm saying, it's like I'm putting myself out there. Nobody knows I'm here, or nobody knows where I am or I exist, so that's what it is. It's people. . . . A lot of girls don't have their green cards as yet, and they don't want to be there [with DWU], but they support it. But they don't want to be there. . . . 'What if I'm at a rally and they come and snatch me.' That's what it is. It's not that the girls don't want to be there, a lot of girls don't have their green cards and they don't want to expose themselves. . . . That's what it's all about, but people support it [the effort being made]. . . . People don't like what's going on."

Irene, the sitter from Trinidad, similarly stated that fear of getting sent back to the islands was a common reason for sitters' nonparticipation in organizing efforts: "No, like you know, people are just scared if something happens. Okay, say you go to a rally and something breaks out and the cops hold you, you don't have anything. You think they're just going to let you go? Half, some of the time they do, half the time they don't, so you don't want to put yourself in that position where you could be in the line of fire then. That's something that, for me, I think they [employers] should do for us [i.e., go to rallies]." But Barbara, another worker at DWU and a childcare provider, scoffed at the idea that the fear of too much public exposure had anything to do with why undocumented women were not organizing: "What we do is public, we're out there every day and most people know that we don't have documents, so that makes no sense. If they wanted to do something to you, they would have a long time ago, but they [employers and policy makers] know that they need us to keep working."

Even workers who had green cards could be afraid to associate with DWU or fight for their labor rights. When, in an interview of Molly, Rachel, and Janet in March 2007, I asked Molly if she had ever heard of DWU, Rachel interrupted and said, "They had a segment on that . . . at the City College . . . on the radio. . . . They were saying that document or not, you have the right to step up to see whether the employer is mistreating you, you have the right to report it."

Molly shook her head, saying, "Yes, right, right." But she noted that even people who did have a green card were afraid to report: they were "still taking the abuse from the bosses," and they endured such circumstances because they needed the money. Janet commented, "I don't get that," and Molly went on, "Yes, but [when] you have your green card, you got to look for something better. . . . Because somebody tell me about a Trinidadian and how somebody make them cry. I said no boss is going to make me cry . . . green card or not."

Just the prospect of getting fired, even if one didn't have to fear deportation, was catastrophic enough to scare many women away from DWU. Deondra, a sitter from Trinidad, confirmed this perception one day while we were chatting with a Panamanian sitter on the front stoop of her employer's brownstone in one of the sites under study. Deondra said, "There are people [DWU] who come around the park to hand out flyers. . . . No one wants to take them, though, because they're afraid to lose their job. If their employers find out, they will lose their job."

Erynn Esposito, a white employer who worked part time with the DWU to organize sitters, discussed this issue in a conversation we had about DWU's attempts to get sitters to ask employers to sign a standard employment contract. When I asked her what obstacles she or DWU had encountered with regard to West Indian sitters in particular, she said not only that they were worried about their legal status but also that they were under the impression that there was more labor supply than demand. Finally, she noted that aspects of their culture of origin made West Indian sitters particularly uncomfortable with the idea of approaching a potential or existing employer.

These attitudes should not be ignored, but rather understood as part of the reality for some West Indian immigrants and part of the forced dependence between employer and employee in general. Some workers were afraid to participate in organizing or unions because in doing so they might jeopardize their relationship with their employer who provided them with their only security. When work takes place in an intimate setting such as a private employer's home, face-to-face encounters create an employer-employee dynamic very different from that experienced by, say, a farmworker or factory worker, who does not meet with his employer each day.

It is fair to say that some employers would be supportive of organizing childcare providers and other domestic workers and standardizing the work relationship that they had with their own childcare provider. Indeed, Erynn, an employer who, with her husband, was in the top 5 percent of income bracket in New York, and who considered herself and her husband part of the "upper class," worked to raise awareness among other employers about this issue.

She told me, "I was shocked at the lack of consciousness of women employers towards women employees. . . . When feminists go to the workplace, they have an idea of how they want or expect to be treated, but then go home and exploit the women that work for them." Erynn said she understood that the race and status difference between herself and West Indian childcare providers would hamper her ability to organize among them; that was why she was "trying to work with employers who were white and of her own status . . . her peers," who would then have their "sitters hand out material to other sitters." Erynn herself passed on information to the sitters (one Puerto Rican and one Trinidadian woman) that she herself employed to care for her two children and that she sent photocopies of DWU flyers for her sitters to hand out in the parks because, in her view, it was more effective to have sitters organize than for a white woman and employer to tell sitters that they should join a group—though she expressed frustration about their tendency not to stand up for themselves. This view was the complete opposite of Jennie's suggestion that white employers would be more effective in substantially changing the condition of West Indian childcare providers than the providers themselves.

But in another discussion, Irene pointed out the problems that made many employers less supportive of domestic workers' organizing efforts. She was talking about how getting a green card for the babysitter was something that employers should take on as their responsibility, "even if it's just a work permit or something so they can work for you. . . . Just do something for them, so they don't have to feel like . . . that crazy feeling. . . . I tell people, I remember a woman I worked for said that 'you know, Irene, I don't know why they [the government] don't give people their stuff [their papers or permits].' [It's] because . . . if we have to pay people who are legal to do this, we couldn't pay them because we'd have to give them medical, we have to give them everything, and if we have to give them everything, how much can we pay them? We can't have childcare. So, why not just help them out [get them papers], you know, so we can do what we have to do."

The employer's remark above exhibits the same contradictions domestic workers have been dealing with for decades, as Irene herself goes on to explain. If the government gave childcare providers temporary work visas, as suggested by Irene's former employer, employers would be forced to pay a certain minimum wage, one that many employers would find too expensive; indeed, that is why they often hire recent immigrants, many of whom are undocumented. By exploiting an undocumented worker in terms of pay rate, employers can afford personal childcare instead of institutionalized day care.

Though West Indian childcare providers' fears arising from their undocumented status are well founded, and though they may present an obstacle to organizing, they are not an insurmountable obstacle. In fact, it is not uncommon for groups of mostly undocumented workers to organize formally for their rights by building coalitions that grow over time, as has occurred with the Justice for Janitors (JfJ) campaign across the United States. With the support of the Service Employees International Union (SEIU), undocumented building workers in the JfJ campaign were able to strategize and use public relations events and protests to help produce successful union recognition.[22]

A final deterrent to DWU involvement, one that was never discussed in my interviews with the DWU workers (who did not themselves have any living children or husbands at the time of the interview), was the difficulties childcare providers faced in balancing the demands of their work and the demands of their own families. Many providers had husbands and children to care for. In his book *Cultures of Solidarity,* Fantasia gives examples of female union activists who had to manage their lives around formal organizing.[23] He talks about one activist who took her husband to union hall meetings simply to ease the "tensions caused by her frantic schedule during the campaign."[24] He also describes the strain on family members as they tried to work out a new division of household tasks. As Fantasia states, "Part of the difficulty in disengaging oneself from private life and becoming more engaged in the public realm lay in feelings of guilt that had to be overcome. Most of these women were also wives and mothers whose sense of value and duty was partly bound up with their family roles. Even the most staunch activists had to deal with the contradiction between their traditional private role and the liberating possibilities of a public one."[25]

Therefore, strategizing how to organize domestic workers requires considering not only their responsibilities at work and in the community but the totality of their home, family, and workplace responsibilities. DWU attempts to accommodate the family lives of workers by offering childcare during monthly meetings and special events. But most workers who said they were reluctant to attend cited, not only fears of employers' retaliation, but also a wish to preserve their off-hours for such private activities as errands, visits with family members, and simple rest.

All these concerns should be taken seriously as conditions that unfortunately hamper some of DWU's efforts. Addressing them will be challenging, but organizers must not only acknowledge their deep-rooted nature (as indeed they do) but also construct their organizing strategies with those concerns in mind, particularly strategies that involve approaching people in the public sphere.

Historically, up to the 1970s, labor organizing in the United States was predominantly led by white men in the industrial sectors. However, since that time, the working class has been predominantly employed in the service sector, where, in New York City, the majority population is immigrant. There is a strong tradition of labor organizing for immigrants in other sectors, such as the garment industry, and in the industrial sectors for white immigrant men—and later their offspring. But only in the last two decades has there been a focus on immigrants of color in the industrial and service sectors. Therefore, the strides being made by groups such as New York taxi drivers and transit workers, janitors, and farmworkers, who are generally isolated, predominantly male, and mostly immigrant, are fairly recent. Labor organizing has been more of a challenge for women workers, and specifically domestics, since they occupy positions in gendered spheres that are typically labeled as "unskilled" labor. A general failure to recognize the importance of this type of work and its effect on the economy has held back change in domestic working conditions. The informal nature of domestic work has been manipulated to such an extent that it is time that the political infrastructure that ignores this sector establish some minimum standards to provide the quality of life that all workers in the United States deserve.

Childcare is an integral component in New York's social infrastructure and a significant contributor to the economic development of the city. While the government has attempted to alleviate some childcare stressors through child tax and child credit relief, it is not nearly enough to cover the expenses of the full-day childcare provision that is required by most middle and upper-middle-class dual-income families, the employers of the childcare providers in this study. The economy depends on the work of upper-middle-class families, yet does not acknowledge by any formal means the changes that this group has seen over the decades. Stable employment as we knew it is disappearing as it becomes more temporary and more flexible. While formal day care centers are not typically unionized, many do offer better benefits such as health care and pension options with sick and vacation leave. None of the workers I interviewed sought out these options, however, because of either lack of legal work documentation or fear of losing the perceived flexibility they had in their current work situations. Workers, especially working women, are not able to maintain the stability that was once assured them; and working mothers, whether they are immigrant childcare providers or the providers' employers, all find themselves repeatedly facing childcare crises. Since this flexible service sector has been built into modern capitalism, we cannot readily resolve the issues of childcare. We need a structural change in how people are connected economically. Government assurance that all employers and employees, regardless of socioeconomic status, will receive adequate coverage for childcare expenses, beginning with appropriate release time from work (as in Canada, where new mothers are allowed one year off work with reduced pay), and government establishment of a better child credit program that gives parents adequate liquid funding for childcare (money that is not simply used against taxes at the end of the year, but money in hand), are only the first step. DWU's attempt to ensure that childcare providers get a fair living wage for New York and their basic human rights is also a good step forward in resolving some of the childcare issues. But while the old union model of contract-based employment that has helped other groups of immigrants may be able to improve the economic situation of domestic workers and is an appealing alternative for employers because of their understanding of or perhaps experience with this model, it is not as grounded as the immediate networks being built among some groups, such as West Indian childcare providers. Providers at times viewed attempts to organize them as an intrusion on their autonomy. Because of the strong community that they had built in public spaces in Brooklyn gentrified neighborhoods, they were reluctant to go outside that circle of trust (i.e., to DWU). Providers preferred to learn about negotiating wages or gaining needed benefits through communication with fellow members of the community, particularly longtime childcare providers who could recount the stories of other workers and then say what they themselves would do in the situation. So we need not only an ongoing dialogue about how New York and the United States in general integrate childcare providers into the larger social and economic structures, but also efforts to alter the structures in ways that respect these workers' *collective autonomy*.[26]

Conclusion

“People don’t care about us, they care about what we can do for them. They want us to do all of the work while they get paid good wages for the work they do outside the house. That is not decency. We just want to be appreciated for the work we do. Pay us so that we can live a decent life. Help us to get our documents, or help us when our children need us to tend to them. . . . Don’t punish us because we have a life outside of working for you. We all want this, not just me, but all of us . . . as a community of sitters.”

This is the message West Indian childcare providers want the public to hear. It is not about giving them the high life, it is about showing appreciation and being decent to a group of people who work to ensure the safety and social integration of the children of Brooklyn.

Is there an ideal childcare work arrangement for Brooklynites? West Indian childcare providers appear to have a good sense of the history of domestic work: they recognize that black women have done this type of private carework for a long time and that the inequalities built into it cannot easily be done away with. But they want their work to be appreciated. Employers can help by offering Metrocards to those who commute, not calling employees several times a day on the cell phone unless they are paying the bill, acknowledging employee birthdays by either offering the day off or having the child under care make a card, allowing for time off when the provider or her child is sick, and not requesting additional duties without compensation—these are employees, not “family” as some might like to think. Some employers choose to foster community among the childcare providers by offering up their homes for playdates in the winter months so that providers along with their charges can have a safe, warm space to socialize. This is not only good for the employees but often good for the children. However, it is important to understand that none of these acts of consideration change the fact that employers maintain a great deal of power over employees; as long as employers hire private childcare there is no ideal childcare arrangement.

Community and Surveillance

Why should we care about West Indian childcare providers and attempt to understand their social, cultural, and economic lives and their uses of public and private spaces? Because such understanding can open up a social world that has been constructed around the care of Brooklyn's, and more broadly, New York's children. The fact that these women, who are under constant monitoring by the public, can create communities of their own speaks to their ability to empower themselves, if only temporarily, in ways that affect how they interact with the children they care for and with their employers. Not only that, but they use the spaces that they move through to provide social opportunities for the children in their care, to extend the parents' social networks, and to deepen a shared sense of cultural commitment among themselves. Food sharing, informal systems of saving money, and technologies like cell phones offer these childcare providers both visible and nonvisible means of expressing West Indianness that ultimately make their subordinated work position more tolerable. Understanding the countercommunity that they create to stave off the isolation within the employer's home is a first step toward understanding how to engage this group of women in organizing efforts like DWU's.

In previous chapters I have argued that the social spaces that the West Indian childcare providers in this study created in public places continuously expressed their culture through their daily work interactions. As exposed as the providers were in public places, this fact did not completely deter them from enacting their collective life. In fact, as Pei-Chia Lan has shown for migrant domestics in Taiwan, their acts of cultural preservation gave them the strength to continue working under a variety of conditions.[1] Food sharing, for example, not only evoked memories of West Indian culture and demonstrated and transmitted cultural skills and knowledge but also strengthened a sense of community within this group of women. Food also became the basis for the women's interactions with their charges, a point of contention between workers and the mothers of the children, and a measure by which providers judged their employer's mothering ability; the sharing of West Indian food with the employer's children was also a way that providers could temporarily assert power within the private workspaces that they occupied during the weekdays while simultaneously disempowering some employers (especially mothers who providers felt were responsible for feeding the children) by excluding them from an act of bonding with the child under care.

Providers were also able to connect as a community through susus or informal savings collectives that acted as a mechanism for building trust among childcare providers as well as providing the benefits of simple savings accounts.[2] Formal banking institutions would do well to acknowledge these practices and determine concrete ways to include such traditional savings organizations in their new business ventures as a way to provide formal credit for low-wage workers. Childcare providers may benefit from the added value of working with such institutions to build credit that mobilizes them economically.

Technology in the form of the cell phone contributed to the collective life and shared culture of West Indian workers because it allowed for communication between the United States and the islands and served as a way for providers to stay in touch with each other during the workday. The cell phone did not always work to providers' benefit, however; it has also served as a new means of surveillance for employers, added to the more traditional means of surveillance, in which neighborhood residents informally observed childcare providers at work and reported back to employers about their behavior. Surveillance took on another form as well—Internet sites where employers could tell other parents what their childcare providers were doing in parks or in other public places. The widespread access to the Internet among the middle class has introduced a new dimension to the work that childcare providers do, one that can undermine any attempt to establish a "normal" and trusting relationship between employer and employee.

Race, Gender, Ethnicity, and Cultural Identity

This study has explored how race, ethnicity, gender, and cultural identity play a role in the domestic occupational arena, whether through the workings of the larger labor market, exemptions of domestic work from labor laws, power relations in the employer-employee relationship, neighborhood surveillance of childcare workers in public places, or tensions between different racial and ethnic groups in public places.

The study has also examined how childcare providers negotiated an identity in relation to racial, cultural, and ethnic categories. The findings of this research indicate that their identity was fluid with regard to these categories and was negotiated mainly through discussion with other childcare providers in public places. Though some providers claimed the term *black* to describe themselves, most seemed to prefer to categorize themselves either by nationality or by a pan-ethnic "Caribbean" or "West Indian" identity.[3] The categorization of West Indians as a collective group determined how relationships were formed and ultimately how the workday was shaped through newly formed communities. Their behaviors and use of language allowed for the control of social spaces in public parks and elsewhere and in large part dictated the social relations that seeped into private lives. Using markers of West Indianness brought these women together in ways that have not been discussed at length by other studies. These social identities were practiced in everyday life: they illuminated both the collegial work relationship between childcare providers and the way employers did or did not fit into the providers' lives.[4]

Larger Implications

Childcare is an important but largely unrecognized part of today's national and local economic infrastructure. The number of childcare providers needed in households to uphold today's economy in the United States far exceeds the aid offered to families to obtain childcare. This leads to questions about organized labor efforts. While nonprofit organizations such as DWU attempt to organize domestic workers and provide them with minimum benefits such as living wages and health care, there are obvious discrepancies between domestic workers' perceptions of these attempts and what organizers believe is going to trigger a labor movement.

My book opened this dialogue by situating the realities of some workers who don't believe their conditions in exploitative work will ever change. For these workers, it is the employer who needs to spearhead the labor movement in order for working conditions to become better, since employers hold the political and financial power to make change. These workers do not want to participate in the public confrontations (marches, recruiting efforts) that nonprofits typically use to organize workers because of fears of losing their job or being deported. The workers' ambivalence toward formal organizing ultimately reproduces their working conditions. However, those involved with organizations such as DWU believe that, with the support of workers themselves and public displays of solidarity, change can come about. Suspicious, fearful, or passively resigned attitudes towards organizing may impede efforts to secure domestic labor rights, or those efforts may get enough momentum that eventually all can and will want to participate.

More pragmatically, domestic workers find it difficult to better their education or improve their chances for economic mobility because of their non-negotiable dependency on childcare work. One day while I was waiting for the subway on my way into Manhattan from Brooklyn, I bumped into Carol, one of the many documented workers employed as a provider in New York. She told me that she had visited a New York City government agency and spoken with a counselor to determine her options, since she was getting older and increasingly tired of caring for small children. She told the counselor that her passion was for cooking, so the agency mentioned that she could take a three-month certification course in catering from seven in the morning to one o'clock in the afternoon and that they would place her in a work environment that matched her interests. Carol worked only part time currently and her rent was $900 a month. After some deliberation, she determined that she could not afford to miss any potential work (she also cared part time for a second child after school for a few hours) because she wouldn't be able to pay her bills.

If funding to subsidize missed wages for skills development were not only made available but advertised through local churches and businesses as well as the employment agencies that these providers frequent, these women might be more likely to take advantage of such employment options. Another option, if there were enough interest, would be to have a nonprofit organization provide these courses at more optimal times. I wondered why Carol didn't consider using her susu money to finance missing wages for the three months, but later concluded that she used that money primarily to fly back to Trinidad in order to see her husband or to meet her own children's financial needs. As she later alluded, her cultural pride had so far kept her from asking members of the susu to help her out in this dire situation, but she admitted that she might eventually have to ask for their financial aid until she found more work.

In New York, public policy has created obstacles for domestic workers to have the security of knowing that they will be compensated and treated fairly. While the small proportion of domestic workers who use placement agencies can get information about their rights and of social services that are available to them, the political system has failed them in several key areas such as health care, proper housing conditions for live-in workers, termination protocol, and minimum wage security.[5] Local advocates such as DWU have managed to get a bill to the New York State Legislature, and it is currently being reviewed for formal passage. This Bill of Rights for domestic workers would provide workers, both documented and undocumented, with the benefits needed to support their own families and work at subsistence levels, allowing for the possibility of greater economic mobility among this group of workers. Since the type of childcare labor they provide is desirable and necessary for families to function in New York's vibrant economy, it makes sense to implement a system that eradicates the economic injustices that are affecting those who are helping to raise the future capitalists of this same economy.[6]

One message that providers directed to me throughout is that this study has constructed bridges between the reader and West Indian childcare providers in Brooklyn. Although I did not focus on the organization of domestic labor, my findings can also be used to inform the work of labor unions and nonprofit agencies. By understanding the collective life of domestic workers, institutions that seek to work on their behalf can come to a better understanding of their concerns. As illustrated by the findings of this research, the concerns of childcare providers are mediated through ethnic identity, work practices, and interactions in public and private places. The needs of these working women may or may not be in line with the reform efforts sought by labor organizations. However this study may aid such organizations in gaining a fuller understanding of these participants and how they understand their place in the larger economy. Such information can assist those who seek to improve the working conditions and lives of domestic workers. I often wondered how my research could contribute to bettering the working conditions of childcare providers and came to realize that I could only attempt to lead by example. My presence as someone who wanted to understand this group of workers more fully and not only through the literature allowed me to participate with them as well as with the DWU organizers. My presence as a "good listener," a student, an employer, a mother, a neighborhood participant, and now a professor who was interested in what West Indian childcare providers had to say might indeed be the only way for me to actively engage them in the efforts being made to better their living conditions. My presence and participation in their daily socializing might be the only way to communicate to a broader audience this unique public display of collective living and culture, which could be used to create a movement of sorts in the domestic sector.

This study offers potential benefits for employers, providers themselves, and the children in their care. It allows employers to see a side of their employees that typically is not shown to them. Employers' perceptions may be broadened through an appreciation of how important food is to providers, how communication with family is sometimes necessary, and how providers may be judged unfairly by those who scrutinize and report their behavior in public spaces without having "the whole story." Employers may see how they can change their own actions when interacting with their employees through a better understanding of the daily struggles of providers. West Indian providers can also benefit from this research by hearing their own voices come together in protest and recognizing that their stories have more profound implications than they may have thought. Further, by bringing together the voices of both those who fear and those who support organizing efforts among domestic workers, this study can hopefully bridge some of the anxiety surrounding that endeavor. Providers may also learn that some employers share their concerns about the welfare of domestic workers, as indicated by Erynn's efforts to bring West Indian providers together. Finally, my hope is that sometime in the future the children that are being cared for by West Indian women will be able to see through this small window into their lives growing up and understand the challenges and celebrations that came along with raising Brooklyn.

Appendix A

Methods

I chose to do an ethnographic book with the hope of finding a lost voice that ethnographers haven't heard in nearly ten years, that of the West Indian childcare provider.[1] This ethnography is one of the first contributions in the twenty-first century to give prominent voice to this group of workers and to their complicated networks that result in a collective life. The intent of this study was to discover if there was any change in the domestic workplace or these women's views on their work. In addition, I wondered if, as a second-generation West Indian researcher, I could add anything to the literature that already existed on these women and their work.

By using ethnographic methods I was able to study what my participants did as well as what they said. In line with Howard Becker's suggestion that qualitative researchers analyze the process of actions—how events unfold, or actions or interactions are sequenced—in the field, I determined that my participants did not always give stable or consistent meaning to their actions; therefore I found myself in the field for a three-year period attempting to piece together what was enacted in public and private spaces and what was said during the interview process. I came to realize over time that what might have appeared as mundane activity to one researcher was the expression of a more profound system of relationships.[2] For example, women eating in public parks or providers offering one another food could be taken for granted as mundane activity and not interpreted as having some deeper purpose of cultural expression or connection. But participating in the field as an observer allowed order and meaning to gradually come together. Like Dorinne Kondo doing research for her book *Crafting Selves,* I wanted to place myself as an ethnographer who could not only write quality descriptions of events but delve into my material with reflection and analysis that would increase the understanding of a multifaceted occupation.[3] In doing so, I was able to create a body of research that demonstrated the ethnographic process. My interpretations of events, relationships, and work function, then, came from an "extended witnessing,"[4] allowing me to find connections during ethnographic encounters that produced more detail as time passed.

While studying West Indian childcare providers working in gentrified neighborhoods, I quickly realized that there was another variable to be evaluated in the field—the researcher. I was deemed the "girl who was writing the book" by many providers, an identity that legitimated my position as a resident in the types of neighborhoods where these women worked. Rather than getting paid to care for children, though, I was positioned as a privileged mom who could afford to stay home caring for her children while attending graduate school. For three years, I endeavored to collect data about the childcare work being carried out in public places and how this contributed to a unique lived experience for West Indian providers. Beyond looking at childcare work, I also analyzed my research experiences with the women in the field.

As an ethnographer, I attempted to ask myself, and my participants, questions that would bring to light the varied social spaces that the childcare providers inhabited and created and how differing roles intertwined to produce enduring work relationships. Although I did not set out to do so, I contributed to an analysis that was consistent with feminist ethnographic methods by using critical reflexivity. Many of the principles of feminist methodology have simply been forgotten or absorbed into what is considered "good ethnography." Earlier ethnographic works and even some later works written by men looked at other men as primary subjects without critically analyzing the role that the women assumed in their lives.[5] Women were studied peripherally in the context of the men. According to Dorothy Smith, however, social scientists, by learning about the everyday lives of oppressed people, can "study up," using a bottom-up approach to critique the structures of power in which those people are embedded and to which they are subject; this approach includes studying the experiences of women, whether mothers, sisters, friends, or wives, in the lives of men.[6] Feminists also suggested that having a female researcher study female participants created a dynamic that allowed for a more open dialogue. Further, as Carol Warren has reminded us, motherhood is a key mutual identification marker that women researchers and participants can share.[7] But even when the researcher and participants are matched by gender, race, language, marital status, and culture, the class differences between them persist.[8] My efforts were intended to present the point of view of a historically ignored group of women who do paid "motherwork" and to offer a new perspective on their lived experiences in both private and public spaces.[9] This type of taken-for-granted domestic work has been written about extensively, but previous writings have often neglected the multiple spaces that organize the lives of the women providers and have not demonstrated some of the deeper cultural connections that these women create.

This ethnography attempts to fill that void in earlier studies by following the lead of other women ethnographers who place themselves as both insiders and outsiders.[10] My research methodology in the field was shaped by the relationships I had with my research participants. These complex relationships were then mediated by similarities and differences in our racial and ethnic identity, social class, and place within the community. Methodologically, it was necessary to be reflexive about my following roles and identities while analyzing my field notes: racial and ethnic identity, social class/education, role as a researcher, and role as a mother. But before examining these, I will describe my research sites and participants.

Fieldwork Sites and Research Participants

For this book, I conducted participation observation over a three-year period, from 2004 to 2007. During this time I observed dozens of childcare providers, the majority of whom were West Indian, in four adjacent gentrified communities. All four neighborhoods have a history of European immigration. Brooklyn became a home for this segment of the working class because men could find employment on the docks along its edge. Later immigrants, including Latino/Hispanics, African Americans, and Caribbeans, brought further diversity to these areas. In total, six parks were part of this study, but three—the parks frequented the most by my participants because they were in close proximity to one another—were observed more consistently. I interviewed in depth twenty-five West Indian childcare providers whom I also regularly shadowed throughout the workday in parks, in employers' homes, during children's lessons, at the public library, and on the neighborhood sidewalks. All were first-generation West Indian women migrants to the United States. Nine were born in Grenada, six in Trinidad, three in Guyana, two in St. Lucia, two in Jamaica, two in St. Vincent, and one in Barbados. The age range of these childcare providers was from twenty-five to sixty-one years old. Exact ages could not be specified, since several women did not feel comfortable disclosing this information,[11] but it is reasonable to estimate that five women were in their thirties, three in their twenties, and the remaining seventeen women over forty years of age at the time of the interviews.

I also conducted interviews with one childcare provider of Hungarian descent and one domestic worker of Mexican descent, and I observed several childcare providers of Filipino, Polish, Latin American, and Nepalese heritage. These interviews and observations may serve as the beginning of what may become future research on childcare providers. Their interactions with West Indian childcare providers were minimal, but their presence was ongoing in the public places I studied, so I included them for a more robust understanding of the public places being used. This book also included interviews and observations of five members of Domestic Workers United, a public librarian, an activist/documentarian, a movement studio owner, and a public parks employee.

All quotations used in the text are direct quotations from either tape-recorded interviews (using a digital or manual recorder) or field notes taken within three hours after my work in the field. When quotation marks are not used, I am recalling events that occurred later and using field notes for reference to provide reasonable accuracy with regard to the points being made by participants.

My Place as an Insider/Outsider

While West Indian childcare providers used the public places found in the neighborhoods where they worked, I sensed that I, as the researcher, didn't quite fit the insider role. Sitters with whom I had not developed relationships peered at me with what felt like curiosity. I neither carried a large notebook around with me nor took notes while in public places. I did not thrust a tape recorder in people's faces when we spoke. The fact that I had two children with me who appeared to be my own (not white) made me an anomaly in the neighborhoods I studied. Curiosity often led to questions between sitters who did and those who did not know me. This eventually led some who didn't know me in the beginning to want to share their stories with me once they discovered what I was researching. For three years, in public places, alongside these childcare providers, I collected data about their work and, more importantly, their collective lives. Beyond observing and asking questions about the lived experiences of these women, I had the unique opportunity to look closely at my own experiences as a researcher, a mother, a resident of Brooklyn, and a person of West Indian heritage. I found that the ability to unpack these kinds of details of the experience was significant for doing ethnographic fieldwork. These details are explored more fully in the body of the book.

I became aware of my presence in a variety of social spaces, of my identity, and of my role as a researcher. I attempted to place myself through cultural identity as an insider, although this did not always appear to be successful. For example, when I would slip into my ever-so-Canadian "eh?" at the end of a statement, or when childcare providers would see me on the street in clothing that somehow marked "employer" status (e.g., carrying a briefcase to school while dressed in heels and a suit), these facts differentiated me from my participants. However, at times I managed to identify simultaneously as an insider and outsider, especially when talking with both employers and employees.

One year into my research I began my in-depth tape-recorded interviews with childcare participants. Providers began calling me "the woman who is writing a book about nannies" instead of the person one of my subjects affectionately had referred to as being "like one of us." The formality of recording voices by a machine meant that I was serious about telling my participants' stories. But the formality of tape recording became at times problematic, in that it appeared to place me more on the side of the employer in the eyes of some childcare providers who had never seen such digital recording devices and who probably wondered how much they cost and whether their voices would be recognized if I allowed their employers listen to my recordings (as I did not).

For the twenty or more employers with whom I spoke over three years, and the ten I interviewed and for the most part lived among, my presence and research was of interest from a networking and surveillance standpoint. Employers often asked me to refer childcare workers to them or their friends. They would also at various points ask me if particular events were considered normal or acceptable. For example, Rose, a mother and employer, once asked me in the park if using a "credit" system (where an employer pays for time that the sitter did not spend working because of an employer emergency but then expects that time to be made up at a later point) was appropriate. She had had a miscommunication one day with her sitter, who did not realize that the time she was working was part of the credit owed to her employer and that therefore she would not get paid for it. I asked Rose if she had told the sitter before her arrival at work that this would be considered the credited time that they had agreed on. She said, "No, she should have just known that." I explained that if you are planning to have an employee work without pay you should probably let her know ahead of time. Employers would often ask me questions of this type.

Employer interviews indicated that employers' perceptions of their working relationship with a provider and their behaviors toward her were distinctly different from what I observed from my research. Often I found myself referring to my field notes based on observed behavior to determine the meanings of interactions that were recounted to me by both employer and employee. These sets of field notes read as moments of truth in cases where casual discussions with some employers were more revealing than those in my more formal interviews with other employers. More often than not, employers would say things to me on the sidewalks or in the parks that related the stresses they felt in their relationships with West Indian childcare providers. They also related several stories about their discomfort with their employees' perceived coldness or distant manner. As Jennie, one childcare provider, explained, "We don't like people knowing our business," a sentiment I heard over and over again in the field among West Indian providers. Although employers' experiences warrant further research, this was not the perspective that I was most interested in as a researcher.

I used employer interviews to ground the experiences of West Indian childcare providers as they moved between public places and to complicate issues about how these providers socialized among themselves. I found my observations and informal interviews with employers to be more informative than formal interviews and thus relied more heavily on them. But I placed the employers' viewpoints in the background, focusing more attention on the childcare providers' accounts of their own daily experiences. In the same vein, the providers wanted to tell the story of how unfairly they were treated as a group. I believe I have been able to capture in this book the unique relationship between employers and employees and the tensions it produced.

Many of my interactions with both employers and employees left me feeling exhausted. Because I lived near three of my public park sites, I'm not sure that I was ever out of the field. Anxiety-producing encounters with sitters as I walked down a local street with their employers often left me wondering what workers really thought of my research. Did they view me as the "other"? Was I being used by employers to gain insights into the workday of their employees? How did West Indian childcare providers view my mothering abilities when they encountered me with my children? And ultimately, did any of this even matter? Martyn Hammersley and Paul Atkinson challenge ethnographers to be aware that they may not in fact be the audience to which participants' actions and behaviors are directed. In other words, participants may expect the ethnographer to discuss what they have divulged with others who could effect change in their lives.[12]

Race and Ethnicity

While exploring the everyday complexities of relationships among the sitters themselves and between sitters and their employers, I realized I had come upon a community that based its identity almost exclusively on work, race, and ethnicity.[13] This group of women defined themselves by their West Indianness, a term I elaborate on in chapter 1. However, my lack of authenticity in expressing West Indianness was apparent to them. For example, at the park one day when I asked Carol, a childcare provider from Trinidad, about the *Naparima* cookbook (a famous cookbook from Trinidad that has exclusively West Indian recipes and that every West Indian woman should have in her kitchen, or so I'm told), she couldn't believe that I didn't have a copy. She told me to get one right away from a relative "back home." She said, "You can't cook without it because it tells you exactly what is what and how to cook every dish you can imagine." When I asked her later on in this conversation about whether to put a hot red pepper on top of pelau (a traditional Trinidadian one-pot meal) for flavoring, she was shocked that I didn't know the correct answer. She rolled her eyes and said, "Of course. . . didn't your mother tell you. . . . It gives the proper flavor, but make sure you don't stir it in too much, just let it sit right on top towards the end, because if it busts, you've ruined the whole thing."

Our social interactions (mine and the providers) were often predicated on my first demonstrating some underlying knowledge of a West Indian custom or tradition. This game, as I like to call it, put me in the position of student. The childcare providers seemed to see me as a learner of West Indian culture, and the elder ones sometimes even seemed to see me as a daughter. They would constantly tell me how I should discipline my children "the proper way," not "like these Americans." Although burdensome at times, my learning about the boundaries of home and community within which my participants worked facilitated my fieldwork in terms of learning more about their collective lives. It also invited a critical analysis of my cultural orientation to the field where meanings are analyzed and people are situated.[14] The development of this cultural orientation, then, was duly reflected in more mature field notes that I wrote as my research progressed.[15]

For example, I noticed that topics such as men and politics came up in conversation sporadically but did not appear to significantly shape the way work or social interactions were carried out during the day. Men were not often spoken about because many of the relationships these women had with men were either severed permanently or tentatively by distance or considered unhealthy or even abusive. As one provider, Grace, bluntly stated, "Men don't work, men don't work, men don't work, men don't work, women work, they don't need men." While she knew that many men did indeed work, she made this assertion to emphasize the hard work that childcare providers endured and that possibly no man could understand. Also, during my conversations and interviews, West Indian women discussed how it was intrusive to ask another worker about her male partner. Privacy with regard to husbands and boyfriends was considered very important. Some of the younger childcare providers would discuss dates they had been on, but not in any detail.

Politics was mostly discussed as it related to disaster or crime in the homeland. U.S. politics did not shape the conversations in public spaces, but when a hurricane hit the islands in the Caribbean or when the crime rate in Trinidad or Jamaica hit an all-time high, there was an abundance of debate and expressions of concern for family and friends. The one time I did notice discussion about a U.S. catastrophe was when Hurricane Katrina hit New Orleans in September 2005. The media portrayed the demise of several thousand black residents of that area as well as the failures of the American government. Discussions centered on the media coverage and how black people were being treated. While my participants were distant from the events (none of them disclosed that they knew people in that area), there was a sense of understanding that came with being "black." This led to empathy and some talk of black people being treated unfairly.

I often wondered how men and politics as silenced topics might have been discussed differently had I been a first-generation West Indian immigrant. Would I have gotten different responses to my questions? Would I have had access to these same women and their employers? Would there have been a social cue that told me of the inappropriateness of my actions during research? What information would these women have held back from me?

Being a Dougla Girl

Once when I attended an Eastern Sociological Society conference I listened to a talk by Dr. Kamini Grahame, an Indo-Trinidadian woman about Trinidadian food, based on her fieldwork there. Upon my asking a few questions after the lecture, Dr. Grahame asked me, "What are you? Where are you from?" I told her that I was from Canada but that my parents were Trinidadian. She then asked, "Are you Indian Trinidadian or Black Trinidadian?" Knowing that there was a long ongoing historical background to this question, I said, "Both and others." She exclaimed, "You're a dougla girl!"[16] Confused at her public use of a West Indian colloquial term (one that some might have considered offensive since at one time it had been a derogatory label), but remembering that my uncles used to tease me and my cousins by calling out to us, "Dougla, go get this" or "Dougla, go get that," I knew what she meant. She was defining me as a Trinidadian with a particular combination of characteristics that included longer wavy hair. Being part black, part Indian, part British, and part European Trinidadian gave me an appearance that was unlike that of some West Indian women. My skin pigmentation and eye color were lighter than those of many black Trinidadians, and my hair was not as tightly curled, but rather wavy, showing that I had traces of "otherness" in me. This comment during the time of my fieldwork made me more aware of how I might be perceived among the women I studied. While many of the sitters that I observed were of either African or Indian Caribbean descent (and probably mostly mixed with other ancestries), none looked quite like me. I wondered if being labeled a "dougla girl" by another outside of my research meant that I was seen as an outsider while in the field. Did I exhibit some form of privilege by being able to "pass" as either Indo-Trinidadian or Afro-Trinidadian? In other words, was I demonstrating that I could cross some of the social barriers between these two groups by emphasizing one or another of my ancestral lineages? Did it matter to these women once I got to know them? Did they see this as part of the reason I was able to live among their employers? How did this affect their responses to me? I never did get to the answers to these questions, but in hindsight I should have considered them before going into the field. Perhaps I was able to uncover things despite my being "dougla," in a phenomenon similar to what Duneier affectionately calls the "Becker principle," Howard Becker's assertion that the daily routines of participants are far more influential than the distractions the ethnographer may bring to the field.[17] For example, the women I interviewed would still go to the parks with their charges, talk on their cell phones, participate in the informal economy, and share food regardless of whatever social impact that I had as a field researcher.

The extensive political discourse surrounding Indo versus Afro ethnicity in Trinidad is too lengthy to explore in depth in this particular book and would require a research project of its own, but it has some significance here. It is important to understand that the racial divide among West Indians, especially those of Trinidadian descent, means that many more gainful employment opportunities, even today, are open to those of "mixed blood." While some argue that Indians in Trinidad do not earn more than blacks, those of African descent have a legacy of being placed in inferior positions both culturally and in business.[18] The women who migrate to the United States must be considered within the context of this racial legacy, and this could be a starting point for further research.

My Role as Researcher

Many West Indian childcare providers seemed to claim our relationship as a reciprocal one. As they became more comfortable with me in the field, they would call on me for small favors, such as watching the child in their care at the park while they grabbed some lunch down the street, or calling me at home to use my bathroom during the day because a local park lacked a public restroom. On colder or rainy days we would gather at my home, where I would cook lunch for everyone or we would cook together, often while listening and dancing to reggae and calypso music. The women also sought me out for counsel in academic matters. Rachel, who wanted to find out more about going to college, once asked me to go with her to meet with a counselor at Hunter College in Manhattan, where I was teaching at the time. After the meeting, where she discovered her options as an undocumented worker, we discussed at length her studies for the General Education Diploma. I acted as part of her support system: other childcare providers and I encouraged her to keep studying and take the exam. In addition, I often supplied sitters with hard-copy college applications. These types of favors, along with the fact that I could often be seen with my two young children, led to a seemingly positive and receptive relationship between the women and me, similar to Carol Stack's experiences as a single mother in her book *All Our Kin*. I had to balance and negotiate how willing I would be to help and how this affected my research and personal life. I felt obliged to do certain things because I came to the field with a form of cultural and social capital (through my education and social networks) that allowed me to easily navigate mainstream institutions. However, I really didn't mind doing these things because I had forged good relationships with the providers. They often gave me the opportunity to run to my home from the park while my children were under their care at no charge for five minutes or would simply be a listening ear to my woes as a student, wife, and mother. This relationship also helped with fact checking as I moved forward with research and had to call providers or meet with them to clarify details of our interviews.

Initially in my research, I felt as though I had to speak with providers each time I passed about how they and their families were doing or to use certain colloquial terms to maintain my legitimacy. At the time I wasn't always sure why I did this, but over the course of several months, and as I began to feel more comfortable in my position as researcher, I engaged less in this conscious behavior and acknowledged them with ease (although I did still ask about families and use colloquial language). I became used to managing impressions of myself and the groups with which I associated.[19]

Months after my book research was complete, I noticed that I was able to maintain relationships with many of the women I encountered. They still came over for playdates with my children and would use my home to heat up their West Indian foods in the microwave, either because their employers didn't use one, they felt the employer's kitchen was filthy, or they did not want to fill the employer's home with the aroma of West Indian food and then risk having to explain why the home smelled a certain way. Molly would invite me to her annual Brooklyn Carnival Day Parade Luncheons, where dozens, if not hundreds, of friends and family members would gather at a buffet restaurant on Utica Avenue (located in a West Indian shopping enclave). She also invited me to cookout parties at her private residence. Although we couldn't attend them all, my husband and children would join me in some of these festivities. Because of this ongoing relationship, I found myself placed in an awkward position while writing my book. I couldn't simply go down my neighborhood street in my shorts and tank top without makeup and feel comfortable because I was still "in the field." While writing, I was constantly bombarded with questions such as "What did your professors think of what you wrote?" "When will the book be finished?" or my favorite, "Aren't you done yet?" The women chose not to understand that it would take years to complete this work. It was their lives that were being documented, and I became their number one resource for "telling the truth about the work."

Social Class

Although my research participants and I shared a racial and ethnic identity, our class status and educational backgrounds were noticeably different. Unlike the participants in my study, who had spent a portion of their lives in the Caribbean and now lived in predominantly urban working-class immigrant communities in Brooklyn, I had been raised in a predominantly white middle class community by parents who were educated professionals. In terms of social class, in many ways I was seen as having more in common with the employers than I did with the sitters. For example, I was married to a professional and could therefore afford living in an upper-middle-class community that was financially inaccessible to the childcare providers that I studied. However, it should be noted that many of my participants came from what would be considered middle-class status (and sometimes upper-middle, given Molly's status as a trader) in the islands, where the population was predominantly black. Although they did not necessarily have a college education, many of them had worked as professionals in positions with the government, in schools, or in business offices after years of schooling. They owned their own homes, had families, owned their cars, traveled, and were financially able to send their children abroad to the United States to continue their education or to find employment. They all had aspirations for their children that included a college education and stable employment. All of these "symbols" created the middle-class status that many of these women upheld. Perhaps, then, West Indian childcare providers were not so different from their employers and maybe, one could argue, this was a reason why some employers felt comfortable hiring such women. I often asked myself, "Is this a case where West Indian providers are experiencing downward mobility once they arrive in the U.S?"

My Role as a Mother

While my relationship with West Indian childcare providers was deepening, I found myself constantly looking for their approval or perhaps even more their disapproval. For example, my clothes often indicated to participants that I was not one of them and accentuated the fact that I was a "mother." When sitting on one of the park benches one day with Molly and another sitter in September 2007, I was wearing denim shorts, running shoes, and a T-shirt. This was not considered appropriate workday attire for a West Indian childcare provider. Although I was not a childcare provider and my participants knew this, the way I dressed was brought up indirectly. Molly commented about my babysitter wearing really short shorts. I said, "If it's ninety degrees out, why would I care if she is wearing what she is comfortable in? I wear similar shorts." Molly, careful not to be critical of me, said, "Yes, and that's okay for you to wear short shorts because you are the mother, but if you are the sitter, you should not have your cleavage showing and your legs bare like that." Molly's comment made me aware of the personal boundaries of appropriate attire for work. She made it clear that I was a "mother" and therefore had a right to wear what I wanted. But she explained that childcare providers had to remain covered and demure because employers often felt jealousy toward their sitters for a variety of reasons. She told me that West Indian sitters should not expose themselves too much, especially if the husband was around, because this exposure could start an argument between the husband and the wife. Again, Molly was clearly marking me as a "mother" and not as a true insider because of my attire. However, in this particular instance, the issue of attire did not simply mark me as "other" but allowed me deeper insight into the West Indian perspective on clothing issues in the employer-employee relationship.

Children in the Field

Often students and professors ask me how I managed to enter the world of West Indian childcare providers. My answer was simple: "I am of West Indian descent and I have two small children whom I brought to the park every day." But the crucial role of my children in my research didn't dawn on me until I read the anthropological work *Children in the Field.*[20]

In this anthology, researchers discuss their experiences with their own children as part of the research process. Renate Fernandez, in her chapter on deciding where to do fieldwork, emphasized how "children influence the choice of field site."[21] This was absolutely true for me. It was while sitting in a public park with my first child that I decided this was the research site for me, since I could envision this as a place that was beneficial both to her upbringing and to my sanity: I could be out in the fresh air with trees and other small children all around us while getting my research done.

My fieldwork, like that of many of the researchers who tell their stories in Cassell's book, was enhanced by the fact that I had two small children. It seemed that the women I encountered viewed my motherhood as a legitimate marker of "caring." Once the women in this study viewed my regular participation in the neighborhood, they appeared to feel more comfortable with me as a researcher, a resident, and a mother. Having children in the field also promoted interactions in my home where sitters could bring their charges: they knew that the house was "child-proof" and that there were ample toys to choose from. The women and I shared event information because of our common interest in "getting out of the house" and finding things to do during the day, such as park fairs, library events, and park birthday parties.

I believe that having my children in the field helped me to understand the position of childcare providers better because I experienced something similar to the monotony of their days and the physical exhaustion they felt from taking care of small children. In addition, many of the complaints I had as a new mother often elicited sympathy from the women who were experiencing similar milestone events with their charges (e.g., tantrums). This allowed me to understand more fully some of the pains and many of the joys these women experienced in taking care of small children.

My children also acted as a hindrance at times in completing this research. In the beginning months of my research I often had to leave the parks, library, or playdates earlier than expected because I chose to nurse my children. Participating in such an intimate activity such as breastfeeding was something that West Indian providers commented on as "not appropriate" for public display even when a cover was used. It was seen as too revealing and as a private matter that should be taken care of at home unless you had pumped milk and were using a bottle to feed. This caused me to have to explain why I couldn't "hang around" as long as I would have liked to and sometimes created long lapses of time between meetings. In addition to nursing calls, I was hampered by my limited hours of childcare. I employed my babysitter (as she labeled herself) anywhere from ten hours a week in the first year to twenty hours a week by the third year in order to finish my in-class studies. This meant time away from the field, but while I was in the field it meant I was always with my children. The problem with having my children with me all of the time was that I constantly had to tend to them, feed them, run after them, and discipline them. My interactions with them also potentially left holes in my research that required me to remain in the field longer than I had anticipated. However, I do feel that their presence enabled this research in ways that would not have been possible without them.

The Husband Factor

Yes, the husband factor. My husband was often part of my research. He supported my position among employers by being college educated and an active community member—he was the president of our condominium board and was often in the parks with our children on the weekends. Also, he demonstrated to the West Indian childcare providers who worked in my neighborhood that he was an involved parent and, even more importantly, of West Indian parentage. He came with me to several parks in the mornings with the children on his way to work. Several mornings he would see the childcare providers on his own and talk with them on the sidewalks. The women seemed to enjoy telling me that they had seen and spoken with him and would confirm that he was a good man. Many of the providers would comment on the fact that he was Jamaican, and, as Molly said, "one of the good ones." This fact legitimized my West Indianness among the women I studied and probably increased the comfort level that I and my participants had with each other.

Evaluating my place in the field allowed me to dissect the realities I was attempting to understand by studying West Indian childcare providers. The three years I spent with these women enabled an ongoing dialogue that I hope will serve as a starting point for further research. Further, understanding my shortcomings while doing fieldwork informed researchers about my personal exchange value (value to others) in the field and how this affected the outcomes of my research.

Appendix B

Demographic Information

TABLE 1

Median Household Income for Carroll Gardens/Red Hook, New York, for the Years 1980, 1990, and 2000

Year	*Median Household Income*
1980	$26,898
1990	$43,070
2000	$45,154

Source: Infoshare Online New York, Community Studies of New York, Inc.
Note: Figures are adjusted for inflation: 1980 and 1990 income figures are in 2000 dollars. That for 1980 was multiplied by 2.44, and that for 1990 was multiplied by 1.43.

TABLE 2

Size of the West Indian Population in New York City (Including Haiti and Guyana, but not Belize or Panama), by Year and Sex

	Decennial Census		
Sex	*1980*	*1990*	*2000*
Male	112,300	146,036	213,145
Female	146,500	180,666	280,223
Total	258,800	326,702	493,368

Source: U.S. Bureau of the Census (2001).

TABLE 3

Brooklyn's West Indian Immigrant Population, 1980–2008

	1980	*1990*	*2000*	*2005–7*	*2006–8*
Total Brooklyn Population	2,239,140	2,228,227	2,452,377	2,521,407	2,539,911
Number of West Indian First-Generation Immigrants	110,280	170,319	232,210	236,444	233,109
Age 0–17	19,560 (17.7)	23,623 (13.9)	21,088 (9.1)	14,077 (6.0)	14,285 (6.1)
Age 18–29	28,100 (25.5)	39,791 (23.4)	42,804 (18.4)	37,422 (15.8)	35,767 (15.3)
Age 30–39	25,380 (23.0)	37,677 (22.1)	48,813 (21.0)	39,812 (16.8)	37,246 (16.0)
Age 40–49	15,160 (13.7)	30,871 (18.1)	49,492 (21.3)	52,742 (22.3)	51,879 (22.3)
Age 50–59	11,260 (10.2)	18,736 (11.0)	35,531 (15.3)	45,897 (19.4)	46,914 (20.1)
Age 60–74	8,380 (7.6)	15,137 (8.9)	26,065 (11.2)	34,508 (14.6)	34,974 (15.0)
Age 75 and over	2,440 (2.2)	4,484 (2.6)	8,417 (3.6)	11986 (5.1)	12,044 (5.2)
Total Females	63,580 (57.7)	98,080 (57.6)	137,238 (59.1)	141,572 (59.9)	138,736 (59.5)
Number of Child Care Workers	980[a]	1,752[b]	7,007[c]	9,805[d]	9,232[e]

Source: Data for 1980, 1990, and 2000 were derived from the respective decennial U.S. censuses, and data for 2005–7 and 2006–8 from the American Community Survey three-year estimates. All were made available through Integrated Public Use Microdata Series: Version 4.0 [Machine-readable database], http://usa.ipums.org/usa. Minneapolis, MN: Minnesota Population Center [producer and distributor], 2009. Analysis was provided by the Center for the Study of Brooklyn.
Note: The West Indian immigrant population includes all Brooklyn residents who reported their place of birth as one of the following: Antigua-Barbuda, Bahamas, Barbados, Belize, Grenada, Guyana, Jamaica, St. Kitts, St. Lucia, St. Vincent, and Trinidad and Tobago.

a. In 1980, occupation was unknown for 33.2 percent of the cases; in addition, "child care worker" was not coded in the original 1980 census data but was recoded by 1990 occupation classifications. As a result, child care worker counts were underrepresented for all years. Child care was the thirteenth most popular occupation among West Indian immigrant women.

b. In 1990, occupation was unknown for 27 percent of the cases; in 1990, child care was the ninth most popular occupation.

c. In 2000, occupation was unknown for 25 percent of the cases; child care was the second most popular occupation and "nurse and home health aide" ranked first.

d. In 2005–7, occupation was unknown for 26.1 percent of cases; child care worker was the second most popular occupation and "nurse and home health aide" ranked first.

e. In 2006–8, occupation was unknown for 23.9 percent of cases; child care was the second most popular occupation and "nurse and home health aide" ranked first.

TABLE 4

Age and Sex of West Indian Child Care Workers in Brooklyn, 1980

Age (Years)[a]	*Number*	%
16–17	20	2.0
18–29	420	42.9
30–39	200	20.4
40–49	140	14.3
50–59	140	14.3
60–74	60	6.1
75 and over	0	0.0
Total	980	100.0

Sex	*Number*	%
Female	860	87.8
Male	120	12.2

Source: Data derived from the 1980 U.S. Census, made available through Integrated Public Use Microdata Series: Version 4.0 [machine-readable database], http://usa.ipums.org/usa. Minneapolis, MN: Minnesota Population Center [producer and distributor], 2009. Analysis provided by the Center for the Study of Brooklyn.

a. Only those aged sixteen and over answered work questions.

TABLE 5

Age and Sex of West Indian Child Care Workers in Brooklyn, 1990

Age (Years)	*Number*	%
16–17	82	4.7
18–29	342	19.5
30–39	612	34.9
40–49	379	21.6
50–59	176	10.0
60–74	124	7.1
75 and over	37	2.1
Total	1,752	100.0

Sex	*Number*	%
Male	76	4.3
Female	1,676	95.7

Source: 1990 U.S. Census data, made available through Integrated Public Use Microdata Series: Version 4.0 [machine-readable database], http://usa.ipums.org/usa. Minneapolis, MN: Minnesota Population Center [producer and distributor], 2009. Analysis provided by the Center for the Study of Brooklyn.

TABLE 6

Age and Sex of West Indian Child Care Workers in Brooklyn, 2000

Age (Years)	*Number*	%
16–17	144	2.1
18–29	1,201	17.1
30–39	1,989	28.4
40–49	2,024	28.9
50–59	1,273	18.2
60–74	367	5.2
75 and over	9	.1
Total	7,007	100.0

Sex	*Number*	%
Male	252	3.6
Female	6,755	96.4

Source: 2000 U.S. Census data, made available through Integrated Public Use Microdata Series: Version 4.0 [machine-readable database], http://usa.ipums.org/usa. Minneapolis, MN: Minnesota Population Center [producer and distributor], 2009. Analysis provided by the Center for the Study of Brooklyn.

TABLE 7

Age and Sex of West Indian Child Care Workers in Brooklyn, 2005–7

Age (Years)	*Number*	%
16–17	0	0.0
18–29	1,640	16.7
30–39	1,738	17.7
40–49	3,264	33.3
50–59	2,406	24.5
60–74	688	7.0
75 and over	69	0.7
Total	9,805	100.0

Sex	*Number*	%
Female	9,343	95.3
Male	462	4.7

Source: 2005–7 American Community Survey three-year estimate data, made available through Integrated Public Use Microdata Series: Version 4.0 [Machine-readable database], http://usa.ipums.org/usa. Minneapolis, MN: Minnesota Population Center [producer and distributor], 2009. Analysis provided by the Center for the Study of Brooklyn.

TABLE 8

Age and Sex of West Indian Child Care Workers in Brooklyn, 2006–8

Age (Years)	*Number*	*%*
16–17	0	0.0
18–29	1,352	14.6
30–39	1,430	15.5
40–49	3,161	34.2
50–59	2,449	26.5
60–74	840	9.1
75 and over	0	0.0
Total	9,232	100.0

Sex	*Number*	*Percent*
Female	8,760	94.9
Male	472	5.1

Source: 2006–8 American Community Survey three-year estimate data, made available through Integrated Public Use Microdata Series: Version 4.0 [Machine-readable database], http://usa.ipums.org/usa. Minneapolis, MN: Minnesota Population Center [producer and distributor], 2009. Analysis provided by the Center for the Study of Brooklyn.

Notes

PREFACE

1. Isolation for childcare providers can mean various things: the experience of social distance in the household hierarchy because of the subservient nature of domestic work, the physical isolation of working within an employer's house with limited opportunities for socializing with other adults throughout the day, or the isolation imposed by employers who do not want their workers to contact family members, friends, or community members while they are being paid to work inside the home (Rollins 1985; Hondagneu-Sotelo 2001; Romero 1992; Lan 2006).

2. I use Simmel's (1964) concept of "sociability" to frame and characterize the micro interactions that were observed, since there was distinct satisfaction derived from the sociation between babysitters that manifested through various social forms. Other sociological studies have used this concept of sociability to problematize other social groups and their community identity in public places (Duneier 1992; Gans 1962; Wacquant 2004). Among West Indian babysitters, the unconscious (and sometimes conscious) use of cultural preservation tactics combated what may be perceived as potential isolation in their daily work routines. They created social spaces in public places, thus transforming their workdays into ongoing interaction.

3. For the purposes of this study, *culture* refers to the West Indian cultural traditions and practices of food, language, economics, and mores.

INTRODUCTION

1. See Sternbergh (2006) for more about this term.

2. Romero (1992); Hondagneu-Sotelo (2001).

3. There are contradictory interpretations of whether places and spaces are different constructs; see Berman (2002), Harvey (2002), and Lefebvre (2002) for discussions of how they differ and are used.

4. See Evans (2003) for more on these associations.

5. Tronto (2002) describes the uniquely intimate workspace of babysitters who work in the private homes of their employers.

6. On the concept of interaction order, see Goffman (1983).

7. See Benardo and Weiss (2006) for more detailed information on Brooklyn's historical development and the significance of cultural street name changes.

8. Census data show a significant decline in Italian- and Spanish-speaking homes over the last three decades and a simultaneous increase in English spoken in the home. This is a common concern among the first-generation immigrant residents of gentrified

neighborhoods in Brooklyn. "Language Spoken at Home for Residents of Carroll Gardens/Red Hook (1980, 1990, 2000)," Infoshare Online, www.infoshare.org.

9. Denitia Smith (1981).

10. See Table 1 in Appendix B to view median household income numbers for one representative research site from 1980, 1990, and 2000: Carroll Gardens/Red Hook.

11. Sharon Zukin was one of the pioneers of the study of gentrification in urban settings and defined the term for use in future studies of urban gentrification. See Zukin (1987:131).

12. Florida (2004, 2005); Wrigley (1999). Florida describes this class of young and talented workers who migrated to metro areas in the 1990s with skills in product design, video editing, consulting, and hedge funding. The higher salaries that they demanded were soon followed by a rise in housing prices and living costs. According to Florida, tensions between this creative class, who tended to be "drawn to new lifestyles and diversity of opinion," and others who professed allegiance to more "traditional virtues" gave rise to the culture wars of the last two decades.

13. See Berman (2002), Mitchell and Staeheli (2005), and Zukin (1995) for more on the social order created in urban public spaces.

14. See Duneier's book *Sidewalk* (1999).

15. Life chances can encompass, but are not limited to, health status, socioeconomic environment, joblessness, educational attainment, and longer life expectancy.

16. See Cassell (1987) for more on how children affect the research process and become enablers of data acquisition.

17. Katz (1997).

18. Rollins (1985); Colen (1989:182).

19. Wrigley (1999).

20. P. Palmer (1989); Rollins (1985).

21. Ann Oakley (1974), for example, has explored how industrial capitalism created a new division of labor by gender in which women's work became "housework" and became increasingly privatized. Evelyn Nakano Glenn (1986) has pointed out how "domestic service . . . functions as a transitional occupation in the shift from unpaid work in the household to wage employment outside it" (99): for some groups, such as certain immigrant groups, it has been a "bridging" occupation fostering social mobility; for others, particularly blacks, it has been a "ghettoizing" occupation that excludes them from the possibilities of other work (102-3). Also see Glenn (1992, 1994:7) on paid reproductive labor and on how the labor of mothering on behalf of middle-class women has been subdivided (wet-nursing, infant and childcare, surrogacy) and parceled out to white, working-class women and women of color.

22. The topic of how nannies create community in public spaces has also been explored by Armenta (2009) in her study of Latina nannies in the parks of West Los Angeles. Her findings are similar to mine in terms of childcare providers' creation of community in public spaces, but my own work includes providers' use of technology and economic strategies to expand the study of community building among nannies.

1. WEST INDIANS RAISING NEW YORK

1. A majority of the women in this study were considered professionals back in their homeland (such as Molly, who had worked as a tradesperson in a variety of countries),

government workers, or teachers. Most West Indian domestic workers came from a variety of class backgrounds and never anticipated or aspired to doing such work. These women did, however, speak English and were used to working outside the home, which perhaps made domestic work seem at least somewhat appealing as a way to enter the U.S. job market.

2. Watkins-Owens (2001).

3. See James (n.d., tables IV, V, and VIII); U.S. Immigration Commission (1911, table 13, p. 101); and U.S. Immigration and Naturalization Service (1913, table X, pp. 66–69; 1914, table X, pp. 62–67).

4. Holder (1980); Walter (1977).

5. U.S. Bureau of the Census (2001).

6. Watkins-Owens (2001).

7. Thomas (1988); Kalmijn (1996).

8. Watkins-Owens (1996); Amott and Matthaei (1996).

9. Bonnett (1990a).

10. U.S. Bureau of the Census (2001).

11. Cancian et al. (2002); Sutton and Chaney (1987).

12. Colen (1995); Foner (1999); Sutton and Chaney (1987).

13. Wrigley (1991).

14. Watkins-Owens (2001).

15. Colen (1995); Foner (1999).

16. On the experiences of West Indian female immigrants from 1900 through the Second World War, see Watkins-Owens (2001).

17. On non-Hispanic immigrants in New York, see Kasinitz, Mollenkopf, and Waters (2002); Foner (1999).

18. On the role that their speaking English played in their getting hired, see Wrigley (1991); on their education level, see Foner (1999); on their acceptance of low wages, see Sutton and Chaney (1987).

19. Wrigley (1991).

20. Colen (1995).

21. Hochschild (1997); Katz Rothman (2001).

22. On the "second shift," see Hochschild and Machung (1989). For this generation of mothers in Brooklyn, guilt over making decisions about opting out of the formal economy or working outside the home is prominent, as evidenced through the various parenting blogs on the Internet and even the observations and interviews conducted as part of this research, and couples are constantly debating the pros and cons of these decisions. Often, this added stress to childrearing is taken out on childcare providers in a variety of forms, including surveillance or lack of appreciation. For more on this subject, see Tronto (2002); Wrigley (1991).

23. On the absence of family assistance and publicly provided childcare, see Katz Rothman (2001); Michel and Mahon (2002). On the recourse to low-wage immigrant help, see Katz Rothman (2001); Tronto (2002); Wrigley (1991).

24. Quote from Cancian et al. (2002); see also Colen (1995); Hondagneu-Sotelo (2001).

25. See Milkman, Reese, and Roth (1998).

26. See Table 2 in Appendix B for West Indian population figures according to the 2001 U.S. Census Tract for 1980, 1990, 2000.

27. See census data from 1980 to 2000.

28. See Kaufman (2000) for additional estimated figures.

29. Hondagneu-Sotelo and Avila (1997).

30. On transnational motherhood among Filipinas, see Salazar-Parrenas (2001); for Latin Americans, see Dreby (2010) and Hondagneu-Sotelo (2001); for the information on the three groups combined, see Dreby (2010).

31. See Appendix A for a discussion about Indo and Afro-Caribbeans/West Indians. Push factors include economic, social, and political hardships that contribute to labor flows from one country to another. See Alejandro Portes and Jozsef Borocz (1989) for a more detailed discussion of this term.

32. Portes and Rumbaut (2006).

33. None of my participants came from Haiti, Belize, Panama, Cuba, or the Dominican Republic; though all of these countries are in or near the Caribbean Sea, their primary spoken language is French as in the case of Haiti, English and Spanish in the case of Belize, and Spanish in the other three cases.

34. According to Waters (1999), "black" in contemporary American folk usage is defined by physical attributes.

35. Kasinitz (1992:4).

36. Kasinitz (1992:4).

37. Waters (1999:45).

38. Denton and Massey (1989); Waters (1999).

39. Bonnett (1981a).

40. Orde Coombs, quoted in Bonnett (1981b:74, 67); Vickerman (2001).

41. Wrigley (1995).

42. See Kasinitz (1992) for a detailed analysis of African American and West Indian employment opportunities.

43. See Vickerman (1999:112-13), as well as Vickerman's detailed analysis in the book of over one hundred interviews with Jamaicans living in New York that explored how they construct their identities from and alongside African Americans.

44. "Kiss-teeth," also termed "chupse" or "suck-teeth," is a Caribbean oral gesture of West African origin produced by sucking in air while placing the tongue against the upper or lower teeth, with lips flat and slightly opened with tension. This generalized marker of negative affect can demonstrate impatience, scorn, disapproval, disgust, disrespect, or disappointment. (Figueroa and Patrick 2001, forthcoming).

45. I am grateful to the sociologist Nancy Foner, who found that the wealthy employees of Manhattan preferred Filipino childcare providers.

46. Providers often spoke of immigrants who were less savvy, in the sense of who did not have working papers and was illegally residing in the United States, and who might have been smuggled in. They did not consider themselves as part of this group although some of them were.

2. PUBLIC PARKS AND SOCIAL SPACES

1. See Rollins for more on maternalism as a concept related to nurturing and "attending to affective needs" (1985:179).

2. Rollins (1985).

3. Rollins (1985); Dill (1994:9).

4. Dill (1994:10-11).

5. Ostrander (1987).

6. Dill (1994:11-12).

7. Dill (1994:4-5).

8. See Wrigley (1995, 2005) on childcare workers for more analysis on the oppression of this subordinated group. Also see Murray (1998) and Salzinger (1991) for in-depth analyses of how the labor of childcare goes unnoticed in private spaces.

9. In the many times I have presented this work, at least one professor has always responded by telling me that her childcare provider "is like family," perhaps to alleviate any guilt she may feel on account of the subordination of the position. But as one colleague reminded me, "Do you ask random family members to come over and wipe your baby's shit, pick up after you, and get basically nothing in return?" When I come across this "like family" comment I wonder if that is a way of saying that the employer simply trusts this person or feels at ease around her when she is in the household. Many of the employers I interviewed did not even know the birthdays of their childcare providers, nor did they ask how the providers' families were back in the homeland or elsewhere.

10. Wrigley (1995).

11. Simmel (1964:119).

12. Live-in work is common among recent immigrants as a strategy for economic incorporation.

13. Colen (1989:174).

14. Rollins (1985, 1989) offers detailed work about the isolation that domestics endure in the private sphere of the employer's home.

15. Hondagneu-Sotelo (2001).

16. P. Palmer (1989).

17. Romero (1992); Wrigley (1991, 1995).

18. Romero (1988).

19. Hondagneu-Sotelo (2001).

20. Dill (1994).

21. Chin (1998) describes some of this private and public dichotomy further in terms of the state and the family.

22. Harvey (1973:24).

23. Harvey (1973:34).

24. Armenta (2009) found the same phenomenon among Latina nannies in L.A. parks who used these public spaces as a way of combating the isolation that is part of doing domestic work.

25. See Duneier (1999). Also see Becker (1989), Charmaz (2001), and Emerson (2001) for more on meaning making in the field.

26. Momsen (1993:60).

27. Carr et al. (1992:190). I use the terms *public places* and *public spaces* interchangeably throughout the book.

28. Carr et al. (1992:190).

29. Lefebvre (1991); Low (1999); Low and Smith (2006).

30. Park and Burgess (1925/1984); Low (1999); Low and Smith (2006); Carr et al. (1992); Harvey (1973).

31. Lofland (1989:457, 459).
32. Lofland (1989:466).
33. Lofland (1989:468–69).
34. Lofland (1989:464).
35. See Lofland (1989).
36. Lofland (1989).
37. New York City Department of Parks and Recreation, [left untitled for purposes of anonymity], n.d., accessed January 11, 2008, www.nycgovparks.org. (2007).
38. J. Palmer (2001).
39. Welfare to Work is a grants program under the Balanced Budget Act that was created in 1997 to provide job opportunities, employment preparation, and job retention services for welfare recipients who are the hardest to employ. In Brooklyn, the WTW program operates under the Park Career Training Initiative (PACT), which assists workers in developing resumes, interview skills, and other coping strategies through clerical, custodial, horticultural, and security work. See Krinsky (2007) for a critical account.
40. My sense was that Marga used the term *babysitter* to indicate a temporary status, since Italian families often had the mother at home with the children, whereas she used the term *nanny* to refer to hired help in a more permanent role during the day. It also seemed during our conversations that for her a nanny was a person of color.
41. According to Colen (1995:391), West Indian childcare providers tend to not play on the floor with children, especially as the providers become older.
42. Hondagneu-Sotelo (2001).
43. Blum (1999).
44. Hochschild and Machung (1989).
45. Wharton (1994); Perkins and DeMeis (1996).
46. Jacobs (1961).
47. See n. 4 in Duneier's (1999:368) for studies that contest Jacobs's findings.
48. See chapter 5 for more about this Web site.
49. Gardner (1980); Feagin and Sikes (1994:60).
50. This is not always the case, and some providers feel that they are treated unfairly when there is indeed an emergency to attend to. For example, Grace's employment as a childcare provider was terminated when she had to go back to the islands for the funeral of her only daughter and then came back to New York, only to have an accident that left her unable to work for weeks.
51. The phrase "one of them" was used to group or isolate West Indian providers from other groups using the parks, such as grandparents, Latina providers, African Americans, or other ethnic groups.
52. This might be more acceptable in societies where all adults are able to watch out for all kids.
53. Feagin (2007:220).
54. This colloquial language, also known as patois or creole, is rooted in English with some African roots, but is typically difficult for non-Caribbeans to decipher.
55. See Marx (1967) and Welch, Tittle, and Petee (1991).
56. Khan (2004); Portes and Rumbaut (2006).
57. Bourdieu (1986) coined the term *social capital*. Portes (1998) expands Bourdieu's definition of its meaning to include involvement and participation in groups that have

positive consequences, but that it should be noted that social capital can have negative consequences because it is exclusionary.

3. INDOOR PUBLIC PLAY SPACES

1. Previous research by Jonathan J. Brower (1979) suggested that participation in organized children's activities such as Little League baseball was often a result of external parental pressures and not intrinsically enjoyed by the child. However, newer research by Mahoney, Harris, and Eccles (2006) reports that it is a fallacy to believe that the scheduling of numerous organized activities for children may undermine family functioning and well-being, so the effect of such activities on the family is unclear.

2. See Alejandro Portes (1998) on social capital and "social chits" for further discussion of how people gain social capital.

3. I initially wanted to speak with Victoria about her studio because she came into contact with many of the women that I had been observing and interviewing over two years. It should be noted that this studio has since closed and been reopened under new ownership.

4. A TASTE OF HOME

1. See Levi-Strauss (1983); Wilk (1999); Long (2004).

2. See Ferguson and Zukin (1995); Massey (1984); E. McIntosh (1995); W. McIntosh (1996); Rozin (1999); Whit (1995).

3. See Lan (2006); Hondagneu-Sotelo (2001); Kaplan (2000).

4. DeVault (1991); Kaplan (2000).

5. Studies of "kitchen culture" include Fine (1996) and Schroedl (1988). Quotes here are from Belasco (2002:2) and Sennett (1992:132).

6. On social space, see Fainstein and Campbell (2002).

7. Harvey (1985:251).

8. On the performance of everyday life in public spaces, see Lefebvre (2002); on food preparation in one private culinary space, see Deutsch (2004).

9. Wilk (2006a); Wilk (2006b); Houston (2005).

10. Sharma and Cruickshank (2001); Stowers (1992).

11. Sharma and Cruickshank (2001).

12. Hondagneu-Sotelo (2001).

13. Hondagneu-Sotelo (2001); Rollins (1985).

14. Hauck-Lawson (1992, 2004).

15. Hauck-Lawson (1992:24, 2004:6).

16. Deutsch (2004).

17. See Deutsch (2004) and Lupton (1996) for a discussion on frequency of food activities as a variable for analysis in food culture studies.

18. Kaplan (2000); Collins (1992:219).

19. Dumplings would probably not be considered kosher by the employers or the children under care, since the ingredients had not been blessed by a rabbi or prepared in any special manner that was consistent with kosher food tradition, which the parents in this case insisted on.

20. Gusfield (1992:75).

21. Sokolow (1983).

22. Houston (2005).

23. The food that one sitter cooked for another was a gift in the Maussian sense: (referring to the anthropologist Marcel Mauss, who studied gift giving in primitive societies): it was voluntarily given without any expectation of being reciprocated, only with the intent that the receiver enjoy it as a nonverbal communicative expression (Mauss 1990). Giving of food among West Indian sitters did not appear to involve the obligation of giving food in return or redistributing it in any form (Davis 2000). As Tarlow (1996) has described for acts of caring, "the gift" is a means of connecting human beings on a more spiritual level. The exchange of food as a gift among West Indian babysitters in Brooklyn parks indeed connected them and created a social community in much the same way as in other societies (Lupton 1996).

24. Kaplan (2000).

25. Hondagneu-Sotelo (2001); Romero (1992); Rollins (1985).

26. Colen (1995).

27. Children this young could participate in a playdate simply by being included in the social space that had been created by the providers. They were spoken to and played with as part of the bonding process that took place outside their time spent with a childcare provider. Many of these children would also see each other when they were with their parents on the weekends. Among more upper-middle-class and professional people, playdates can sometimes be more formal, structured events as opposed to simply "playing."

28. See Blum (1999).

29. Lupton (1996).

30. Katz Rothman (2001); Lan (2006).

31. Hondagneu-Sotelo (2001).

32. Hochschild (1997).

33. Hochschild (1997:51).

34. Kaplan (2000).

35. Mennell (1985:261).

5. MOBILITY FOR THE NONMOBILE

1. See Gumpert and Drucker (1998) for a detailed analysis of how technological advances change the living environment.

2. Lofland (1989); Gumpert and Drucker (1998).

3. Gumpert and Drucker (1998:424); Caronia (2005); Katriel (1999); Lee Humphreys (2005b).

4. Lee Humphreys (2005a).

5. Caronia (2005).

6. Gumpert and Drucker (1998:422); Caronia (2005).

7. Katriel coined the phrase "despatializing communicative action" to define continuous communication across places (1999:96).

8. Lan (2006:198) discusses cellular phone use among South Asians and the complexities of the functions available within the context of Goffman's frontstage/backstage analogy.

9. This reliance was further evidenced by the fact that several providers could be seen wearing cell phone earpieces for most of the day while walking about the neighborhoods they worked in.

10. Katriel (1999); Lee Humphreys (2005b).

11. Rheingold (2002:27).

12. Leung and Wei (2000); Rakow and Navarro (1993:145).

13. Hochschild and Machung (1989) were the first to discuss the phenomenon of parallel shifts within the home and at work.

14. Gumpert and Drucker (1998).

15. Rakow and Navarro (1993).

16. Remote mothering has been discussed in Rakow and Navarro (1993) and Leung and Wei (2000).

17. Gumpert and Drucker (1998).

18. Horst (2006:143).

19. Caronia (2005:99); Lee Humphreys (2005b).

20. See Lee Humphreys (2005a).

21. Lee Humphreys (2005b:367).

22. Cell phone sharing plans allow two or more people to access a shared number of minutes with a single bill, which is typically paid by the employer.

23. Hollander (1998).

24. McLaughlin and Kraus (2006).

25. Nelson and Garey (2009:113).

26. See Nelson and Garey (2009) for more details about how nannies are constructed as characters on the I Saw Your Nanny Web site and how these constructions give meaning to the behaviors being posted.

27. See Nelson and Garey (2009) for a comment analysis on how parents who work from home compare to parents who work outside the home and how this affects their decision to defend their nanny.

6. WHERE'S MY MONEY?

1. See Bonnett (1981a) for a more detailed analysis of the susu system.

2. See Feagin and Feagin (1999), Kasinitz (1992), Watkin-Owens (2001), Foner (1979), and Bonnett (1981a) for how various immigrant groups have used rotating credit associations in their communities.

3. Ardener (1964:201).

4. Sassen-Koob (1979).

5. Rabinovitch (2005).

6. Geertz (1962:242).

7. Bonnett (1981a).

8. Geertz (1962); Huggins (1997).

9. Biggart and Castanias (2001).

10. Biggart and Castanias (2001:480).

11. Ardener (1964).

12. Gerber (1982).

13. Light (1972). Light also notes, however, that African Americans faced more discrimination and that more West Indians possessed, on arrival in the United States, the liquid money and high educational levels that would favor their obtaining bank loans to facilitate business ventures.

14. Foner (1979:288); Garcia (1986).
15. Bonnett (1981a); Kasinitz (1992).
16. Aldrich and Waldinger (1990:128).
17. Bonnett (1981b:347); Bonnett (1990b).
18. Some providers kept the list of participants and the amount owing by each in their heads. They relied on this memory of who owed to the pot in case they encounter a delinquent payer in the park and wanted to remind her to pay her portion.
19. Castells and Portes (1989).
20. Bonnett (1981b:351).
21. Biggart and Castanias (2001:481).
22. None of the childcare providers whom I observed/interviewed ran or currently participated in a susu that had male members. However, in general and in many groups, susus are not exclusive to women.
23. Bonnett (1981a).
24. Bonnett (1981a:39).
25. Bonnett (1981a).
26. On the term *lenders,* see Bonnett (1981a).
27. Susus can run as long as a community of people exists who are interested. The longest-running susu that I was aware of among the providers I studied had lasted five years.

7. ORGANIZING RESISTANCE

1. Van Raaphorst (1988); Weiner (1989).
2. Poo and Tang (2005:113).
3. See Savage (1996).
4. Poo and Tang (2005:113).
5. Mishel and Voos (1992).
6. Ness (2005:58).
7. Needleman (1998:73).
8. Needleman (1998:71–72).
9. Mitra (2005).
10. Ness (1998).
11. Needleman (1998).
12. Colen (1986).
13. Other groups are attempting to organize domestic workers represented in these ethnic groups, but no other organizations concentrate solely on domestic workers.
14. Zinn and Dill (1994). The book also discusses how conservatives have blamed the poverty of black families on the U.S. government's support, via welfare programs, of "pathology" in the black family, specifically female-headed households, which have been stigmatized as "dysfunctional."
15. The Bill of Rights that DWU has been working on over the past few years was recently passed by the New York State Assembly Labor Committee by a vote of 25 to 1 and was also passed by the Senate on June 2, 2010. Under New York State law, domestic workers would be protected from being fired for attempting to organize.
16. Friedman and McAdam (1992:157).

17. Waldinger et al. (1998:114); Fantasia (1988).

18. Lewis (2006:13). The originator of the "free rider" concept is Mancur Olson (1965).

19. Friedman and McAdam (1992:159).

20. Friedman and McAdam (1992:167).

21. For West Indians, getting deported from the United States is considered a disgrace to the peoples of the respective islands. Throughout my current research on aging Jamaicans in Kingston, I have found that deportees are treated as less than capable and are not received well by their families or their former comrades. When West Indians speak of isolation in the context of deportation, they mean that they will have nothing if they go back to the islands because people will assume they are lazy and couldn't make life work in the United States.

22. Erickson et al. (2002).

23. Fantasia (1988).

24. Fantasia (1988:165).

25. Fantasia (1988:166).

26. *Collective autonomy* here means the freedom childcare providers feel once their collective lives are expressed, whether through participating in their culture's foodways, using technology such as cell phones to connect with each other, or simply congregating at various public spaces such as parks. Having the freedom to go about the day's work with a group or in an effort to connect with a social group gives childcare providers a sense that they are in control. They can also have a sense of control if they can set their own wage and determine a schedule that they themselves set without a signed contract with an employer (something they only rarely have).

CONCLUSION

1. Lan (2006).

2. Bonnett (1981a).

3. On the use of the term *black* and black identity among West Indian immigrants, see Kasinitz (1992); Waters (1999).

4. A critical analysis of how an ethnic/racial group of childcare providers becomes "the group of choice" among employers in a variety of areas in Brooklyn would be insightful and lead to a more nuanced body of research on childcare providers and hiring practices as a form of conspicuous consumption. Ethnographic studies in Brooklyn focusing on Tibetan and Nepalese childcare providers, who are especially sought after by white upper-middle-class employers in other newly gentrifying neighborhoods such as Williamsburg and Greenpoint, would be useful to researchers as well as to labor organizing groups that may be overlooking some ethnic immigrant groups of domestic workers. Organizers, parents, and providers themselves would benefit greatly from this type of investigation, and it would add to the growing literature on childcare providers.

5. In 2003 New York City created a "Nanny Bill" (Local Law 33) that required employment agencies to inform workers of their rights and labor laws.

6. According to DWU (2006), an estimated 40 percent of employed women in New York City benefit from the labor of domestic workers.

1. Cohen (1991); Colen (1995, 1986); Foner (1979, 1999); Rollins (1989); Wrigley (1991, 1999).

2. See Becker (1996) for more about mundane activity as the basis for routine and systems of consistent behavior that can be analyzed for sociological purposes.

3. Kondo (1990).

4. Thorne (1993).

5. See, e.g., Duneier (1992); Laud Humphreys (1970); Liebow (1967); Wacquant (2004).

6. Dorothy Smith (1987).

7. Warren (2001).

8. Wolf (1996); Lal (1996); Warren (2001).

9. On "motherwork," see Naples (1992).

10. See, e.g., Lan (2006); Joseph (1996); Stack (1996); Hondagneu-Sotelo (2001); Naples (2003).

11. Some of the younger sitters told me that they had lied about their age in the beginning of their careers in order to get a job. There was an ongoing joke about some sitters not revealing their ages. After years in the field I wasn't able to get them to divulge this information.

12. Hammersley and Atkinson (1991).

13. See Regis and Lashley (1992) for a more elaborate discussion of connections between Caribbean immigrants.

14. See Wolcott (1999) and Sanjek (1990) for more on constructing meaning in the field.

15. See Venkatesh (2000), on the Robert Taylor Homes in Chicago, which examined the relations and social production between the fieldworker and observed participants. Stack (1974) also suggests that biases from both fieldworker and the observed tend to mold views and the quality of interactions.

16. According to its use in the Mighty Dougla's calypso, *dougla* is a word for "a person of mixed Negro and East Indian descent" (Lowenthal 1968: n. 74).

17. Duneier (1999:338).

18. On Afro- versus Indo-Trinidadians' income, see Sudama (1994). From the time that Indians were brought into Trinidad as indentured servants in the late nineteenth century, there was a distinct notion that they were inferior to the black residents, since they were considered uneducated and found themselves at the bottom of the social order that they were entering (Sudama 1994). In addition, because of their distinct culture and strong identity formation, Indians were seen as a separate people from the black Trinidadians (Ryan 1972; Singh 1994). However, once the Indian population (mostly the offspring of the indentured laborers) began to educate themselves and gained economic strength through their cultural separation from the black natives, they became the "model" minority in a country that was predominantly black (Ryan 1972). Over the last twenty years, Afro- and Indo-Trinidadians have attained parity in positions in the civil service, teaching, the police force, and the armed forces. However, Indians predominate in the legal and medical professions.

19. See Goffman (1959) for more on impression management.

20. See Cassell (1987).

21. See Fernandez (1987:186).

References

Aldrich, Howard E., and Roger Waldinger. 1990. "Ethnicity and Entrepreneurship." *Annual Review of Sociology* 16:111–35.

Amott, Teresa, and Julie Matthaei. 1996. *Race, Gender, and Work: A Multi-cultural Economic History of Women in the United States*. Boston: South End Press.

Ardener, Shirley. 1964. "The Comparative Study of Rotating Credit Associations." *Journal of the Royal Anthropological Institute* 94 (2): 201–29.

Armenta, Amada. 2009. "Creating Community: Latina Nannies in a West Los Angeles Park." *Qualitative Sociology* 32 (3): 279–92.

Becker, Howard. 1989. "Tricks of the Trade." *Studies in Symbolic Interaction* 10: 481-90.

———. 1996. "The Epistemology of Qualitative Research." In *Ethnography and Human Development: Context and Meaning in Social Inquiry*, 53-71. Chicago: University of Chicago Press.

Belasco, Warren. 2002. "Food Matters: Perspectives on an Emerging Field." In *Food Nations: Selling Taste in Consumer Societies*, edited by Warren Belasco and Philip Scranton, 2-23. New York: Routledge.

Benardo, Leonard, and Jennifer Weiss. 2006. *Brooklyn by Name*. New York: New York University Press.

Berman, Marshall. 2002. "A Marxist Urban Romance." In *Metromarxism: A Marxist Tale of the City*, edited by Andrew Merrifield, 157-74. New York: Routledge.

Biggart, Nicole Woolsey, and Richard P. Castanias. 2001. "Collateralized Social Relations: The Social in Economic Calculation." *American Journal of Economics and Sociology* 60 (2): 471–500.

Blum, Linda M. 1999. *At the Breast: Ideologies of Breastfeeding and Motherhood in the Contemporary United States*. Boston: Beacon Press.

Bonnett, Aubrey W. 1981a. *Institutional Adaptation of West Indian Immigrants to America: An Analysis of Rotating Credit Associations*. Washington DC: University Press of America.

———. 1981b. "Structured Adaptation of Black Migrants from the Caribbean: An Examination of an Indigenous Banking System in Brooklyn." *Phylon* 42 (4): 346–55.

———. 1990a. *In Search of a Better Life: Perspectives on Migration from the Caribbean*, edited by Ransford W. Palmer. New York: Praeger.

———. 1990b. "The New Female West Indian Immigrant: Dilemmas of Coping in the Host Society." In *In Search of a Better Life: Perspectives on Migration from the Caribbean*, edited by Ransford W. Palmer, 139-50. New York: Praeger.

Bourdieu, Pierre. 1986. "The Forms of Capital." In *Handbook of Theory and Research for the Sociology of Education*, ed. J. R. Chardson, 241-58. New York: Greenwood.

———. 1989. "Social Space and Symbolic Power." *Sociological Theory* 1 (Spring): 14–25.
Brower, Jonathan J. 1979. "The Professionalization of Organized Youth Sport: Social Psychological Impacts and Outcomes." *Annals of the American Academy of Political and Social Science* 445:39–46.
Cancian, Francesca M., Demie Kurz, Andrew S. London, Rebecca Reviere, and Mary C. Tuominen, eds. 2002. *Child Care and Inequality: Rethinking Carework for Children and Youth*. New York: Routledge.
Caronia, Letizia. 2005. "Mobile Culture: An Ethnography of Cellular Phone Uses in Teenagers' Everyday Life." *Convergence* 11 (3): 96–103.
Carr, Stephen, Mark Francis, Leanne G. Rivlin, and Andrew M. Stone. 1992. *Public Space*. New York: Cambridge University Press.
Cassell, Joan. 1987. *Children in the Field: Anthropological Experiences*. Philadelphia: Temple University Press.
Castells, Manuel, and Alejandro Portes. 1989. "World Underneath: The Origins, Dynamics, and Effects of the Informal Economy." In *The Informal Economy: Studies in Advanced and Less Developed Countries*, edited by Alejandro Portes, Manuel Castells, and Laura A. Benton, 11-40. Baltimore: John Hopkins University Press.
Charmaz, Kathy. 2001. "Grounded Theory." In *Contemporary Field Research: Perspectives and Formulations,* edited by Robert M. Emerson, 335-52. Prospect Heights, IL: Waveland Press.
Chin, Christine B. N. 1998. *In Service and Servitude: Foreign Female Domestic Workers and the Malaysian "Modernity" Project*. New York: Columbia University Press.
Cohen, Rina. 1991. "Women of Color in White Households: Coping Strategies of Live-In Domestic Workers." *Qualitative Sociology* 14 (2): 197–215.
Colen, Shellee. 1986. "With Respect and Feelings: Voices of West Indian Workers in New York City." In *All American Women: Lines That Divide and Ties That Bind*, edited by Johnetta B. Cole, 46-70. New York: Free Press.
———. 1989. "'Just a Little Respect': West Indian Domestic Workers in New York City." In *Muchachas No More: Household Workers in Latin America and the Caribbean*, edited by Elsa M. Chaney and Mary Garcia Castro, 171-96. Philadelphia: Temple University Press.
———. 1995. "'Like a Mother to Them': Stratified Reproduction and West Indian Childcare Workers and Employers in New York." In *Conceiving the New World Order: The Global Politics of Reproduction,* edited by Faye D. Ginsburg and Rayna Rapp, 78-102. Berkeley: University of California Press.
Collins, Randall. 1992. "Women and the Production of Status Cultures." In *Cultivating Differences: Symbolic Boundaries and the Making of Inequality*, edited by Michele Lamont and Marcel Fournier. Chicago: University of Chicago Press.
Davis, Natalie Zemon. 2000. *The Gift in Sixteenth-Century France*. Madison: University of Wisconsin Press.
Denton, Nancy A., and Doreen B. Massey. 1989. "Racial Identity among Caribbean Hispanics: The Effect of Double Minority Status on Residential Segregation." *American Sociological Review* 54 (5): 790–808.
Deutsch, Jonathan. 2004. "'Eat Me Up': Spoken Voice and Food Voice in an Urban Firehouse." *Food, Culture, and Society* 7 (1): 27–36.
DeVault, Marjorie L. 1991. *Feeding the Family: The Social Organization of Caring as Gendered Work*. Chicago: University of Chicago Press.

Dill, Bonnie Thornton. 1994. *Across the Boundaries of Race and Class: An Exploration of Work and Family*. New York: Garland.
Domestic Workers United. 2006. *Home Is Where the Work Is: Inside New York's Domestic Work Industry*. New York: Domestic Workers United. www.domesticworkersunited.org/media/files/9/homeiswheretheworkis.pdf.
Dreby, Joanna. 2010. *Divided by Borders: Mexican Migrants and Their Children*. Berkeley: University of California Press.
Duneier, Mitchell. 1992. *Slim's Table: Race, Respectability, and Masculinity*. Chicago: University of Chicago Press.
———. 1999. *Sidewalk*. New York: Farrar, Straus and Giroux.
Emerson, Robert M., ed. 2001. *Contemporary Field Research: Perspectives and Formulations*. 2nd ed. Prospect Heights, IL: Waveland Press.
Erickson, Christopher L., Catherine L. Fisk, Ruth Milkman, Daniel J. B. Mitchell, and Kent Wong. 2002. "Justice for Janitors in Los Angeles: Lessons from Three Rounds of Negotiations." *British Journal of Industrial Relations* 40 (3): 543–67.
Evans, Graeme. 2003. "Hard-Branding the Cultural City: From Prado to Prada." *International Journal of Urban and Regional Research* 27 (2): 417–40.
Fainstein, Susan, and Scott Campbell, eds. 2002. *Readings in Urban Theory*. London: Blackwell.
Fantasia, Rick. 1988. *Cultures of Solidarity: Consciousness, Action, and Contemporary American Workers*. Berkeley: University of California Press.
Feagin, Joe R. 2007. "The Continuing Significance of Race: Antiblack Discrimination in Public Places." In *Rethinking the Color Line*, edited by Charles A. Gallagher, 161-71. New York: McGraw-Hill.
Feagin, Joe R., and Clairece Booher Feagin. 1999. *Racial and Ethnic Relations*. 6th ed. Upper Saddle River, NJ: Pearson Education.
Feagin, Joe R., and Melvin P. Sikes. 1994. *Living with Racism: The Black Middle Class Experience*. Boston: Beacon Press.
Ferguson, Priscilla P., and Sharon Zukin. 1995. "What's Cooking?" *Theory and Society* 24 (2): 193–99.
Fernandez, Renate. 1987. "Children and Parents in the Field: Reciprocal Impacts." In *Children in the Field: Anthropological Experiences*, edited by Joan Cassell, 185-215. Philadelphia: Temple University Press.
Figueroa, Esther, and Peter L. Patrick. 2002. "Kiss-Teeth." *American Speech* 77 4 (2002): 383–97.
———. Forthcoming. "The Meaning of Kiss-Teeth." In *Black Language in the U.S. and Caribbean: Education, History, Structure, and Use*, edited by Arthur K. Spears and James Dejongh.
Fine, Gary. 1996. *Kitchens: The Culture of Restaurant Work*. Berkeley: University of California Press.
Florida, Richard. 2004. "Creative Class War: How the GOP's Anti-elitism Could Ruin America's Economy." *Washington Monthly*, January-February, 30-37.
———. 2005. *The Flight of the Creative Class: The New Global Competition for Talent*. New York: Harper Business.
Foner, Nancy. 1979. "West Indians in New York City and London: A Comparative Analysis." *International Migration Review* 13 (2): 284–97.

———. 1999. "Benefits and Burdens: Immigrant Women and Work in New York City." *Gender Issues* 16 (4): 5–24.
Friedman, Debra, and Doug McAdam. 1992. "Collective Identity and Activism: Networks Choices, and the Life of a Social Movement." In *Frontiers in Social Movement Theory*, edited by Aldon D. Morris and Carol McClurg Mueller, 156-73. New Haven: Yale University Press.
Gans, Herbert J. 1962. *The Urban Villagers: Group and Class in the Life of Italian-Americans*. [New York]: Free Press of Glencoe.
Garcia, John A. 1986. "Caribbean Migration to the Mainland: A Review of Adaptive Experiences." *Annals of the American Academy of Political and Social Science* 487:114–25.
Gardner, Carol Brooks. 1980. "Passing By: Street Remarks, Address Rights, and the Urban Female." *Sociological Inquiry* 50:328–56.
Geertz, Clifford. 1962. "The Rotating Credit Association: A 'Middle Rung' in Development." *Economic Development and Cultural Change* 10 (3): 241–63.
Gerber, David A. 1982. "Cutting Out Shylock: Elite Anti-Semitism and the Quest for Moral Order in the Mid-Nineteenth-Century American Market Place." *Journal of American History* 9:615–37.
Glenn, Evelyn Nakano. 1986. *Issei, Nisei, War Bride: Three Generations of Japanese American Women in Domestic Service*. Philadelphia: Temple University Press.
———. 1992. "From Servitude to Service Work: Historical Continuities in the Racial Division of Paid Reproductive Labor." *Signs: Journal of Women in Culture and Society* 18 (1): 1–39.
———. 1994. "Social Constructions of Mothering: A Thematic Overview." In *Mothering: Ideology, Experience and Agency*, edited by Evelyn Nakano Glenn, Grace Chang, and Linda Rennie Forcey, 1-32. New York: Routledge.
Goffman, Erving. 1959. *The Presentation of Self in Everyday Life*. New York: Anchor Books.
———. 1983. "The Interaction Order: American Sociological Association, 1982 Presidential Address." *American Sociological Review* 48 (1): 1–17.
Gumpert, Gary, and Susan J. Drucker. 1998. "The Mediated Home in the Global Village." *Communication Research* 25 (4): 422–38.
Gusfield, Joseph R. 1992. "Nature's Body and the Metaphors of Food." In *Cultivating Differences: Symbolic Boundaries*, edited by Michèle Lamont and Marcel Fournier, 75-103. Chicago: University of Chicago Press.
Hammersley, Martyn, and Paul Atkinson. 1991. *Ethnography: Principles in Practice*. New York: Routledge.
Harvey, David. 1973. *Social Justice and the City*. London: Edward Arnold.
———. 1985. *Consciousness and the Urban Experience*. Baltimore: John Hopkins University Press.
———. 2002. "The Geopolitics of Urbanization." In *Metromarxism: A Marxist Tale of the City*, edited by Andrew Merrifield, 133-56. New York: Routledge.
Hauck-Lawson, Annie. 1992. "Guest Editor Introduction." *Food, Culture, and Society* 7 (1): 24–25.
———. 2004. "Hearing the Food Voice: An Epiphany for a Researcher." *Digest* 12 (1–2): 6–7.
Hochschild, Arlie Russell. 1997. *The Time Bind: When Work Becomes Home and Home Becomes Work*. New York: Metropolitan Books.

Hochschild, Arlie Russell, and Anne Machung. 1989. *The Second Shift: Working Parents and the Revolution at Home*. New York: Penguin Books.
Holder, Calvin. 1980. "The Rise of the West Indian Politician in New York." *Afro-Americans in New York Life and History* 4 (1): 45–59.
Hollander, Ricki. 1998. "Spy or Wary Eye? Nannies on Camera." *Christian Science Monitor*, May 1.
Hondagneu-Sotelo, Pierette. 2001. *Domestica: Immigrant Workers Cleaning and Caring in the Shadows of Affluence*. Berkeley: University of California Press.
Hondagneu-Sotelo, Pierette, and Ernestine Avila. 1997. "I'm Here but I'm There: The Meanings of Latina Transnational Motherhood." *Gender and Society* 11 (5): 548–60.
Horst, Heather A. 2006. "The Blessings and Burdens of Communication: Cell Phones in Jamaican Transnational Social Fields." *Global Networks* 6 (2): 143–59.
Houston, Lynn Marie. 2005. *Food Culture in the Caribbean*. Westport, CT: Greenwood Press.
Huggins, Sheryl E. 1997. "Pooling Community Dollars: A 'Susu' Can Mean Money for Your Business." *Black Enterprise*, October 1, 1–2.
Humphreys, Laud. 1970. *Tearoom Trade: Impersonal Sex in Public Places*. Hawthorne, NY: Aldine de Gruyter.
Humphreys, Lee. 2005a. "Cellphones in Public: Social Interactions in a Wireless Era." *New Media and Society* 7 (6): 810–33.
———. 2005b. "Social Topography in a Wireless Era: The Negotiation of Public and Private Space." *Journal of Technical Writing and Communication* 35 (4): 367–84.
Jacobs, Jane. 1961. *The Death and Life of Great American Cities*. New York: Random House.
James, Winston. n.d. "The History of Afro-Caribbean Migration to the United States. In Motion: The African-American Migration Experience," www.inmotionaame.org/migrations/resources.cfm?type=text.
Joseph, Suad. 1996. "Relationality and Ethnographic Subjectivity: Key Informants and the Construction of Personhood in Fieldwork." In *Feminist Dilemmas in Fieldwork*, edited by Diane L. Wolf, 107-21. Boulder, CO: Westview Press.
Kalmijn, Matthijs. 1996. "The Socioeconomic Assimilation of Caribbean American Blacks." *Social Forces* 74 (3): 911–30.
Kaplan, Elaine Bell. 2000. "Food as a Metaphor for Care: Middle-School Kids Talk about Family, School, and Class Relationships." *Journal of Contemporary Ethnography* 29 (4): 474–509.
Kargman, Jill. 2007. *Momzillas*. New York: Broadway.
Kasinitz, Philip. 1992. *Caribbean New York: Black Immigrants and the Politics of Race*. Ithaca: Cornell University Press.
Kasinitz, Philip, John Mollenkopf, and Mary C. Waters. 2002. "Becoming American/Becoming New Yorkers: Immigrant Incorporation in a Majority Minority City." *International Migration Review* 36 (4): 1020–36.
Katriel, Tamar. 1999. "Rethinking the Terms of Social Interaction." *Research on Language and Social Interaction* 32 (1-2): 95–102.
Katz, Jack. 1997. "Ethnography's Warrants." *Sociological Methods and Research* 25 (4): 391–423.
Katz Rothman, Barbara. 2001. *Recreating Motherhood*. New Brunswick: Rutgers University Press.

Kaufman, K. 2000. "Outsourcing the Hearth: The Impact of Immigration on Labor Allocation in American Families." In *Immigration Research for a New Century: Multidisciplinary Perspectives*, edited by Nancy Foner, Ruben G. Rumbaut, and Steven J. Gold, 345-68. New York: Russell Sage Foundation.

Khan, Aisha. 2004. *Callaloo Nation: Metaphors of Race and Religious Identity among South Asians in Trinidad*. Durham: Duke University Press.

Kondo, Dorinne K. 2001. *Crafting Selves: Power, Gender, and Discourses of Identity in a Japanese Workplace*. Chicago: University of Chicago Press.

Krinsky, John. 2007. *Free Labor: Workfare and the Contested Language of Neoliberalism*. Chicago: University of Chicago Press.

Lal, Jayati. 1996. "Situating Locations: The Politics of Self, Identity, and "Other" in Living and Writing the Text." In *Feminist Dilemmas in Fieldwork*, edited by Diane L. Wolf, 185-214. Boulder, CO: Westview Press.

Lan, Pei-Chia. 2006. *Global Cinderellas: Migrant Domestics and Newly Rich Employers in Taiwan*. Durham: Duke University Press.

Lefebvre, Henri. 1991. *The Production of Space*. Translated by D. Nicholson-Smith. Oxford: Blackwell.

———. 2002. "The Urban Revolution." In *Metromarxism: A Marxist Tale of the City*, edited by Andrew Merrifield, 71-92. New York: Routledge.

Leung, Louis, and Wei Ran. 2000. "More Than Just Talk on the Move: Uses and Gratifications of the Cellular Phone." *Journalism and Mass Communication Quarterly* 77 (2): 308-20.

Levi-Strauss, Claude. 1983. *The Raw and the Cooked: Introduction to a Science of Mythology*. Chicago: University of Chicago Press.

Lewis, J. Scott. 2006. *The Function of Free Riders: Toward a Solution to the Problem of Collective Action*. Bowling Green: Bowling Green State University.

Liebow, Elliot. 1967. *Tally's Corner: A Study of Negro Streetcorner Men*. Boston: Little, Brown.

Light, Ivan H. 1972. *Ethnic Enterprise in America: Business and Welfare among Chinese, Japanese, and Blacks*. Berkeley: University of California Press.

Lofland, Lyn H. 1989. "Social Life in the Public Realm." *Journal of Contemporary Ethnography* 17 (4): 453–82.

Long, Lucy, ed. 2004. *Culinary Tourism: A Folkloristic Perspective on Eating and Otherness*. Lexington: University Press of Kentucky.

Low, Setha M. 1999. *Theorizing the City: The New Urban Anthropology Reader*. New Brunswick: Rutgers University Press.

Low, Setha, and Neil Smith. 2006. *The Politics of Public Space*. New York: Routledge.

Lowenthal, David. 1968. "Race and Color in the West Indies." In *Color and Race*, edited by John H. Franklin, 302-48. Boston: Houghton Mifflin.

Lupton, Deborah. 1996. *Food, the Body and the Self*. Thousand Oaks, CA: Sage Publications.

Mahoney, Joseph L., Angel L. Harris, and Jacquelynne S. Eccles. 2006. "Over-scheduling Children: Organized Activity Participation, Positive Youth Development, and the Over-scheduling Hypothesis." *Social Policy Report: Giving Child and Youth Development Knowledge Away* 20 (4): 3–15.

Marx, Gary T. 1967. "Religion: Opiate or Inspiration of Civil Rights Militancy among Negroes." *American Sociological Review* 32 (1): 64–72.

Massey, Doreen B. 1984. *Spatial Divisions of Labor: Social Structures and the Geography of Production*. New York: Methuen.
Mauss, Marcel. 1990. *The Gift: The Form and Reason for Exchange in Archaic Societies*. New York: W. W. Norton.
McIntosh, Elaine N. 1995. *American Food Habits in Historical Perspective*. Westport, CT: Praeger.
McIntosh, William Alex. 1996. *Sociologies of Food and Nutrition*. New York: Plenum Press.
McLaughlin, Emma, and Nicola Kraus. 2006. "Spying on Nanny." *New York Times*, November 19.
Mennell, Stephen. 1985. *All Manners of Food: Eating and Taste in England and France from the Middle Ages to the Present*. New York: Basil Blackwell.
Michel, Sonya, and Rianne Mahon. 2002. *Child Care Policy at the Crossroads: Gender and Welfare State Restructuring*. New York: Routledge.
Milkman, Ruth, Ellen Reese, and Benita Roth. 1998. "The Macrosociology of Paid Domestic Labor." *Work and Occupations* 25 (4): 483–510.
Mishel, Lawrence, and Paula B. Voos, eds. 1992. *Unions and Economic Competitiveness*. New York: M. E. Sharp.
Mitchell, Don, and Lynn Staeheli. 2005. "The Complex Politics of Relevance in Geography." *Annals of the Association of American Geography* 95 (2): 357–72.
Mitra, Diditi. 2005. "Driving Taxis in New York City: Who Wants to Do It?" In *The New Urban Immigrant Workforce: Innovative Models for Labor Organizing*, edited by Sarumathi Jayaraman and Immanuel Ness, 33-56. New York: M. E. Sharpe.
Momsen, Janet Henshall. 1993. *Women and Change in the Caribbean: A Pan-Caribbean Perspective*. Bloomington: Indiana University Press.
Murray, Susan B. 1998. "Child Care Work: Intimacy in the Shadows of Family-Life." *Qualitative Sociology* 21 (2): 149–68.
Naples, Nancy A. 1992. "Activist Mothering: Cross-generational Continuity in the Community Work of Women from Low Income Urban Neighborhoods." *Gender and Society* 6 (3): 441–63.
———. 2003. *Feminism and Method: Ethnography, Discourse Analysis, and Activist Research*. New York: Routledge.
Needleman, Ruth. 1998. "Building Relationships for the Long Haul: Unions and Community-Based Groups Working Together to Organize Low-Wage Workers." In *Organizing to Win: New Research on Union Strategies*, edited by Kate Bronfenbrenner, Sheldon Friedman, Richard W. Hurd, Rudolph A. Oswald and Ronald L. Seeber, 71-86. Ithaca: Cornell University Press.
Nelson, Margaret K., and Anita Ilta Garey. 2009. *Who's Watching? Daily Practices of Surveillance among Contemporary Families*. Nashville: Vanderbilt University Press.
Ness, Immanuel. 1998. "Organizing Immigrant Communities: UNITE's Workers Center Strategy." In *Organizing to Win: New Research on Union Strategies*, edited by Kate Bronfenbrenner, Sheldon Friedman, Richard W. Hurd, Rudolph A. Oswald, and Ronald L. Seeber, 87-101. Ithaca: Cornell University Press.
———. 2005. "Community Labor Alliances: Organizing Greengrocery Workers in New York City." In *The New Urban Immigrant Workforce: Innovative Models for Labor Organizing*, edited by Sarumathi Jayaraman and Immanuel Ness, 57-70. New York: M. E. Sharpe.

Oakley, Ann. 1974. *Woman's Work: The Housewife, Past and Present*. New York: Random House.
Olson, Mancur. 1965. *The Logic of Collective Action: Public Goods and the Theory of Groups*. Cambridge, MA: Harvard University Press.
Ostrander, Susan A. 1987. "Women Using Other Women." *Contemporary Sociology* 16 (1): 51–53.
Palmer, Joy A. 2001. *Fifty Key Thinkers on the Environment*. London: Routledge.
Palmer, Phyllis. 1989. *Domesticity and Dirt: Housewives and Domestic Servants in the United States, 1920–1945*. Philadelphia: Temple University Press.
Park, Robert E., and Ernest W. Burgess. 1925/1984. *The City*. Chicago: University of Chicago Press.
Perkins, H. Wesley, and Debra K. DeMeis. 1996. "Gender and Family Effects on the 'Second-Shift' Domestic Activity of College-Educated Young Adults." *Gender and Society* 10 (1): 78–93.
Poo, Ai-jen, and Eric Tang. 2005. "Center Stage: Domestic Workers Organizing in the Global City." In *The New Urban Immigrant Workforce: Innovative Models for Labor Organizing*, edited by Sarumathi Jayaraman and Immanuel Ness, 105-18. New York: M. E. Sharpe.
Portes, Alejandro. 1998. "Social Capital: Its Origins and Applications in Modern Sociology." *Annual Review of Sociology* 24:1–24.
Portes, Alejandro, and Jozsef Borocz. 1989. "Contemporary Immigration: Theoretical Perspectives on Its Determinants and Modes of Incorporation." *International Migration Review* 23 (3): 606–30.
Portes, Alejandro, and Ruben G. Rumbaut. 2006. *Immigrant America: A Portrait*. 3rd ed. Berkeley: University of California Press.
Rabinovitch, Ari. 2005. "Money Pools Float Immigrant Dreams." *Columbia News Service*, November 26.
Rakow, Lana F., and Vija Navarro. 1993. "Remote Mothering and the Parallel Shift: Women Meet the Cellular Phone." *Critical Studies in Mass Communication* 10 (2): 144–57.
Regis, Humphrey A., and Leroy L. Lashley. 1992. "The Editorial Dimensions of the Connection of Caribbean Immigrants to Their Referents." *Journal of Black Studies* 22 (3): 380–91.
Rheingold, Howard. 2002. *Smart Mobs: The Next Social Revolution*. Cambridge, MA: Perseus.
Rollins, Judith. 1985. *Between Women: Domestics and Their Employers*. Philadelphia: Temple University Press.
———. 1989. Review of *Union Maids Not Wanted: Organizing Domestic Workers, 1870-1940*, by Donna L. Van Raaphorst. *Women's Studies International Forum* 12 (4): 480-81.
Romero, Mary. 1988. "Chicanas Modernize Domestic Service." *Qualitative Sociology* 11 (4): 319–34.
———. 1992. *Maid in the USA*. New York: Routledge.
Rozin, Paul. 1999. "Food Is Fundamental, Fun, Frightening, and Far-Reaching." *Social Research* 66 (1): 9–13.
Ryan, Selwyn D. 1972. *Race and Nationalism in Trinidad and Tobago: A Study of Decolonization in a Multiracial Society*. Toronto: University of Toronto Press.

Salazar Parrenas, Rhacel. 2001. *Servants of Globalization: Women, Migration and Domestic Work*. Stanford: Stanford University Press.

Salzinger, Leslie. 1991. "A Maid by Any Other Name: The Transformation of 'Dirty Work' by Central American Immigrants." In *Ethnography Unbound: Power and Resistance in the Modern Metropolis*, edited by Michael Burawoy, Alice Burton, Ann Arnett Ferguson, and Kathryn J. Fox, 139-60. Berkeley: University of California Press.

Sanjek, Roger, ed. 1990. *Fieldnotes: The Makings of Anthropology*. Ithaca: Cornell University Press.

Sassen-Koob, Saskia. 1979. "Formal and Informal Associations: Dominicans and Colombians in New York." *International Migration Review* 13 (2): 314–32.

Savage, Lydia A. 1996. "Negotiating Common Ground: Labor Unions and the Geography of Organizing Women Workers in the Service Sector." PhD diss., Clark University.

Schroedl, Alan. 1988. "The Dish Ran Away with the Spoon: Ethnography of Kitchen Culture." In *The Cultural Experience: Ethnography in Complex Society*, edited by James P. Spradley and David W. McCurdy, 177-90.Prospect Heights, IL: Waveland Press.

Sennett, Richard. 1992. *The Conscience of the Eye: The Design and Social Life of Cities*. New York: W. W. Norton.

Sharma, S., and J. K. Cruickshank. 2001. "Cultural Differences in Assessing Dietary Intake and Providing Relevant Dietary Information to British African-Caribbean Populations." *Journal of Human Nutrition and Dietetics* 14:449–56.

Simmel, Georg. 1964. *The Sociology of Georg Simmel*. Edited and translated by Kurt H. Wolff. New York: Free Press.

Singh, Kelvin. 1994. *Race and Class: Struggles in a Colonial State, Trinidad, 1917–1945*. Calgary: University of Calgary Press.

Smith, Denitia. 1981. "Squeezed Out of Manhattan? New Places to Live." *New York*, September 7.

Smith, Dorothy. 1987. *The Everyday World as Problematic: A Feminist Sociology*. Boston: Northeastern University Press.

Sokolow, Jayme. 1983. *Eros and Modernization*. London: Associated University Press.

Stack, Carol B. 1974. *All Our Kin: Strategies for Survival in a Black Community*. New York: Basic Books.

———. 1996. "Writing Ethnography: Feminist Critical Practice." In *Feminist Dilemmas in Fieldwork*, edited by Diane L. Wolf, 96-106. Boulder, CO: Westview Press.

Sternbergh, Adam. 2006. "Up with Grups: The Ascendant Breed of Grown-Ups Who Are Redefining Adulthood." *New York*, March 26.

Stowers, S. L. 1992. "Development of a Culturally Appropriate Food Guide for Pregnant Caribbean Immigrants in the United States." *Journal of the American Dietetic Association* 92 (3): 331–36.

Sudama, Trevor. 1994. "Speech on Ethnic Relations in a Plural Society: The Case of the Indians in Trinidad and Tobago." In *Race Relations in Trinbago: Afro and Indo-Trinbagonians and Basdeo Panday*, edited by Frankie B. Ramadar. New York: Caribbean Diaspora Press.

Sutton, Constance R., and Elsa M. Chaney, eds. 1987. *Caribbean Life in New York City: Sociocultural Dimensions*. New York: Center for Migration Studies of New York.

Tarlow, Barbara. 1996. "Caring: A Negotiated Process That Varies." In *Caregiving: Readings in Knowledge, Practice, Ethics, and Politics*, edited by Suzanne Gordon, Patricia Benner and Nel Noddings, 56-82. Philadelphia: University of Pennsylvania Press.

Thomas, Bert J. 1988. "Historical Functions of Caribbean-American Benevolent/Progressive Associations." *Afro-Americans in New York Life and History* 12:45–58.
Thorne, Barrie. 1993. *Gender Play: Girls and Boys in School.* New Brunswick: Rutgers University Press.
Tronto, Joan C. 2002. "The 'Nanny' Question in Feminism." *Hypatia* 17 (2): 34–51.
U.S. Bureau of the Census. 2001. "Foreign-Born Population." In *Statistical Abstract of the United States 2001.* Washington, DC: U.S. Bureau of the Census.
U.S. Immigration and Naturalization Service. 1913. *Annual Report of the Immigration and Naturalization Service.* Washington, DC: Government Printing Office.
———. 1914. *Annual Report of the Immigration and Naturalization Service.* Washington, DC: Government Printing Office.
U.S. Immigration Commission. 1911. *Abstracts of Reports of the Immigration Commission.* Vol. 1. Washington, DC: Government Printing Office.
Van Raaphorst, Donna L. 1988. *Union Maids Not Wanted: Organizing Domestic Workers, 1870–1940.* New York: Praeger.
Venkatesh, Sudhir Alladi. 2000. *American Project: The Rise and Fall of a Modern Ghetto.* Cambridge, MA: Harvard University Press.
Vickerman, Milton. 1999. *Crosscurrents: West Indian Immigrants and Race.* New York: Oxford University Press.
———. 2001. "Tweaking a Monolith: The West Indian Immigrant Encounter with Blackness." In *Islands in the City: West Indian Migration to New York*, edited by Nancy Foner. Berkeley: University of California Press.
Wacquant, Loic J. D. 2004. *Body and Soul: Notebooks of an Apprentice Boxer.* Oxford: Oxford University Press.
Waldinger, Roger, Christopher L. Erickson, Ruth Milkman, Daniel J. B. Mitchell, Abel Valenzuela, Kent Wong, and Maurice Zeitlin. 1998. "Helots No More: A Case Study of the Justice for Janitors Campaign in Los Angeles." In *Organizing to Win: New Research on Union Strategies*, edited by Kate Bronfenbrenner, Sheldon Friedman, Richard W. Hurd, Rudolph A. Oswald, and Ronald L. Seeber, 102-20. Ithaca: Cornell University Press.
Walter, John C. 1977. "Black Immigrants and Political Radicalism in the Harlem Renaissance." *Western Journal of Black Studies* 1 (2): 131–41.
Warren, Carol B. 2001. "Gender and Fieldwork Relations." In *Contemporary Field Research: Perspectives and Formulations*, edited by Robert M. Emerson, 203-23. Prospect Heights, IL: Waveland Press.
Waters, Mary C. 1999. *Black Identities: West Indian Immigrant Dreams and American Realities.* New York: Russell Sage Foundation; Cambridge, MA: Harvard University Press.
Watkins-Owens, Irma. 1996. *Blood Relations: Caribbean Immigrants and the Harlem Community, 1900–1930.* Bloomington: Indiana University Press.
———. 2001. "Early Twentieth Century Caribbean Women: Migration and Social Networks in New York City." In *Islands in the City: West Indian Migration to New York*, edited by Nancy Foner, 25-51. Berkeley: University of California Press.
Weiner, Lynn. 1989. Review of *Union Maids Not Wanted: Organizing Domestic Workers, 1870–1940*, by Donna L. Van Raaphorst. *Journal of Economic History* 49 (2): 512–13.
Welch, Michael, Charles R. Tittle, and Thomas Petee. "Religion and Deviance among Adult Catholics: A Test of the 'Moral Communities' Hypothesis." *Journal for the Scientific Study of Religion* 30 (2): 159-72.

Wharton, Carol S. 1994. "Finding Time for the 'Second Shift': The Impact of Flexible Work Schedules on Women's Double Days." *Gender and Society* 8 (2): 189–205.
Whit, William C. 1995. *Food and Society: A Sociological Approach*. Lanham, MD: Rowman and Littlefield.
Wilk, Richard R. 1999. "'Real Belizean Food': Building Local Identity in the Transnational Caribbean." *American Anthropologist* 101 (2): 244–55.
———. 2006a. *Fast Food/Slow Food: The Cultural Economy of the Global Food System*. Lanham, MD: Rowman and Littlefield.
———. 2006b. *Home Cooking in the Global Village: Caribbean Food from Buccaneers to Ecotourists*. New York: Palgrave Macmillan.
Wolcott, Harry F. 1999. *Ethnography: A Way of Seeing*. Walnut Creek, CA: AltaMira Press.
Wolf, Diane L. 1996. "Situating Feminist Dilemmas in Fieldwork." In *Feminist Dilemmas in Fieldwork*, edited by Diane L. Wolf, 1-55. Boulder, CO: Westview Press.
Wrigley, Julia. 1991. "Feminists and Domestic Workers." *Feminist Studies* 17 (2): 317–29.
———. 1995. *Other People's Children: An Intimate Account of the Dilemmas Facing Middle-Class Parents and the Women They Hire to Raise Their Children*. New York: Basic Books.
———. 1999. "Hiring a Nanny: The Limits of Private Solutions to Public Problems." *Annals of the American Academy of Political and Social Science* 563:162–74.
———. 2005. "Migration, Domestic Work, and Repression." *New Politics* 10 (3), http://newpolitics.mayfirst.org/node/261.
Zinn, Maxine Baca, and Bonnie Thornton Dill, eds. 1994. *Women of Color in U.S. Society*. Philadelphia: Temple University Press.
Zukin, Sharon. 1987. "Gentrification: Culture and Capital in the Urban Core." *Annual Review of Sociology* 13:129–47.
———. 1995. *The Cultures of Cities*. Oxford: Blackwell.

Index

About the Author

TAMARA MOSE BROWN is Assistant Professor of Sociology at Brooklyn College, City University of New York.

9 780814 791431

CPSIA information can be obtained at www.ICGtesting.com
Printed in the USA
BVOW07s1410091014

370200BV00001B/4/P

9 780814 791431